Putting Participation into Practice

Putting Participation into Practice

Edited by

David Guest and Kenneth Knight

GOWER PRESS

Published by
Gower Press, Teakfield Limited,
Westmead, Farnborough, Hants., England.

ISBN 0 566 02086 6

Typeset by Inforum Ltd., Portsmouth
Printed and bound in Great Britain by
The Pitman Press, Bath

Contents

Preface

The aim of this book is to be of practical help to those —
managers, trade unionists, personnel practitioners, consultants and teachers — who are taking initiatives, making decisions or providing advice on the development of employee
participation. It provides a representative cross-section of
experience of the main forms of participation at present operating in the UK, described by those involved in their introduction. A group of selected case histories is presented within a
descriptive and analytic framework which clarifies the social
and organisational origins of the recent growth of interest in
the subject, the aims and attitudes surrounding it and the different forms which participation can take. The individual case
histories are also supplemented by comprehensive reviews of
developments at each level of participation and by a more general examination of the implications and problems of implementing these systems.

The book had its origin in a series of seminars at Brunel
University, directed by the two editors under the auspices of
the Brunel Management Programme. Most of the contributors to this book also contributed to these seminars, which
were aimed at providing decision-makers with a practical
insight into the options available and the thinking behind
them. Our discussions of the issues of participation with the
many executives who attended this series of seminars between
1974 and 1977 has been of great help to us in the preparation
of this book and we gratefully acknowledge their assistance.

Bearing in mind the practical aims of the book we have deliberately restricted the choice of case histories to those which are
comparatively recent — that is, where the main developments

have taken place in the last ten years — and to British examples. This explains the absence of such well-known cases as the Glacier Metal Company, the John Lewis Partnership and the Scott-Bader Commonwealth, as well as of the very significant developments in various forms of participation that have taken place in other countries, notably in Germany, Holland and Scandinavia, in Yugoslavia and Israel, and in the USA. Apart from the fact that these developments have been very fully documented in other publications, they are liable to be met with the objection from practising managers and trade unionists that they relate to different cultures and systems of industrial relations and, in the case of the earlier British cases, to a different industrial climate. At the other end of the scale, we have not included any detailed description of the latest developments in the UK of worker co-operatives on the one hand and parity representation on boards, as in the new Post Office experiment, on the other, as these seem to us too new for a balanced assessment.

While we have attempted to provide a coherent framework for an understanding of the forms and issues of participation in the introductory, linking and concluding chapters, we have deliberately refrained, in the selection and editing of the chapters by the other contributors, from any attempt to impose our own views in order to arrive at a consistent or uniform perspective. The field of employee participation is one in which a wide divergence of views is based on an equally wide range of experiences, and for anyone wishing to take new initiatives in this field it is more useful to be made aware of this range of views and to have access to the first-hand experience of those who have confronted the issues in practice, than to be presented with an artificially created illusion of consensus.

The structure of the book is based on the idea of 'levels' of participation, explained in Chapter 2. The book is in five parts. Part I is concerned with the context or background to participation, with Chapter 1 reviewing the origins of the current interest in the subject, Chapter 2 providing an analytic framework for an understanding of the many forms of participation and Chapter 3 looking at the evidence about the wishes of the people involved. Parts II, III and IV are concerned with participation at shop-floor, plant and company level respectively, and consist of a set of first-hand accounts of specific cases, prefaced, in each section, by a chapter which provides an overview of the relevant forms of participation and their implications. Part V is concerned with the more general issues and practical implications which arise in implementing employee participation and concludes with a look at the likely course of future developments.

DAVID GUEST
KENNETH KNIGHT

Notes on the Contributors

John B. Benson is Personnel Director of Scottish & Newcastle Beer Company Limited.

Chris W. Clegg is a Research Fellow in the Medical Research Council Social and Applied Psychology Unit at the University of Sheffield.

John Davis was Manager of Management Training with B.L. Cars Ltd., and was responsible for participation training in the company. He is now working as a private consultant.

Denis Gregory is with the Trade Union Research Unit at Ruskin College, Oxford, and is currently working with the Wales TUC research unit.

David Guest is Lecturer in Personnel Management at the London School of Economics and Political Science.

Ken Jones was a senior personnel manager in the British Steel Corporation from 1967 to 1976. He has also been a national trade union official and university teacher in industrial relations. He is now an independent consultant.

Kenneth Knight is Director of the Management Programme within the Brunel Institute of Organisation and Social Studies (BIOSS) at Brunel University; he is the author of *Matrix Management*, Gower Press, 1977.

Geoffrey Richards is Works Manager of the Grangemouth works in the Organics Division of ICI.

Kirsty Ross is currently Head of the Employment Section at the Equal Opportunities Commission and was formerly an internal consultant with Philips at Mullard, Blackburn.

Jeoffrey Screeton is Manager of the Quick-Vision Cathode Department, Component Division, Mullard, Blackburn.

David Searle is Managing Director of Morgan & Grundy Limited.

Toby D. Wall is a Research Fellow with the Medical Research Council Social and Applied Psychology Unit at the University of Sheffield.

Derek Williams is Personnel Director of the Drinks Division of Cadbury Schweppes Limited.

Part I
The Context of Participation

This section sets the scene for the specific approaches to participation described in Parts II, III and IV. After discussing the reasons for the sudden upsurge in interest in the subject over the last ten years (Chapter 1), we set out a framework for distinguishing between different forms, subjects and levels of participation in relation to their context (Chapter 2). But does anyone in industry really *want* more participation? Chapter 3 not only reviews some of the evidence on the general question, but also shows how it can be answered for specific organisations, and how the answers one gets can be used as a basis for developing a scheme to satisfy these wants. In the process it provides a first example of shop-floor participation — an area treated more fully in Part II.

1 Participation: Why the Interest?

David Guest

Lecturer in Personnel Management, London School of Economics and Political Science

Introduction

In 1968 the Donovan Report[1] devoted a mere three and a half pages to the subject of worker directors and supervisory boards, concluding that they were likely to be of marginal value and attracted little or no support amongst management and trade unions in the UK. Yet ten years later, in 1978, following a committee of inquiry,[2] a government White Paper[3] has proposed a major extension of worker participation at company level, including the appointment of worker representatives to company boards.

It would seem reasonable to assume that some significant changes had occurred in the intervening years to produce such a turnabout of views. Whatever the causes, one result is that from being a topic of minority interest until the mid-1970s, like it or not worker participation is now something which few managers or trade unionists can afford to ignore. This brief chapter explores some of the changes which have led to this interest in participation and then outlines some of the reasons why managers, in particular, should be interested in the topic.

Reasons for the increased interest in participation

One dominating factor during the years between 1968 and

1978 was the continuing economic and industrial decline of the UK. A variety of explanations and solutions to this problem have been and continue to be sought. One of the recurring if controversial explanations has been the country's poor industrial relations and more particularly the level of industrial conflict and the impact of high wage settlements on inflation. Though this explanation has often been called into question, a variety of means have been devised in an attempt to reduce conflict and control wages. Central to such attempts is an assumption that free collective bargaining, long regarded by the unions as their major basis for participation, is no longer serving the interests of the country, of industry and even of the workers. However, alternatives have proved no more successful. Unilateral government control of wages was tried, but failed, and the attempt to impose legislation, in the form of the 1971 Industrial Relations Act, to regulate negotiation and conflict behaviour, succeeded only in provoking confrontation and proving unworkable. In the search for alternative solutions, it was perhaps inevitable that worker participation would come to be viewed as another strategy that was at least worth a try. One manifestation of a more participative approach at national level, albeit without industry representation, has been the joint government-TUC shaping of the Social Contract.

An interest in participation has been reinforced by a knowledge that several of the countries in Europe with the most successful economies and the lowest levels of industrial conflict have well established systems of participation. This leads on to the second main point, which is the influence of membership of the European Economic Community. One consequence of this has been a greater interest in industrial relations policies and practices in the EEC countries and indeed throughout Europe, since developments in Scandinavia have also attracted attention. A second consequence has been the need to consider the implications for company law of the draft Fifth Directive[4] which at present envisages some kind of system whereby worker representatives would sit on the boards of large companies.

A third and particularly important stimulus to the current debate has been a change towards a more positive attitude to participation at board level among certain senior and influential members of the trade union movement. An explanation of this change can be found in the TUC's 1974 report on industrial democracy.[5] This points out that, while collective bargaining has been and should remain the chief means of participation, there are certain crucial topics at company level which have an important influence on the welfare of the workforce but are normally outside the scope of collective bargaining. On the one hand the growth of plant bargaining has given unions a voice at a lower level in many organisations, and the legislation of the mid-1970s, particularly the Health and Safety at Work Act and the Employment Protection Act, has been seen as providing a legislative framework for participation at shop-floor and plant level.[6] On the other hand, at national level the TUC has represented the workers' interests through discussions on the Social Contract and incomes policy as well as through established mechanisms such as the National Economic Development Corporation. A gap can therefore be seen to exist at company level. The limited impact to date of planning agreements and disclosure of information has only served to highlight this gap. It is not surprising that unions should begin to demand a voice at company level and that this demand should focus the debate on the rather narrow issue of board-level participation.

A further point which is frequently stressed in discussions of participation is the need to meet the rising expectations of the workforce, particularly expectations in relation to what is sometimes called the quality of working life.[7] The argument, briefly, is that workers are no longer prepared to accept authoritarian management, arbitrary treatment, stressful working conditions, boring jobs and an insecure future, all of which they can do little to influence. In addition the workforce is becoming increasingly well educated and therefore more articulate in its demands. As a result, workers are demanding participation at all levels of the enterprise, from day-to-day decisions about how to do their job to board decisions on future investments and plant locations.[8]

A fifth issue stimulating an interest in participation is concern about the concentration of power in industry. There is a view, which not all industrialists would oppose, that as organisations have tended to become larger senior management has become more remote from the concerns of the shop-floor worker. At the same time, more sophisticated control systems have enabled power to become concentrated in the hands of a small number of senior managers. To combat this, it is argued, senior management and industrial decision-makers should become more responsive to the employees as a whole. One step in this direction may be to alter the present law whereby board members are accountable solely to the shareholders.

A linked criticism of industrialists is that they give too low a priority to social considerations. The implication is that the conventional goals and priorities of the enterprise, usually defined in terms of profit, growth or return on capital, may need to be amended. The first priority may be participation by workers who are a part of the organisation. A further step may be the development of participation by those affected by the organisation, either as members of the local community in which it exists, or as consumers of its products. Steps in this direction have already been taken with respect to public corporations in the energy and transport industries.

A final feature of the current interest in participation is a reawakened interest in the concept of democracy. This is reflected in concern about the EEC and the sovereignty of Parliament, in discussion of devolution within the UK and in debates on electoral reform. It has also led to a search for a link between parliamentary democracy and industrial democracy, with industry sometimes described as one of the last bastions of undemocratic behaviour in British society.

While the concern for industrial democracy finds a ready echo, the analogy with parliamentary democracy is not really valid. The concept of democracy is highly problematic, but one of the aims of parliamentary democracy is usually rule by representatives of the majority of voters.[9] This is seldom the intention of schemes of industrial democracy, except perhaps in socialist states such as Yugoslavia.

The concept of majority rule in industry runs foul of the issues of ownership and control and of how, in our present mixed economy, to take account of the potentially competing demands of capital and labour. In practical terms, therefore, bearing in mind the kind of schemes advocated, participation is probably still the more useful and realistic concept.

A concern for issues of democracy does imply that in a democratic society participation should be viewed as an end in itself rather than as primarily a means to other ends. This raises questions about the nature and meaning of participation, questions which are explored in the next chapter.

So far we have outlined six reasons which might help to explain the current interest in worker participation, an interest which has grown dramatically in the last ten years. While most of the factors, such as trade union attitudes, reflect a powerful short-term source of pressure, others, such as concern for the quality of working life, might have limited short-term impact but considerable long-term significance.

Most of these points were raised, directly or indirectly, in the Bullock Report.

On the surface, there would seem to be good reasons for industrialists, understandably on the defensive, to oppose an extension of participation. Yet such a view would be short-sighted, for there seems to be much that management could gain by adopting a positive and flexible approach to the subject.

Management interest in participation

Employer and management organisations have bitterly opposed the majority findings of the Bullock Report and, indeed, have consistently objected to the original terms of reference[10] given to the Committee. The initial reactions of the CBI to the White Paper on industrial democracy continue this highly critical stance.[11] However, this should not lead to the conclusion that they are necessarily opposed to any extension of participation. As subsequent chapters will show, in recent years senior management in several organisations has taken the initiative in introducing various forms of participation. The advantages of participation are also implicit in the fact that it already exists, in one form or another, in many organisations, where management would be strongly opposed to its removal. The Bullock Report, in partially accepting the logic of the CBI argument that participation should grow from the bottom up, then went on to say:

> The evidence we received convinced us that the process of development is in fact already advanced, particularly in larger companies, and that a wide range of participation already exists below board level. Employee participation may take many forms, from improved communication to joint responsibility for decisions, to experiments in job enrichment and participative management, and it may range from unwritten but accepted codes of practice within companies to formal structures such as representative councils with constitutions, officers, etc.[12]

Building on this, the CBI, in common with a number of other bodies, has advocated the concept of a 'participation agreement' which could include any form of participation but would be able to meet the needs of a particular organisation. The White Paper also accepts the need for flexibility and would seem to go a long way towards meeting CBI objections on this issue.

Given the existence of various management-initiated forms of participation and an advocacy, by the CBI of an extention of participation albeit enforced in the face of a less palatable alternative, what does management stand to gain?

The first and possibly the most controversial reason for a management interest in participation is that it could lead to a significant increase in efficiency and a major improvement in the quality of decision-making. Indeed the White Paper reflects this view by suggesting that 'where decisions are mutually agreed both sides of industry must then share the responsibility for them. Such shared responsibility will improve the efficiency of British industry . . .' (p.1). There is, of course, a danger that the outcome may not always be positive and much depends on choosing the most appropriate form of participation and upon the way in which it is introduced. These two issues, which represent the central concerns of this book, will be recurring themes in subsequent chapters. Leaving them aside for the present, there are underlying reasons why a link between participation and efficiency could exist.

One of these reasons, again recognised in the White Paper, is that there is a considerable resource of untapped potential among the workforce, including management, in most organisations. Many people are operating at well below their intellectual capacity and with the improvement in educational opportunities this number is likely to increase. There are, broadly speaking, two kinds of participation which might tap some of this potential. One is sharing in the process of decision-making, where the ultimate decision is taken at a fairly senior level. The broader perspective afforded by wider involvement might help to improve the quality of decision-making. A second approach is to delegate decision-taking by giving workers more control over their own jobs.

There are those who argue that delegation of control will be an inevitable consequence of technological developments towards automation. Davis (1972), for example, believes that in highly automated systems important events occur in a random and unpredictable way and require an immediate response. The workers must possess a variety of skills to meet the range of contingencies, they must be able to respond swiftly without supervision and they must therefore be committed to the organisation and to their job.[13]

If this is true then traditional supervisory and managerial

control systems will be both inappropriate and inefficient. But while Davis's arguments may have validity for technologists, professionals and a number of others involved in automated processes and sophisticated services, there is contradictory evidence for many other jobs in offices, in traditional and mechanised production units and in service industries where the process of work simplification seems to be continuing.[14] In such contexts a more positive step by management would be required to reverse the trend, and gains in efficiency will only be readily apparent where flexibility of operations is a requirement or an advantage.

A second reason for a management interest in participation is that it may help to facilitate the process of change. British industry in general faces considerable difficulties in understanding how to introduce change of any sort, and resistance from the workforce is only one of a number of inhibiting factors. Evidence from a recent comparison of approaches to industrial change in various organisations in West Germany and Britain (Jacobs et al., 1978) highlighted a number of interesting contrasts. The British typically adopt an adversary approach, with reluctance on the part of management to involve the unions at an early stage, a fear of union reactions and use of collective bargaining to negotiate progress. In Germany, unions are more involved in the planning process, and, although there may be considerable tensions, there is more focus on joint problem-solving. Involving workers in the planning and implementation of change may sometimes slow the initial discussions, but it can help to highlight the pitfalls, anticipate problems and remove some sources of opposition. In the long term, therefore, the goals of the change may have been clarified and the process of change eased. A participative approach to change has often been advocated in the past,[15] one successful manifestation of this being some of the productivity bargains of the 1960s (see Chapter 15 for a more detailed discussion of participation and change).

A third reason for a management interest in participation is that it may improve industrial relations. Both sides are likely to gain from a better understanding of the context in which they are negotiating and the goals and expectations of the other party. Providing shop stewards with an opportunity to understand and explore the long-term and short-term implications of allocation of profits is one example of this. Joint formulation of policy and early anticipation and discussion of issues likely to produce strongly felt differences of interest can also help to minimise the various forms of industrial conflict.

The White Paper quite clearly sees this as a major objective of industrial democracy: 'The objective is positive partnership between management and workers, rather than defensive coexistence' (p.1); and 'The objective of participation is understanding and co-operation and it is obvious that the chances of success are improved where employers and employees agree together on the procedures for involvement which suit their wishes and circumstances' (p.2).

A fourth possible reason for management interest in participation is that, where it takes a form that is relevant to the worker, it may lead to an increase in job satisfaction and well-being. It would be a serious mistake, however, to believe that the introduction of participation is sufficient in itself to guarantee job satisfaction, since job satisfaction is made up of a number of factors, among the more important of which are pay, job security and social relations. A high level of job satisfaction should, of course, be an end in itself, but it can sometimes have other indirect benefits such as lower labour turnover and possibly lower absenteeism. On the other hand, the link between job satisfaction and work performance is extremely complex and the range of intervening variables, such as the technology and the flow of work, may mean that these two factors are unrelated.

A further possibility which cannot be totally ignored is that an interest in participation can help the image of an organisation, by indicating a concern for the workforce and a sense of social responsibility. In certain markets this can be a saleable factor; for example, Volvo, despite occasional criticism, seems to have gained considerable positive publicity from its concern with autonomous work groups. In Britain, recent 'image' advertisements for ICI have publicised the company's achievements in the field of participation.

There are, we feel, powerful positive reasons for a management interest in participation. In addition there are the more negative arguments which also have to be taken into account. The prospect of possible statutory imposition of participation makes it wise to be prepared either with a satisfactory alternative or with a framework which will ensure that any changes brought about by statute will have a positive impact.

Historically, workers have been extending their 'frontier of control'[16] by gradually eroding managerial prerogatives. This process, which has been accelerating rather than slowing in recent years, means that it is now more than ever true that effective management is only possible with the consent of the managed. Both positive and negative arguments can therefore be advanced for a management interest in participation.

Trade union interest in participation

The reasons for a trade union interest in participation are in one sense straight-forward and obvious. Trade unions seek to enhance their power and control in the workplace to enable them more effectively to protect and advance the interests of those they represent. The TUC view is that this power is weakest at the level of the company board.

While many trade unionists would accept the objective of increased power, there are deep divisions as to how it should be attained. The traditional view, still held, though for different reasons, by the electricians (EEPTU) and, with respect to private industry, by the engineers (AUEW) is that the adversary relationship of collective bargaining is the most appropriate for all issues. Any alternative would be likely to compromise trade unionists, who would find it difficult to oppose policies they themselves might have helped to formulate. Left-wing groups tend to endorse this view on the grounds that participation in the private sector helps to bolster capitalism, but it seems to find sympathy in most sections of the trade union movement.

The more recent view adopted by the TUC and supported most notably by the transport workers (T&GWU) is that, while collective bargaining will remain the major form of participation, an alternative is required to exert influence at board level. The implication of such a policy is that representatives of shareholders and workers can operate together and that the differences between capital and labour are therefore not irreconcilable. This is a major break with tradition and a marked contrast to a sole concern with collective bargaining.

A third approach, which in many respects comes closer to the CBI view, is that while an extension of participation is to be encouraged the form it takes should be left to negotiation between management and unions in each organisation. The General and Municipal Workers (GMWU) is the largest union to support this approach.

There is little doubt that the union movement is deeply divided on the subject of participation. While there is general agreement on the desirability of more power for the unions, there is far less agreement or even clarity of view on the ultimate objective, be it joint control, worker control or a continuing adversary relationship of mutual dependence. As a result of this lack of clarity, the disagreement about whether or not certain forms of participation are appropriate is likely to remain.

Some managers might welcome disagreement within the union movement. However, it can present problems in achieving managerial goals, since it will be necessary to anticipate the varieties of possible reaction; there may be differences between unions and, within any one union, between the views at national and local level. It is also important to remember that some unions are likely to oppose certain forms of participation, such as job enrichment or works councils, which, while potentially attractive to both individual workers and management, may be seen as a threat to an extension of union power and, more particularly, through fragmentation, as a threat to the maintenance of the existing power base.

Summary and conclusions

This opening chapter has outlined some of the main reasons why there has been a growing interest in participation. Six general reasons were identified. These were: the search for a new means of overcoming industrial and economic problems; the influence of membership of the European Economic Community; a change of attitude in the TUC; the rising expectations of the workforce; concern about the concentration of power in industry; and an interest in the concept of industrial democracy.

Management interest was justified on the grounds that participation could lead to improved efficiency, an easier introduction of change, improved industrial relations, greater job satisfaction and an improved organisational image. The union interest stems from a desire to extend union power and influence, but deep divisions among trade unionists about the appropriate means and ends of participation were identified.

The range of pressures and interests is such that worker participation is likely to continue as a topic for discussion and action for some time to come. However, it is clear that there is considerable confusion over means and ends in participation. There is also a danger that too much attention will be paid to participation at board level at the expense of other levels. Given the variety of forms of participation and the range of contexts and conditions within which it might be introduced, a broader perspective on the subject would seem to be desirable. A framework for such a perspective is offered in Chapter 2.

Notes

[1] *Report of the Royal Commission on Trade Unions and*

Employers' Associations 1965-68, HMSO, London, 1968.

[2] *Report of the Committee of Inquiry on Industrial Democracy*, Cmnd 6706, HMSO, London, 1977.

[3] *Industrial Democracy*, Cmnd 7231, HMSO, London, 1978.

[4] Both the Draft Directive and the draft statute for the European Company envisage worker directors on boards of large companies. However, the Fifth Directive has remained in draft form for many years due to the inability of member countries to agree its content and in 1975 a Green Paper outlining a more flexible approach was produced in an attempt to make progress.

[5] TUC, *Industrial Democracy*, London, 1974.

[6] In practice the unions have been highly suspicious of the development of shop-floor participation, particularly where it is not introduced through collective bargaining, and it remains relatively underdeveloped. For a further discussion of union views, see Chapter 14.

[7] See, for example, a report by Wilson (1973) 'On the Quality of Working Life'. Partly as a result of this report, the Work Research Unit within the Department of Employment was set up. This has a tripartite steering group and is involved in research, consultancy and advice in the broad area of job satisfaction and aspects of the quality of working life.

[8] The evidence from within the UK for this claim is rather limited. Most of the surveys suggest that many workers would like more control over factors affecting their immediate job. However this is seldom a top priority. For a fuller discussion, see Chapter 3.

[9] In theory, this is, of course, what already happens with shareholders under present company law. Employees are excluded, unless they are also shareholders and even there their influence may be extremely limited.

[10] The main sentence of the terms of reference was:

Accepting the need for a radical extension of industrial democracy in the control of companies by means of representation on boards of directors, and accepting the essential role of trade union organisations in this process, to consider how such an extension can best be achieved, taking into account in particular the proposals of the Trades Union Congress report on industrial democracy as well as experience in Britain, the E.E.C. and other countries.

[11] The nature of the CBI opposition to the White Paper seems to centre on three issues: fears about the extension of union power into the boardroom; the potential exclusion of non-union members; and the use of law to impose worker representatives on a supervisory board in the face of opposition by an employer.

[12] Op.cit., p. 41.

[13] Davis is one of several writers who would adopt a 'socio-technical systems' perspective which accepts that there is a degree of choice about how work is organised; but, at the same time, he is implying that under automated systems the choice is very limited and control must be developed.

[14] See, for example, Braverman (1974).

[15] See, for example, Walton and McKersie (1965) and their notion of integrative bargaining. From a slightly different perspective, many Organisation Development specialists would advocate a similar approach. Another kind of participative approach, albeit with a greater focus on bargaining, is offered by McCarthy and Ellis (1973) with their concept of 'predictive bargaining'.

[16] For the original development of this concept, see Goodrich (1975).

2 A Framework for Participation[1]

David Guest

Lecturer in Personnel Management, London School of Economics and Political Science

The meaning of participation

Attempts to define worker participation have often led to confusion and difficulty. Reviewing the subject, Walker and de Bellecombe (1967) noted that 'workers' participation in management is an old persistent idea with many meanings'. They go on to add that 'the basic idea is obviously that the people who are managed should have some say about the decisions that affect them'. Terms such as 'involvement', 'say', 'participation in decision-making' and 'control' abound in the many definitions that have been offered.

A further complication is a tendency to use the terms 'worker participation' and 'industrial democracy' interchangeably. In what is perhaps a fairly typical view, the British Institute of Management, in its evidence to the Bullock Committee wrote: 'Accepting the terms "industrial democracy" and "employee participation" as synonymous, we would define industrial democracy as the practice in which employees take a part in management decisions'.[2] The Bullock Report, which consistently uses the term industrial democracy, does not explore the concept in any detail but says that it is concerned with 'the need to involve employees to a greater extent in company decision-making' (p.20).

19

While one can accept the spirit and general intention of these various definitions, they do present operational problems due to their imprecision. How, for example, is it possible to demonstrate that workers are 'involved' or 'having a say'? At what point can workers be said to be taking part in management decisions? Does joint consultation, the major goal of which may be to involve the workers, count as participation? A frequent criticism is that involvement may be a means of obtaining compliance, a kind of pseudo-participation, unless it quite explicitly involves an element of control. Indeed, the concept of control is rather more precise than most of the alternatives. It is the term favoured by the TUC and can be understood in a negative form as the ability to exercise an effective veto,[3] or in a positive sense as being in a position to initiate action. Of course, participation can exist where the power of veto control is not available; however there is always the possibility of management using its dominating position to overrule opposing views. It is not surprising, therefore, to find that many workers are suspicious of schemes which do not provide them with any degree of real control.

A further issue complicating any definition of participation is the problem of participation in what? Here the concern is not just with particular substantive issues, but with a distinction which is sometimes made between decision-making and decision-taking. In practice this becomes a question of whether workers exert influence or control. Managers and their spokesmen have often expressed concern that participation might compromise the position of the manager. To maintain his accountability, it is argued, it is legitimate to encourage participation in the formulation of decisions through presentation of information and argument, but the manager alone should finally take the decision. In this sense, workers may influence management decisions through participation but they would not exert control, as management can choose whether or not to be influenced.

There are at least three forms of participation which in various ways enable workers to exert control over decisions. The example probably being most widely discussed currently is worker representation, and in particular parity representation, on a company board. A second and rather different example is found in those forms of shop-floor participation where management retains responsibility for successful operation of the plant but, for one reason or another, has delegated control of certain activities to individual workers or to groups of workers. (The management implications of these different forms of control are examined in Chapter 13.) The third and rather more complicated example is collective bargaining. It is complicated in the sense that management retains control over its decisions but joint agreement is necessary, and consequently joint control is involved in reaching a settlement. Because of this, union proposals and responses are likely to have a very real influence over related management decisions.

The debate on the problem of definition can be extended at length but the point which should emerge clearly from this short discussion is that considerable confusion has been created by imprecise definition. It will also be clear from this analysis that we are attracted to a definition of participation in terms of control. Worker participation may then be defined as the process whereby an employee is able to exert some degree of control over decisions. Both the nature of the decisions and the amount of control must be kept open for the present. The crucial point to bear in mind is that control implies some veto power.

A definition of participation in terms of control will not be popular with those who, often considering the subject from an employer's perspective, feel that the essential feature of participation is the element of 'working together', which implies a primary focus on the development of trust, co-operation and involvement in a common concern. The use of control does not deny the validity of this perspective, but it does seek to provide it with a more concrete and specific basis. Furthermore, any definition in terms of control which focuses on shared rather than unitary management control does in fact imply an inevitable interdependence: the various parties must come together to achieve their goals. Where it departs from the unitary perspective is in accepting that while there are some common interests, not all the goals of those representing capital and labour, employer and employee will be mutual or compatible.

Whatever the advantages of defining participation in terms of control, it does have limitations because it would exclude from debate a number of approaches that commonly fall within a looser definition of the concept and which, at the very least, deserve some consideration. One way which has sometimes been used to get round this is to present a participation continuum. The various forms of participation can be presented along this continuum which, using control as its dimension, can range from total managerial control at one extreme to total worker control at the other.

The use of a participation continuum has been advocated in the past by a range of writers with rather different views on the subject as a whole.[4] Some observers have noted that, while a continuum is a useful way of conceptualising participation, it does not in itself provide a definition. Furthermore, if a definition does use a concept such as control, then some of the approaches falling on the continuum could not be classified as genuine participation. Pateman (1970), for example, uses the term 'pseudo-participation' to refer to information-giving and other forms of activity where worker influence is minimal and which, at worst, might therefore be little more than sophisticated schemes of management manipulation.

Despite these limitations, a continuum does have advantages in helping to point to distinctions between forms of participation and in showing how the various forms may relate to one another along at least one relevant dimension. Using control as the dimension, it is possible to identify seven distinct points along a continuum. These can be listed as follows:

1 Total management control.
2 One-way communication from management to the workforce.

3 Two-way communication, discussion and exchange of views.

4 Limited joint decision-making over a range of topics at the discretion of management.

5 Delegated control.

6 Joint control.

7 Total worker control.

A continuum can provide a view along one dimension. However, in this context it is insufficient in itself because it fails to draw out some of the important distinctions between the various forms of participation, distinctions which are likely to have a bearing on any plans to introduce greater participation in an organisation. These distinctions relate to variations in the form, level and content of participation, each of which is examined in the next section.

The analysis of participation

The form of participation

A fundamental distinction can be made between individual and representative forms of participation. Individual participation, also known sometimes as direct or immediate participation, occurs when each worker participates by using the control available to him in his job. Representative participation, also known sometimes as indirect participation, occurs when a representative acts on behalf of a group of workers. The workers only participate through him, although they will usually have direct control over his election. The main forms of participation falling within these two categories are listed in Table 2.1.

Direct forms of participation fall into two sub-groups. First there are those primarily concerned with communication, which may be predominantly downward, as in the case of briefing groups, or predominantly upward, as in the case of attitude surveys. Out of either of these, or possibly independ-

Table 2.1

The main forms of participation

Individual	Representative
Briefing groups	Collective bargaining
Attitude surveys	Joint consultation
Problem-solving groups	Works council
Job enrichment	Worker directors
Autonomous work groups	

ently, problem-solving groups may arise. The second type of direct participation is concerned with job design, typically through the introduction of job enrichment, which provides a worker with greater control over his job, or autonomous work groups, which do the same for an interrelated set of jobs. All of these forms of individual participation are defined and discussed in some detail in Chapter 4.

One value of a focus on direct participation, particularly when it relates to job content, is that it reminds us that participation can relate to one's own job and does not necessarily need to extend to wider issues. It is also worth remembering that workers already participate, if only to a very limited extent, through the discretion provided in their job. Where the scope is felt to be too limited the worker will usually find other, often negative, means of exerting his control. Typically these may include poor quality and quantity of output, restrictive practices, individual acts of sabotage and individual forms of withdrawal such as poor time-keeping, absenteeism or even leaving the organisation.

Individual forms of participation are often designed to meet the claim that the restrictive nature of jobs or the way in which the organisational bureaucracy funtions means that many workers are not and cannot be expected to be fully involved in what they do. Furthermore, as the next chapter highlights, most surveys of attitudes towards participation show that, while workers will often favour an extension of participation through representative forms, they are nevertheless most interested in those issues directly affecting their day-to-day work, many of which might best be dealt with through individual forms of participation.

A major problem with individual forms of participation is that they can often represent a break with tradition within an organisation and can therefore be difficult to introduce. An organisation that has never had briefing groups or autonomous work groups is quite likely to need outside help in getting them off the ground. The very fact that they are novel may lead to strong opposition; and the time involved in planning, implementing and maintaining such systems may be considerable.

It will often be wise to involve relevant unions in the planning and implementation of schemes for direct participation. Nevertheless unions are often highly suspicious and sometimes strongly opposed to direct participation for two main reasons. First, it is usually introduced by management and this initiative may be sufficient in itself to raise doubts about the goals of the exercise. Second, it may appear to divert the interest of workers away from representative forms of participation and from the sources of dissatisfaction from which the unions draw part of their strength. Linked to this, the gains to be derived from direct participation are more likely to accrue to management and the workforce than to the unions as such. In short, therefore, it represents a potential wedge between the workers and their unions, raising genuine fears of a fragmentation of collective worker power and influence.

Some time has been spent discussing the implications of individual forms of participation because most of the attention of management and unions is normally directed towards the representative forms, which will consequently be more familiar. There are several reasons for the focus on representative participation. First, it deals with what both management and unions believe to be more significant issues, including many over which management will often seek to retain unilateral control. A second, closely related, reason is that it provides the unions with their major opportunity to extend their power and influence. Third, it is a more straightforward and more familiar form of participation for both sides in the sense that it often involves only the process of sitting around a table. Of course the people at that table and the nature of the issues discussed may vary considerably, but the innovations associated with an extension of representative participation may seem less complex to introduce and in a sense less strange for those involved in the representative system.

The level of participation

Three principal levels at which participation can occur in an organisation of any size can be identified. These are the levels of the shop-floor, the plant or site and the company. The distinction is useful in further highlighting the range of approaches to participation, although it is not intended to suggest that these levels are in any way mutually exclusive. Indeed, it could be argued that a comprehensive approach to participation should deliberately seek to ensure that all three levels are included. However, in practice the choice of level is likely to be determined by the goals and the content of the participation. Once the level has been decided, this in turn will help to point to the particular forms of participation that are feasible.

The use of levels to analyse participation is partly clouded by the fact that a limited number of forms of participation — including, most notably, collective bargaining — can occur at more than one level. Another obvious constraint is that not all organisations have three levels. Smaller organisations, but also some which are quite large, may have only one plant; therefore plant and company levels become merged. In contrast, large organisations may have more levels. For example, a large plant may appear to have relatively autonomous sections and large organisations may have both a central headquarters and a number of quite independent subsidiary companies or divisions. The issues thrown up by this kind of situation have been taxing the minds of those interested in participation on company boards. Organisations in the public sector may have numerous levels and there the use of 'company' level is inappropriate. One way round the problem of definition may be to use the vaguer terms, adopted by Wall and Clegg in Chapter 3, of local, medium and distant levels of participation. On the other hand the use of shop-floor, plant and company levels will be familiar to many people and in most cases will help to identify the intended distinction more precisely.

The content of participation

The final important distinction to be made in the analysis of participation helps to identify the kinds of subject-matter that might be covered. It is worth emphasising again that in practice the topics will be influenced by the goals of the various parties involved; since these are quite likely to conflict, the question of what is to be included may be a major source of contention.

A distinction can be made between what might be termed policy and executive issues. Policy issues in this sense are intended to include such things as the goals of the enterprise, what markets the company should be in, what share of the market should be achieved, what sources of financing are appropriate, where manufacturing units should be located and what sort of personnel policies on issues such as employment, equal opportunity, redundancy and, indeed, participation should be pursued. Typically, of course, such matters are settled at board level and once decided will have a considerable impact on the future direction and success of the organisation. Such decisions will have a significant, if sometimes indirect impact on the workforce but, with the exception of the personnel policies, fall within that range of issues to which management often feels worker representatives are incapable of making a useful contribution.

Within the context of these policies, executive decisions will be made. These will be concerned with ensuring the success of the policy decisions and would include issues such as the organisation and allocation of roles and the terms and conditions of employment. A further distinction may be made between executive decisions with long-term implications, such as those relating to terms and conditions of employment, and those which are directly related to task performance. In this latter category will be items arising from routine or non-routine events and often requiring an immediate response. They may arise infrequently or many times a day and will often relate to specific tasks about which a worker or a group of workers will have detailed knowledge.

Obviously hard and fast distinctions between classes of decision cannot be maintained. Nevertheless the conceptual distinction should help to clarify further the issues involved in participation. Accepting, therefore, that distinctions can be made in terms of the form, level and content of participation, and given that these are inevitably interrelated, Table 2.2 identifies and summarises the typical interrelationships.

Having looked at four separate elements in the analysis of participation, namely the dimension of control, and the form, level and content of participation, we are now able to combine these themes by locating the various forms of participation along the control continuum, as is done in Table 2.3.

Most examples of a participation continuum do not provide this level of detail.[5] However it can be argued that each category is distinct, in terms of the degree of control implied. Some confusion may arise over terminology; in particular, 'works council' is a term with many different meanings. Here it is used, in the context of the UK, to refer to a number of schemes, developed in recent years, which tend to fall somewhere between joint consultation and collective bargaining.[6]

Table 2.2

The level, content and form of participation

	Policy issues	Long-term executive issues	Immediate task-related executive issues
Company level	Worker directors; supervisory boards	Collective bargaining	
Plant level		Collective bargaining; joint consultation; works councils	
Shop-floor level		Briefing groups	Problem-solving groups; autonomous work groups; job enrichment

A continuum, while highlighting the range of forms of participation, does not, in itself, necessarily imply that one form is better than another. Also, it is perfectly possible for various forms of participation, often falling at different points on the continuum, to co-exist side by side in one organisation — for example, collective bargaining, joint consultation and information-giving are frequently to be found together. Two general historical trends may be noted, however. The first is for a greater number of forms of participation to be found in any one organisation; the second is a tendency, under growing pressure from the workforce, for the scope of participation to move towards the right of the continuum, either through the adoption of new forms, or through widening the scope of collective bargaining, or both.

This analysis of participation in terms of control over management decisions has deliberately excluded any discus-

Table 2.3

The forms of participation on the participation continuum

	I	II	III	IV	V	VI	VII
	Total management control	Unilateral communication	Bilateral communication and discussion	Limited joint decision-making	Delegated control	Joint control	Total worker control
Representative forms	The military	Information meetings	Joint consultation; minority worker directors	Works council		Parity worker directors; collective bargaining	Worker co-operatives
Individual forms	The military	Briefing groups	Attitude surveys	Problem-solving groups	Autonomous work groups; job enrichment		Worker co-operatives

sion of what is often termed financial participation. The basic aim of financial participation is for workers to share in the wealth of the company and a number of schemes have been devised to make this possible. Some of these are outlined in Chapter 10. The reason why they have been excluded from the present analysis is that such schemes do not, in practice, have anything to do with control or even involvement in decision-making. Within the definition of participation used here, they only become significant when workers own enough shares to influence the outcome of shareholders' meetings. Nevertheless there is evidence of a growing interest in financial participation among employers, employees and government.

The influence of context[7]

For practical purposes, the analysis of participation must be taken a step further. Anyone contemplating the introduction of new forms of participation is faced with a number of choices and, in considering what approach is likely to be most appropriate, there are a number of contextual factors that he should take into account. These may turn out to be facilitators or constraints, depending on the circumstances; furthermore, each situation will be unique and there may well be a number of special points which have to be taken into account in one organisation but not in others.

Three main types of contextual factor may be identified. First, there are those concerned with the nature of the organisation, including its size, structure and markets. Second, there are those represented by the individuals who constitute the potential participants. And, third, there may be certain legal influences. Each of these requires rather more detailed explanation.

Organisational factors

There are several organisational features which can point to certain approaches to participation being more or less feasible and appropriate. There is space here to consider only some of them briefly.

A first and fairly obvious influence is the size of the organisation, which can affect both the practicality and potential outcome of attempts to introduce new forms of participation.

In the first place, of course, many of the reasons for introducing or extending participation are more powerful in large organisations than in small ones, which tend to afford more freedom of action, more personal involvement and more job satisfaction. (See, e.g., Ingham, 1970.) On the one hand the large organisation is more likely to have to resort to methods of indirect participation through representatives for a wide range of important decisions, but, at the same time, there is a need to provide means of direct involvement at the workgroup level, so as to regain some of the advantages of the small organisation.

Unfortunately, both these needs can also be more difficult to fulfil effectively in a large organisation. One danger is that, in seeking to impose a uniform system of participation across several units, it succeeds only in setting up a bureaucratic and over-rigid system. It may be difficult to ensure that contact between representatives and the workforce is maintained, particularly if participation occurs at board level. In West Germany, the problem of communication between worker representatives on supervisory boards and the workforce has sometimes meant that special jobs have been created with the primary objective of maintaining some sort of contact and dialogue. A planned extension of participation at board level also raises questions about whether the scheme should involve both main and subsidiary boards and how inter-union problems should be tackled. Finally, anxieties about precedents and comparisons across the organisation might lead some large companies to resist flexible forms of shop-floor participation, particularly if pay increases are involved. Several of the cases which follow highlight the problems and issues faced by large organisations in seeking to develop worker participation and point to different ways of seeking to resolve them.

A second influence, which may be linked to size, is the nature of the technology. Mass production assembly lines, for example, have often been viewed as a significant constraint on the development of shop-floor participation. The classic example of this is the car production line, with its repetitive and highly prescribed jobs. Even a company like Volvo, which made a determined attempt to alleviate some of the constraints of the production line in an effort to reduce labour turnover and absenteeism, found that a significant increase in shop-floor participation entailed building a completely new factory.

Over the years there have been many studies of the impact of technology on job satisfaction and alienation (see for example Blauner, 1964) and on organisation structure (Woodward, 1965, 1970). The danger of both these approaches is that they can lead to a form of technological determinism, which encourages the view that the technology is the dominant organisational influence, should be taken as given and should determine the nature of jobs in the organisation. In practice there is no need for this view; the car production line is an extreme and untypical example of the production process and in most circumstances there is scope for flexibility both in the organisation structure and in the design and allocation of tasks. A rather small and decreasing proportion of the workforce work on production lines; indeed, it may be more relevant to focus attention on the newer problem of the office 'production system'.

Those particularly concerned with technology as a constraint have usually focused on the problem of shop-floor participation. It does not pose the same kind of constraint in the case of participation at other levels. However, while technology may limit the opportunity to take decisions on the shop-floor, at plant and board levels it may influence the range of possible policy decisions. Furthermore, from a slightly different perspective, technical knowledge or the lack of it may impose limitations on the opportunity for many people, at all levels, to participate.

Technology can clearly be an important influence on the scope for developing participation, but rather than accepting the technology as given, a more useful approach is to view both the technology and the social organisation of work as flexible but interdependent. Known as the socio-technical systems approach, this is discussed in more detail in Chapter 4.

A third organisational influence on participation is the nature of the product, be it goods or services, and therefore the nature of the product market. Burns and Stalker (1961) have drawn a distinction between what they term mechanistic and organic organisations. With a stable product market, a conventional bureaucratic or mechanistic structure seems to work well. But with a volatile, swiftly changing market, a formal bureaucracy is too slow to respond, and they argue therefore that a flexible and loosely structured organisation is more effective.

The implications for participation are that in certain market conditions a formal system of participation through representative committees may not be able to deal with a range of issues which require a swift response. Indeed, no management committee, meeting at fixed intervals, would be able to deal with this type of situation. On the other hand it may encourage devolved decision-making and an extension of direct forms of participation. In short, the product market may influence and constrain the form of participation that is likely to be most effective in dealing with certain types of decision.

A fourth set of influences covers a range of social factors. For example, account must be taken of the goals and values of the various interest groups within an organisation. Apart from senior management and the different groups which make up the workforce, these will usually include shareholders, middle and junior managers and various unions. External interest groups, such as customers and government and its agencies, may also have to be considered. Each, from its own point of view, may have a valid interest in supporting various approaches to participation and opposing others. For example, as the case studies from Philips (Chapter 6) and ICI

(Chapter 9) indicate, the often powerful group of craft workers may be opposed to forms of individual participation which allow less skilled workers to encroach on some of their traditional tasks. The interest groups will have various sources of power and the realities of the distribution of power will be an important influence in the success of any innovations.

Quite apart from the distribution of power, there are a number of cultural factors which may influence what is feasible. The history of the organisation and its image in the eyes of its employees and the public at large may make certain developments more or less likely. For example, traditions of paternalism or conflict cannot be changed overnight. Linked to these factors, the current organisational climate, and more particularly the industrial relations climate, will influence the amount of confidence, openness and trust that exists. These in turn can help to explain why in one organisation works councils, for example, are welcomed by the workforce as a genuine attempt to increase participation on the part of management, while in another they are viewed as yet another illustration of management manipulation and are probably doomed to failure.

Individual factors

Individual influences on participation can be divided into two types: those associated with the capacity of individuals to participate, and those associated with their inclination or motivation to participate.

While there is little doubt that the majority of workers are quite capable of tackling jobs which make greater demands on their intellectual capacity than those they are engaged in, there are obviously limits to this. Quite clearly not all shop-floor workers or even all trade union representatives are equally capable of making a contribution to discussions at board level. It is at the more familiar level of their own job that most workers would probably want to participate more. But here, too, there are limits. For example a study by Pym (1965) of the introduction of a form of work flexibility in shoe manufacturing, which meant that each worker had to be able to produce several different types of footwear instead of just one or two, showed that some workers were unable to cope with these demands.

Under the second category of individual constraint, certain types of worker can be identified who, because of their personality, attitude or motivation, may not want to participate. The evidence is by no means clear or consistent, and measurement is always difficult, but it does suggest that those who prefer strong leadership and clear authority, those who believe that they personally cannot exert much influence over their lives and those lacking in self-confidence may be less willing to participate at any level in the organisation. The evidence also indicates that, for whatever reason, interest in participation has in the past been lower among women and among the less well-educated.[7]

The question of motivation is more complex, but in general it can be argued that workers will only be motivated to participate when they feel that they will derive some benefit from so doing. This raises the question of the goals and values held by the workers. Before seeking to involve workers in any form of participation, advocates of the scheme, amongst both management and unions, would be well advised to find out, through interviews, attitude surveys or whatever means seem appropriate, what these goals and values are. Second, they should try to find out whether the scheme significantly increases or decreases their chances of attainment. In this way it should become easier to anticipate whether the scheme will be supported, opposed or regarded with apathy.

Legal influences

The issue of legal influences does not need much development. The simple point is that existing and potential legislation may require participation to develop in certain ways. Already legislation such as the Health and Safety at Work Act limits participation on safety committees in many organisations to union members.

The EEC Fifth Directive, if it ever reaches the statute books, seems likely to require some sort of action at board level. The 1978 government White Paper, while being fairly flexible, may lead to legislation requiring some positive action on participation. There is little doubt that the possibility of legal enforcement has been one of the more potent factors stimulating the current debate on participation.

The practical implications of the framework for participation

One reason for presenting the analysis and framework described in this chapter is that it can help to clarify many of the issues involved in any attempt to understand what participation is. At the same time it may provide a broader view of the potential forms of participation.

A second and more practical purpose is to provide a framework within which to analyse the potential for the extension or introduction of participation in an organisation. It is impossible to provide any clear and specific guidelines because each situation is unique and often, in practice, several choices are available and feasible. Furthermore the development of schemes for participation is usually evolutionary, adapting to changing circumstances and to the enthusiasms and goals of the major interest groups. There is therefore no 'right' answer to the questions of whether to extend participation and, if so, in what form.

There are, nevertheless, a number of issues which it will usually be helpful to consider in any organisation. A useful first step is for those initiating change to clarify their goals and to identify the range of goals which other influential interest groups are likely to possess. This in turn will help to identify the potential subject matter or content of any participation. At the same time it is essential to analyse the current organisational context and the range of factors described in the previous section. This will highlight existing forms of participation; where these are working well it would be unwise to consider new forms which undermine them in any way. In general, radical innovations will be treated with suspicion and it will be safer and easier to build on existing good practices. In this sense, the process whereby the appropriate forms of participation are decided and the process of implementation, which forms one of the themes of this book, are inevitably interlinked. The range of choices — including, of course, the possible decision not to extend participation — can only be fully understood in the context of specific cases, a number of which are presented in the following chapters. However, without some framework for analysis and diagnosis it will be more difficult to decide, on a sensible basis, whether participation is an appropriate strategy, and the outcome may well fail to live up to expectations.

Summary

The first section of this chapter examines the meaning of participation, arguing that many of the conventional definitions are too loose and that there are advantages in using a definition based on the concept of control. A continuum of participation, using control as its dimension and outlining seven points from total management control to total worker control, was presented.

The second section presents an analysis of participation, using three major distinctions. The first distinction is between individual and representative forms of participation, the second between shop-floor, plant and company levels and the third between policy and executive issues which constitute the content of participation. The various forms of participation are placed along the continuum.

The third section explores some of the factors influencing the decision to extend participation. Four organisational issues are identified; size, technology, product market and social and cultural factors. Individual factors are also emphasised and in particular the influence of capacity to participate and willingness to participate. Finally, the role of law is briefly discussed.

The final section raises some issues concerning the practical steps involved in the introduction of participation. It argues that, although each situation is unique and there is invariably a choice of feasible approaches, use of a framework for analysis and diagnosis can assist in identifying the most appropriate means by which to put participation into practice.

Notes

[1] A further exploration of many of the issues discussed in this chapter can be found in Guest and Fatchett (1974).

[2] BIM evidence to the Bullock Committee, paragraph 4.

[3] This is close to the participative role for unions advocated by the Electricians and Plumbers Union (EEPTU), which believes that the strength of participation is reflected in the ability, through collective bargaining, to say 'No', and thereby have an impact.

[4] See for example McGregor (1960), Likert (1967), Blumberg (1968) and Fox (1971).

[5] There are notable exceptions to this. See for example the six-step continuum used by Clarke, Fatchett and Roberts (1973).

[6] For a fuller account see Chapter 8.

[7] For a more detailed account of these influences, particularly the individual influences, see Guest and Fatchett (1974), Chapter 8 and 9.

3 Who wants participation?

Toby D. Wall

Research Fellow, Medical Research Council Social and Applied Psychology Unit, University of Sheffield

Chris W. Clegg

Research Fellow, Medical Research Council Social and Applied Psychology Unit, University of Sheffield

The main political parties, the TUC, individual trade unions, the CBI, and many significant national lobbies have made public their respective positions on the question of participation. Doubtless theirs will be the major influence on future legislative developments in this area. Less well understood, however, are the positions of workers, shop stewards and managers. Yet these are the people who will implement and live with any participative system and who will determine the quality of its operation. In this chapter we consider the views of these three groups, and explore how enabling them to make their opinions explicit may be used as a vehicle for putting participation into practice.

Employee attitudes towards participation

Shop-floor attitudes

From a fact-finding mission to several countries, including England, Israel and Australia, M. Derber, a Professor of Labour and Industrial Relations in America, reported that 'in none of the countries I visited was there much evidence of widespread or intense worker interest in participation in management decision-making, even at the shop floor or departmental level' (1970, p. 133). In contrast, an analysis of empirical evidence led Pateman (1970) to conclude that 'there is, at present, a widespread desire among many different categories of workers for [shop-floor] participation' (p. 56). Paradoxically, both statements contain a strong element of truth. On the one hand there is little evidence of an *active* grass-roots *demand* for participation making its presence felt. On the other hand, participation involves certain values to which the majority of employees subscribe and which are often accompanied by a general awareness that the old-fashioned autocratic ways of managing work are no longer appropriate. In broad terms, the answer to the question, 'Are workers demanding participation?', is no; while the answer to the question, 'Would workers like participation?', is yes. Indeed the idea that management (or workers) should have complete control over all decision-making is typically rejected. This is well illustrated in a study by Brannen et al. (1976), who found that only 11.3 per cent of their sample of British Steel employees agreed with the statement that 'management alone should make decisions', and only 2.2 per cent with the proposition that 'workers should control the plant'. More than four out of five felt control should rest between these two extremes, with the majority giving management the balance of power.

It should not be concluded, however, that this is simply a manifestation of some general prevailing democratic ethic. A more specific analysis reveals that the extent of individuals' desires for control varies *depending on the particular decision in question*. Not surprisingly the strongest desire is for shop-floor participation. Studies have repeatedly shown that most individuals want considerable control over their day-to-day work and the decisions which affect it (see for example Hespe and Wall, 1976; Ramsay, 1976). Indeed recognition of this interest has formed the basis of many approaches to management and organisation theory (e.g., Likert, 1967; McGregor, 1967; Argyris, 1964), as well as to job design (e.g. Herzberg,

1966). It is at this level that workers feel they have the know-ledge to contribute and can see the immediate relevance of par-ticipation. Nevertheless, many workers also favour participation at higher organisational levels. Here there typi-cally exists less emphasis on personal involvement and con-trol, and more on representation. Many individuals like to know that access to company- or corporate-level decision-making exists, and that some of their number are watching over their interests at this level.

Within these boundaries, however, there is little possibility of reaching finer judgements about the nature of workers' atti-tudes. Different investigations have yielded conflicting find-ings. There is in fact more evidence of variability than consensus. In part this is because participation is not an issue about which many have extensive knowledge, nor one on which they have developed detailed and consistent opinions. In short, it is not high on the list of priorities. But complexity also results from the fact that individuals' views, quite under-standably, vary from situation to situation, and from decision area to decision area. Those in jobs severely constrained by technology, for example, may see little scope for personal con-trol over their work and therefore may not express a desire for it. At the same time, interest in top-level participation may be heightened when the poor commercial performance of a plant threatens its future. The point is that local circumstances and conditions affect the nature of workers' views on participation and this, from a practical point of view, is more important than any number of generalisations. We develop this theme later, but first some comments on the views of shop stewards and managers are appropriate.

Shop stewards' and managers' opinions

Two recent, as yet unpublished, surveys serve to confirm a num-ber of generalisations about shop stewards' attitudes towards participation (Bye and Fisher, 1977; Ursell et al., 1977). For many stewards there exists a dilemma. On the one hand they support the objective of increasing control for non-managerial employees, and welcome initiatives on participation for this reason. On the other hand, they are anxious that current industrial relations machinery should in no way be weakened or compromised, and feel that participation in management might represent such a threat. Most, therefore, opt for participation in terms of extending the range of issues encompassed by collective bargaining at the same time as increasing the amount of information available to them through greater consultation, both of which they see as strengthening the union's position. Consistent with this is their hostility to non-unionised workers being represented in any participative system. As with workers, however, there exists a wide range of opinions within this broad framework. These vary according to existing union-management relations, the policy of the union in question and the issues and individuals involved. Once again this level of variability leads to the conclusion that for practical purposes more detailed knowledge of local conditions is essential.

Nor are managers' attitudes as easy to characterise as some stereotypical descriptions might have one believe. A recent survey in England and Wales (Clegg et al., 1977) reveals that there is no such thing as a single managerial perspective on participation. Instead, three general orientations emerge, each of which covers approximately one-third of the managers sampled. The first holds that participation is an unwarranted intrusion upon managerial prerogatives and is to be avoided, since it will have no substantial effect on efficiency. For managers holding this view, demands for participation are seen as attempts to wrest more power from its 'rightful owners', anything more than consultation being anathema to them. A second perspective holds participation to be an essential means of improving communications and of achieving such pragmatic goals as increasing efficiency and reducing conflict. The focus of participation here is on shop-floor activities such as production-oriented meetings between groups of workers and their management and supervision, as well as on job-redesign schemes aimed at utilising the untapped skills and knowledge of the workforce. The third perspective goes one stage further: Not only is participation seen as a means to various practical ends on the shop floor, but also as a way of sharing power (and responsibility) at higher levels in the organisation. Managers of this persuasion believe that workers, through their representatives, have a right to a say in the decisions made at plant and corporate level. Whilst these three managerial groups hold significantly different perspectives on participation, one view is common: that non-unionised workers have the same rights to representation as do union members, a view conflicting directly with that held by shop stewards.

From opinion to practice

In our cameos of worker, shop steward and manager attitudes towards participation we have emphasised the wide range of opinion usually found. Such trends as one is able to discern are too general to be of much practical significance for those wishing to develop a more participative method of management. This range of attitudes both within and between the different interest groups suggests that no simple universal approach to participation can be successfully adopted. It is our contention, therefore, that legislative initiatives will not be able to cover all organisational contingencies except in the broadest terms. This means that the realities of participation will depend to a large degree on *organisations developing their own way forward within the framework of law and additional to it.* In the remainder of this chapter we argue that a survey-feedback exercise provides a useful starting point for the development of such organisation-specific participative systems, using illustrations from a case study.

The survey-feedback approach

The very notion of participation is one which encompasses the principle of interested parties joining in the decision-making which guides their collective activities. It seems axiomatic, therefore, that the introduction of a participative system should be a joint venture from the outset. The imposition of a system by any one interest group, from inside or outside an organisation, is not likely to encourage the commitment required to overcome the difficulties it will encounter, especially during its formative period.

The problem, of course, is how to initiate the debate on participation. One strategy is to conduct an organisation-wide survey in order to establish the principal interests of those likely to be involved, and to identify common ground on which participation can be developed. Such a survey, if carried out with the explicit aim of trying to develop a participative system, can provide very rich data about people's views, as they respond in the knowledge that what they say may have practical significance, rather than being of purely 'academic' interest. This will only be the case, of course, if the survey itself it seen as open and above-board, and one to whose results all will have access. Here the involvement of a 'third party' trusted by all interest groups can be invaluable. More than just publicising the issue and obtaining information, however, a well-designed survey can serve an *educational function*. On a subject such as participation this is an important point requiring further elaboration.

Few people, especially those working on the shop floor, have a clear idea about which decisions are made at what levels within their employing organisations. Nor are their ideas on participation well developed, particularly with respect to alternative modes of involvement. These knowledge deficiencies can to some extent be overcome by a survey which asks for people's views on specific decisions (identified as being made at different levels within *their* organisation) and which provides a shortlist of participative approaches. In other words, the survey is designed to reflect the important areas of decision-making and the alternative methods of participation which are feasible. There are dangers. It is clear that such a survey *could* omit reference to issues on which its designers did not want or recognise the need for answers. To ensure that no single party has ultimate control over the range of issues to be covered, the design of the survey must itself be a matter involving representatives of all the interested parties.

Thus a survey can effectively serve three purposes: (a) raise the issues for debate; (b) provide the information necessary for people to express their views; and (c) yield a picture of respondents' opinions which can guide the design of a participative system, or at least provide a framework for further debate. Moreover, if all parties collaborate in its design as suggested, such a method can be a fine example of collective action with which to begin.

Survey feedback: a case study

A case study using this survey-feedback approach serves to put flesh on the skeleton. The organisation in question was the recreation department of a local authority which the researchers approached, along with a number of other organisations, outlining their interest in participation. In fact these research interests closely matched the needs of the department and both parties anticipated a mutually beneficial relationship. Following exploratory discussions and interviews, workers, supervisors and managers[1] helped in the design of a questionnaire, advising on the terminology to be employed and the issues of interest and controversy to be included. The questionnaire was designed to cover a representative sample of decisions made at three clearly identifiable organisational levels, local, medium and distant, which correspond approximately to those of shop-floor, plant and company level as described in Chapter 2 (pp. 26-7). Each decision area chosen for the questionnaire was accompanied by a number of specific examples.

For each of the decisions respondents were asked to indicate:

(a) the level of influence workers *should* have compared with management;
(b) the level of influence workers in practice had compared

with management; and

(c) which of several alternative methods of participation they preferred.

The results of the first part of the survey are summarised in Table 3.1. They show the average amount of influence workers desired and perceived at each of the three levels of organisational decision-making, as well as in relation to a particular issue of interest to this group, the bonus scheme. Looking first at local-level decisions, most respondents expressed a preference for 'considerable' or 'complete' control. With respect to current practice there existed a divergence of opinion, but it is evident that the degree of influence workers perceived themselves as exerting over these decisions fell below the level they would like.

Workers' attitudes towards their influence at medium level were extremely consistent across the different decisions sampled, the majority seeking equal influence with management but reporting that in practice they had none. The discrepancy between actual and desired participation was much greater at this than at local level. Much the same pattern was revealed for distant-level decisions. Regarding the bonus scheme, a comparable picture emerged, though both the degree of participation sought and the amount seen as existing were higher. It is apparent that most of these employees wished for more influence in decision-making than they had in practice.

The next question concerned the way such influence should be exercised. At the medium and distant levels a number of alternatives were available, three of which were sufficiently familiar to the respondents to be included in the questionnaire. The three methods were: through direct personal contact, using the works committee, and through the shop stewards. The choices made by the respondents are summarised in Table 3.2.

At medium level the most popular method was through direct contact between workers and managers, whilst the works committee was favoured most for distant-level decisions. Not surprisingly, collective bargaining through the

Table 3.1*

Workers' desired and perceived influence in organisational decision-making

	Desired influence					Perceived influence				
	None	Slight	Moderate	Considerable	Complete	None	Slight	Moderate	Considerable	Complete
LOCAL-LEVEL (Average across 5 decision areas)	4%	5%	21%	29%	41%	24%	15%	25%	18%	17%
MEDIUM-LEVEL (Average across 5 decision areas)	None	Hardly any	Less than management	Same as management	More than management	None	Hardly any	Less than management	Same as management	More than management
	15%	6%	13%	55%	11%	78%	9%	7%	5%	1%
DISTANT-LEVEL (Average across 4 decision areas)	None	Hardly any	Less than management	Same as management	More than management	None	Hardly any	Less than management	Same as management	More than management
	14%	4%	18%	60%	4%	81%	8%	8%	4%	0%
BONUS SCHEME	None	Hardly any	Less than management	Same as management	More than management	None	Hardly any	Less than management	Same as management	More than management
	5%	4%	9%	64%	18%	53%	21%	8%	18%	0%

*Adapted from Wall and Lischeron (1977).

Table 3.2*

Desired form of participation in organisational
decision-making

| | Direct | Indirect | |
	Personal contact	Works committee	Union stewards
MEDIUM-LEVEL (Average across 5 decision areas)	% 50	% 27	% 23
DISTANT-LEVEL (Average across 4 decision areas)	26	46	28
BONUS SCHEME	21	23	56

*Adapted from Wall and Lischeron (1977).

shop stewards was seen by most as the appropriate way of dealing with issues related to the bonus scheme.

The attitudes of the supervisors and managers serve to complete the picture. They were asked to indicate the degree to
which workers should have influence in each of the specified
decision areas, as well as the level of influence currently
exerted in each. Their views closely mirrored those of their subordinates, their conclusions being that workers should have a
strong influence in decision-making at all levels. In particular
they recognised that involvement in medium- and distant-
level decisions fell well below that which should obtain. When
asked for a choice of method their preference was for direct
contact between themselves and workers for both medium
and distant participation.

In general, then, the survey revealed a commitment to participation from all interested parties and general agreement that
current practice was far removed from their ideal. At this stage

the problem became one of deciding what action should be taken. The results of the survey were used as a starting point in discussions held between groups of workers, their supervisors and managers. Initially these served to substantiate the survey findings, with all parties reaffirming their support for participation in decision-making. Support also emerged for the view that it was at the medium and distant levels of decision-making that worker influence should be increased. Discussion shifted to consideration of the form most appropriate for this type of participation. Few thought informal day-to-day personal contact would suffice; instead preference was expressed for regular meetings between small groups of workers and relevant members of management. It was intended that such meetings would complement the existing shop steward organisation by allowing easier access to all types of information. The term coined to denote this participative system was 'Action Planning Groups'.

It is not our intention to describe in detail the terms of reference for this system although a brief summary is appropriate. In practice fifteen groups were instituted, meeting for an average of one hour every three weeks during work time. Meetings comprised 6-14 men, their immediate supervisor, the area manager, other members of the organisation as invited, and a 'third party' (one of the research team) in the role of advisor, counsellor and arbiter. Initially people were given *carte blanche* to raise any item they wished on the understanding, agreed by management, that any question would receive an answer either on the spot or at the very next meeting. The meetings avoided personality issues and, with some effort, moved away from individual grievances. Items that were appropriate to the role of the trade union were re-channelled into the industrial relations system, to the satisfaction of the shop stewards. Once the new system had settled down, meetings more or less fulfilled the purpose for which they were designed: i.e., giving workers access to higher levels of decision-making. For example, groups asked for and received information about the maintenance of machinery, the supply of equipment and raw materials, the bonus scheme, protective clothing, training for new recruits, the possibilities for and policies on promotion, and so on. As newly disclosed information became available to groups, many novel suggestions were proferred, many of which were implemented. A number of policy and budget decisions were also altered as a result of discussions in the groups.

In this context the important feature of this system was that it was jointly developed by the interested parties *to meet their own requirements*. This is not to imply that all was plain sailing. Feelings within the department polarised in terms of 'them' and 'us' and such a joint diagnosis of the problems required more effort on the part of all concerned than would have been the case with an imposed system. In particular it required substantial commitment in the face of considerable uncertainty. On the positive side this type of approach did increase the chances of success. For this system the most obvious successes were that it actually started (how many don't), it achieved a voluntary attendance rate of over 90 per cent, and the method was subsequently adopted by another part of the same organisation. Examination of the topics discussed reveals interest in a wide range of decision areas, many of which were acted upon to improve the work-life of the participants and the effectiveness of the organisation.

Unfortunately three years after Action Planning Groups were instituted in the recreation department, the system had decayed to the extent that meetings were almost never convened. Nevertheless it fared better in the other department, where the system was still functioning two years after it was implemented, with either management or the shop floor having the right to call a meeting and using it. There are a number of factors contributing to the long-term failure of one system and the success of another: the rate of change of personnel, the personal commitment of the managers involved, the integration of the new system with other decision-making institutions, and the 'ownership' of the problems and the system.

(For a detailed analysis of the problems the systems encountered, their successes and failures, and the various ways in which they developed, see Wall and Lischeron, 1977.)

Two final points need stressing. The first is that the outcomes of this kind of approach are likely to be quite varied, based as they are on the unique mix of strengths and weaknesses to be found in different situations. For example, in a more strongly unionised organisation, one can expect a stronger emphasis on the trade union as the main channel of communication, and as a main instrument of problem-solving. The second point is equally important. We implied earlier that people's attitudes to participation tend to be general and rather passive. After experience of participation schemes, however, their views become clearer (though not necessarily stronger). For example, in the case described above, the majority of the participants became committed to and positive about their new system, 91 per cent of them recommending that other groups in the local authority should institute Action Planning Groups.

Summary

We have argued that whilst the political process may lay down the rules for participation, the quality of the game lies in the hands of the players: the managers, shop stewards and workers. This will be the case however prescriptive the legislation, in that there will always be room for local initiatives, either in choosing how to meet legislative requirements or in developing new practices over and above them.

Our brief review of attitudes has revealed considerable variety both within and between groups of workers, shop stewards and managers. Whilst surveys on participation may be an appropriate way of testing the range of opinion, they do not solve the practical problems for particular organisations of what to do next.

Recognising the variety of attitudes expressed, we have described one way of using the situation to initiate discussions on participation within individual organsations. In our example a detailed and highly specific attitude survey was used to help diagnose the problems of employees in one part of a large organisation. The results of the survey, which itself was designed co-operatively, were used as the basis of discussions among the interested parties that led to the design and implementation of a system tailored to meet their needs.

This process has three principal characteristics. First, the emphasis is as much on *how* changes are achieved as on *what* is changed. Next, it is highly *pragmatic*, by being based on the problems existing in the organisation at that time. And, third, it is liable to lead to *incremental* changes in so far as it builds on shared ground. To those seeking more fundamental changes, this strategy might seem conservative and would probably only be acceptable within the context of government legislation laying down a stringent set of minimum requirements. The point here is that in either event the strategy we have successfully employed would still be an appropriate way of finding out who wants participation, together with what they mean by it.

Note

[1] The organisation was only partially unionised, and at this stage shop stewards did not feel the need to contribute other than as ordinary members of the workforce.

Part II
Shop-floor participation

This section deals with ways of establishing participation directly at the place of work. Chapter 4 reviews the different forms such participation can take and some of the issues raised by them. The range of environments covered in the next three chapters highlights the diversity of contexts in which shop-floor participation can operate: Chapter 5 shows that briefing groups, often seen purely as a means of downward communication, can provide a useful way in to other forms of participation through a 'bottom-up' approach; job design and autonomous work groups are exemplified by Chapters 6 and 7. The Philips case in Chapter 6 is typical of many such applications in being concerned with manufacturing and assembly work — less typically it gives a full and frank account of the problems and obstacles which such an application can come up against in practice. Chapter 7 helps to provide a broader perspective by showing that job design need not be confined to basic manufacturing and clerical operations, but can encompass a much wider range, including selling, estimating, design and installation. All three of these examples underline the importance of the personal initiative of a manager in getting a scheme under way.

4 Participation at shop floor level

David Guest

Lecturer in Personnel Management, London School of Economics and Political Science

Introduction

Participation at the level of the shop or office floor has been rather overshadowed, in the public debate, by the current concern of government, TUC and CBI for the seemingly larger stakes involved in company-level participation. There is, however, considerable evidence[1] that workers are more interested in participation as it affects their own jobs and working environments than in the less tangible and less immediate issues of the boardroom. It therefore seems both sensible and potentially beneficial to consider introducing participation at this level.

An essential feature of shop-floor participation is that it is individual, or direct, in the sense that each worker has an opportunity to participate for himself rather than through a representative. The best-known forms of participation falling into this category are autonomous work groups and job enrichment, both concerned with the design of jobs. Most countries in Western Europe and North America now have semi-official bodies concerned with the general issues of job satisfaction and the quality of working life and these have placed considerable emphasis on job design. In the UK this role is filled by the Work Research Unit, located in the Department of Employment, but with a tripartite steering group.

Apart from changes in job design, other forms of individual participation which deserve consideration include opinion surveys, briefing groups, problem-solving groups and suggestion schemes. As Chapter 2 indicated, it might also be sensible to consider restrictive practices as a form of individual participation, albeit of a protective rather than a positive kind. But since it is unlikely to be a tactic which management would seek to develop it will not be considered here; those interested may find a discussion of restrictive practices and participation in Guest and Fatchett (1974), Chapter 5.

Although opinion surveys, briefing groups, problem-solving groups and suggestion schemes are, as we have said, individual forms of participation in the sense that every worker has a chance of expressing his own views and participating for himself rather than through a representative, the kind of issues they cover may relate to policy and practice at shop-floor, plant or company level. This is particularly true of information passed down by briefing groups or the views passed up in opinion surveys. However, since many of the concerns arising in these forms of participation do relate to the work process and conditions of work and, since the location of the participative activity is at or very near the work-station, these forms of participation are discussed here in the chapter on approaches at the level of the shop floor.

The next section of this chapter offers a short analysis of opinion surveys, problem-solving groups, and briefing groups. Suggestion schemes are not discussed, but it is worth noting in passing that many organisations find them useful as a means of encouraging direct contributions from the workforce. A variation which is sometimes used is a form of 'speak up' programme through which people may give opinions, anonymously if they prefer, on company policy and practice.

The second half of the chapter examines job enrichment and autonomous work groups in rather more detail. This is justified on the grounds that changes in job design may often have considerable significance for workers since they imply permanent alterations to working patterns. In this sense they provide a permanent extension of participation. Other forms of participation may result in permanent and significant change, but the *process* of participation is always temporary. Furthermore changes in job content are the only uniquely shop-floor forms of participation.

Opinion surveys

Opinion surveys provide a swift, systematic and inexpensive means of obtaining views from the workforce on a range of issues. They can be used, for example, to consult the workforce on a particular issue. A company which was about to move its office from one part of the country to another used an opinion survey to find out how many employees were likely to move, what factors they were taking into account in deciding whether or not to move and what the issues were to which they would like the company to give special attention. While some organisations use an opinion survey only once, others, of which the best known is probably IBM, have used them over a number of years as a means of monitoring employee satisfaction.

The case for using an opinion survey needs careful consideration; in particular the objectives should be clear. Some of the reasons for using an opinion survey have already been hinted at, but a fuller list might include the need to:

(a) gather information on reactions to plans and policies;
(b) monitor job satisfaction and morale;
(c) identify problems;
(d) consult employees on a wide range of matters;
(e) obtain information as a basis for problem-solving, participation and change.[2]

From this list, it can be seen that opinion surveys are essentially a means of information-gathering and consultation. The use to which that information is put determines how far they are used as a form of participation. In most cases, it is likely that they will be used as a complementary form of participation rather than as a substitute for something that already exists. Indeed, any attempt to use them as a substitute is likely to meet opposition and possibly limit their validity.[3]

Organisations considering the use of opinion surveys should take account of a number of important factors:

1 Unions and worker representatives should be consulted, otherwise there is danger of resentment and opposition to what may look like an attempt to usurp their role. This may lead to non-co-operation, resulting in a low and biased response.

2 The design of opinion surveys requires expertise, in particular as regards method (interview versus questionnaire), content, layout, length, analysis and interpretation.[4] Sometimes it will be necessary to bring in help from outside and this can have the additional advantage of ensuring impartiality.

3 Opinion surveys raise expectations. The objectives should therefore be made absolutely clear, as should the uses to which the information will be put. Feedback of results should be provided wherever possible, since failure to meet expectations can have a damaging impact on morale and possibly on industrial relations.

4 It is often possible to obtain reliable information by sampling a proportion of the workforce. But where the primary aim is consultation or feedback discussions as a basis for participation, there are advantages in including everyone in the survey.

In conclusion, opinion surveys can be a useful means of information-gathering and consultation. However, like most kinds of information, their chief value for participation will often lie in the use which is made of the results, as is illustrated by the case study in Chapter 3.

Problem-solving groups

A number of organisations have taken steps to involve workers in the identification, analysis and solution of a range of job-related problems. A total work group may be involved or, when this results in too large a number, sub-groups may be created.[5] Out of these groups, a representative group may be formed to tackle issues at plant level. The central aim of a problem-solving group is to provide a forum for communication, problem-identification and discussion, so that varying points of view may be better understood and a climate created in which problem-resolution is tackled constructively. Although almost anything which does not impinge too directly on collective bargaining may be raised and discussed, the focus will normally be on the day-to-day shop-floor problems which make the worker's job more difficult and less satisfying. This is based on the assumption that the individual who carries out a job is in a good position to comment on it. Since many of the problems and issues raised are likely to affect performance, managers obviously hope that improved efficiency will be one of the outcomes. Normally, another management objective will be to provide an opportunity to discuss the kinds of changes which are more or less feasible and desirable. Once workers understand the reasons for changes and are able to help in shaping them and once managers understand workers' fears and anxieties, it is hoped that both the process whereby the changes are discussed and introduced and their outcomes will be more effective.

Typically, meetings will occur at regular intervals as appropriate. Initially, fairly frequent meetings may be required as a mass of issues are raised, but after a while they may be reduced from perhaps once every two weeks to once every one or two months. The meetings can take place at either the beginning or end of the work day or perhaps for a period of one hour over lunch. Some retail shops have a regular day each week on which they open an hour late. This hour may be used for training, communication or for problem-solving meetings.

An initial difficulty in setting up this kind of participation can be the identification of problems and the development of useful discussion in the early meetings. One way of overcoming these problems may be to use an opinion survey at the outset and to use the groups to feed back and discuss the results and their implications. It may be profitable in the early stages to use some sort of outside help; certainly it is important, as the experience at Philips described in Chapter 5 indicates, to give considerable attention to the way in which the group develops in the early stages, when patterns of behaviour and the expectations associated with them become established.

Whether or not outside help is used, once those involved become accustomed to the way in which the groups work, sufficient issues are likely to be raised from within the group. The type of issues raised will normally relate to production problems, problems of equipment and working conditions and the difficulties created by various rules, regulations and procedures. Additionally there are likely to be many requests for information.

Examples of this kind of approach or variations on it are presented in Chapters 3 and 6. Another fairly widely known illustration is the work of the National Ports Council in Fred Olsen Limited and the Port of London Authority.[6] It may well be an approach which is particularly suited to the kinds of job which contain elements of variability and unpredictability, both because of their intrinsic content and because of contact with customers, clients or the general public.

A brief outline of this form of participation is sufficient to indicate that its roots lie to some extent in the human relations approach to change. It assumes an integrative view of worker-management relations — that is, that workers and management can work together, constructively, to solve mutual problems. Trade unions might claim that this weakens their bargaining position by removing delays to production without providing a financial return. For this reason it is vital that the unions should be involved in setting up these groups. At the very least the groups should have union approval and care should be taken to avoid getting involved too deeply in issues more properly settled through collective bargaining. The involvement might usefully go further since experience suggests that shop stewards are normally very helpful group members.

In addition to union approval, the other crucial factor for the success of this approach is management support. Some managers feel that supervisors should obviate the need for problem-solving groups by identifying and resolving the kind of issues they throw up. While this may occasionally be true, and while supervisors should always be closely involved in these groups, in practice they seldom have the time, the ability or the authority to go far enough on their own. One reason why management support is needed is that managers may find that group meetings can be quite painful, since they are required to explain and justify their actions, provide information and keep to promises of action. To facilitate this, and further to ensure the success of the groups, an outside third-party may be useful to provide initial input, to help the groups get used to problem-solving, to assist in breaking the established pattern of relationships where workers may defer to and be unwilling to contradict management, and even occasionally to act as a possible arbiter, should there be disagreement. He can also help to ensure that there is a feeling that some sort of visible progress is being made, an essential ingredient of most innovative forms of participation.

Evidence on the impact of problem-solving groups indicates that they can be very successful in raising and solving a wide range of job-related issues.[7] They invariably highlight the workers' wealth of knowledge and ideas about their jobs. However, they do not tackle central issues like pay and job security and one of the difficulties can be that of obtaining and retaining the enthusiasm of a whole group rather than just the more active participants.

Briefing groups

Briefing groups are essentially a swift and systematic means of transmitting information throughout an organisation. As a specific approach, the briefing group in the UK has been developed by, and is particularly associated with, the Industrial Society.

The aim of briefing groups is to transmit information, of any kind, through the management system, by holding regular meetings of fairly short duration. In addition it may be possible to call special meetings to communicate particular and important items of information. One advantage of this approach for management is that the information is communicated through formal management channels, represented by the management hierarchy, and in this way can bolster junior management and supervision, who can easily be by-passed by other means of communication. Another advantage is that, owing to the control system — the preparation of written briefs — the information is unlikely to become distorted as it moves from senior management to shop floor.

The rationale underlying briefing groups is that effective communication is central to the maintenance of morale and satisfaction. Effective communication to the advocates of briefing groups ideally means face-to-face communication between a supervisor and his subordinates, but it also means regular and controlled transmission of information.

It is easy to criticise briefing groups, in their simplest form, as nothing more than devices for the managerial control of information. Even managers have often found it difficult to maintain enthusiasm for them in this form, since the preparation of briefs can be time-consuming and, although the time taken to carry out a briefing is normally short, its disruptive effect for little apparent return means that it is often time begrudged.

Briefing groups become more significant as a potential form of participation when the communication becomes two-way, not just in terms of a shop-floor reaction to management information, but also as a vehicle for suggestion, ideas and requests for information initiated by the shop floor. This in turn can lead to further developments. In the sense, therefore, that briefing groups can provide a way into other forms of participation, as well as filling a possible information gap, they can fulfil a useful function. Their potential as a way into participation is outlined in some detail in Chapter 5.

Job design

Introduction

There are various approaches to the redesign of jobs and the terminology used to describe them can be confusing. Job enrichment is usually used to refer to the redesign of jobs to build in more scope for achievement, autonomy and the exercise of responsibility. Job enlargement refers to the process of building a wider range of tasks into a job, thereby providing more variety. Job rotation occurs when a worker moves from one task to another. Each of these three approaches — job enrichment, job enlargement and job rotation — is concerned with the design of the job of an individual worker. Autonomous work groups, on the other hand, focus on a range of jobs, which can be linked together in some meaningful way, perhaps because they are concerned with a specific part of the production process. They are intended to provide work groups with control over what they do and how they organise themselves, within certain predetermined parameters. In the sense that virtually no work group is completely independent, the term semi-autonomous work group might be more appropriate.

From this brief description it will be apparent that job enrichment and autonomous work groups are the more significant forms of job design in the sense that they extend the control exercised by workers into areas previously regarded as the responsibility of their manager. In general terms these two approaches share the same rationale; namely, that the redesigning of jobs to provide more control for workers leads to greater involvement and satisfaction and also to greater motivation, and hence to greater productivity.[8] In practice, however, they differ in certain important respects. In particular, they differ in their view of the way in which job design changes should be carried out. To understand these differences requires some understanding of the underlying theories in each case. These will be examined briefly together with their practical implications.

Job enrichment

The name probably most closely associated with job enrichment is that of Herzberg. In two widely read books (Herzberg, Mausner and Snyderman, 1959; Herzberg, 1966) and numerous articles, as well as through lecture tours and consultancy activities, he has publicised his two-factor or motivator-hygiene theory of motivation. This theory argues that job satisfaction operates along two separate dimensions, with one set of conditions creating dissatisfaction unless they are adequately catered for and the other set leading to positive satisfaction and high motivation. The dissatisfiers, which he terms hygiene factors, include pay, interpersonal relations, job security and working conditions. The satisfiers, or motivators, include responsibility, achievement, interesting work and advancement. Since, in Herzberg's view, only the motivators can lead to satisfaction and motivation, jobs should be redesigned and 'enriched' by building in more of the motivator factors.

The major distinction in Herzberg's theory is between the intrinsic job content factors, closely associated with actually doing the job, and the extrinsic factors surrounding the job. This distinction, which has been quite frequently made by writers other than Herzberg, is useful. Furthermore, by focusing on the importance of the task, Herzberg provided a counter to the human relations movement, still dominant in the late 1950s. However, Herzberg's theory has been heavily criticised on three main grounds: first, that the research method on which it is based is weak; second, that the nature of his theory is unclear and imprecise; and, third, that his own research data, and that of many others, do not wholly support the theory.[9]

It is not necessary to accept Herzberg's theory, in order to advocate job enrichment. However, it is important to recognise the contribution made by Herzberg and by his theory in drawing management attention to job enrichment. An alternative approach, providing a more useful analysis of the motivating factors in tasks and better researched although far less well-known in management circles, has been developed by Hackman and Oldham. They argue (Hackman and Oldham, 1975) that worker motivation will be increased if more autonomy, feedback, variety, significance and opportunity for personal identification are built into the job. They have developed a formula to explain how these variables interrelate and also identify certain individual differences in motivation which are likely to result. What their theory amounts to, in practical terms, is still an advocacy of job enrichment.

As well as outlining the nature of job enrichment and the justification for it, Herzberg also has something to say about how job enrichment should be introduced. He emphasises that management should control the change process. Since interpersonal relations, and therefore many consultative/participative processes, are 'hygiene'-based, Herzberg feels that they are unlikely to increase motivation and need not be used. Therefore, while the outcome may be redesigned jobs permitting more day-to-day control and participation, the process whereby they are introduced need not be participative. Similarly, since pay is a hygiene factor, Herzberg argues that an increase in pay will not increase motivation and should not be an essential part of the process of introducing job enrichment. For some managers this approach to change has obvious attractions; others, however, recognise that in practice it is likely to antagonise employees. Such an assumption is usually correct, as Denis Gregory points out in his discussion of union attitudes and policies in Chapter 14. Quite apart from this, in most job evaluation schemes, more responsibility would result in an upgrading and therefore more pay. Failure to meet this expectation could produce a hostile reaction.

In practice job enrichment introduced in the manner advocated by Herzberg appears to have had its greatest success in a number of mainly non-union American organisations. The best-known examples of this can be found in the books by Ford (1969) and Maher (1971).

Herzberg himself has reported successful application in a military context (Herzberg and Rafalko, 1975). Elsewhere, including the UK, there have been successes with managerial, professional, supervisory and clerical groups.[10] However, in Europe, including the UK, there have been a fairly large number of applications where the manner of introducing the change fits in more closely with the existing industrial relations structure. In practice this means either that job enrichment comes about as an unplanned result of technological change or that its introduction is controlled by a joint management/union team. In this context, the dividing line between the autonomous work group and individual job enrichment becomes blurred. Nevertheless some jobs, by their very nature, are generally more suited to job enrichment — the job of the salesman is one example.

A review of these studies is obviously beyond the scope of this present chapter. The Work Research Unit (1978) has produced bibliographies of both job enrichment and other forms of job-design change in specific industries, including engineering and food manufacturing. These are available on request. Other reports have reviewed progress in specific organisations [11] or more generally. [12] Typical benefits which emerge from these projects include increased job satisfaction, involvement and commitment, better industrial relations, reduced labour turnover and absenteeism and often improved quality and quantity of work. How far these changes in quality and quantity can be attributed to improved motivation and how much to the effects of improved organisation of work and manpower utilisation is seldom easy to establish.

Autonomous work groups

The concept of the autonomous work group is similar to job

enrichment in many respects, but the focus is on a group of jobs rather than on an individual job, and a measure of inter-dependence is often sought, so that the group of workers has to decide how to allocate tasks among its members. Autono-mous work groups can be used in a variety of contexts, but they seem to be particularly suited to situations where there is an uneven workflow and where, without them, manpower uti-lisation might be rather poor.

The basic aims of the autonomous work group are usually much the same as those of job enrichment, namely to increase motivation, job satisfaction and productivity. However, autonomous work groups are also designed to make better use of the social system and, linked to this, one of the objectives of Norwegian developments in this area has been to extend 'industrial democracy'. Furthermore, the underlying rationale for autonomous work groups is rather different, resulting in a different approach both to the way in which jobs should be designed and to the way in which changes should be intro-duced. A theoretical basis for autonomous workgroups can be found in what is normally termed 'socio-technical systems' the-ory. Put at its simplest, this theory suggests that organisations are only likely to be successful in achieving their major goals if they take account of both the social and technical require-ments within the organisation. Too much emphasis on either the technical aspects of production or on people and human relations in isolation is likely to be counter-productive; what is needed is an ability to take account of both and to 'jointly opti-mise' or balance them. Autonomous work groups are an attempt to achieve this balance and some of the best-known cases are ones where they have replaced the traditional produc-tion line, which advocates of this approach would normally regard as an illustration of an overemphasis on technical requirements.[13]

An early example of the success of the 'socio-technical' the-ory and of a form of autonomous work group was provided in the 1940s by a study in the Durham coal mines (Trist and Bam-forth, 1951). During the 1950s, further studies were carried out (Trist et al., 1963; Rice, 1958) demonstrating the value of the approach, but limited interest in the UK meant that several of the leading exponents from the Tavistock Institute, who were associated with this approach, went to work overseas. Much of the best-known work has subsequently been carried out in Scandinavia, although recently there has been renewed interest and an increasing amount of work in both the UK and the USA.

One element of socio-technical theory which has received some emphasis in the advocacy of autonomous work groups is an underlying set of assumptions about human motivation. On the basis of experience, a list of six important needs has been produced.[14] These are the needs for:

(a) job content to be reasonably demanding in terms other than sheer endurance, yet providing some variety;

(b) the opportunity to learn on the job and to go on learning;

(c) an area of decision-making an individual can call his own;

(d) some minimum degree of helpfulness and recognition in the workplace;

(e) an ability to relate the job and the product to one's social life;

(f) a feeling that the job leads to some sort of desirable future.

In fact this list is rather vague and general and its derivation and validity are unclear. Nevertheless, in conjunction with other elements of socio-technical theory it leads to a list of guidelines for the design of jobs. This list seems to be fairly flexible, but generally includes the following.[15] Jobs should be designed to contain:

(a) an optimum level of variety;

(b) a single overall task;

(c) an optimum work cycle;

(d) some personal control over quality and quantity standards;

(e)   feedback of performance through knowledge of results;

(f)   some demands on skill and knowledge;

(g)   some control over auxiliary and boundary tasks;

(h)   provision for 'interlocking' tasks, job rotation or physical proximity where jobs are necessarily independent, where individual jobs entail a relatively high degree of stress and where an individual job does not make an obvious contribution to the end product;

(i)   some prospects of advancement.

As with the list of 'needs', this list may be intuitively attractive but it also seems rather arbitrary and no clear indication is given of whether particular elements are more important than others or whether omission of any is likely to have serious consequences. It is probably best to use it as a kind of checklist of features towards which the design of jobs should aspire. As such it can be useful; but, on this basis, no specific item is sacrosanct.

When it comes to introducing shop-floor participation, advocates of autonomous work groups generally prefer a highly participative process with detailed worker involvement from an early stage in the design of the new jobs. They also expect unions to be closely involved and seem to expect that changes in both the system and level of pay may have to be negotiated. In general terms this approach seems likely to be far more acceptable to trade unions and to many managers than that recommended by Herzberg. A straightforward and brief introduction to this form of participation has been presented by Klein (1976) but the most detailed description of case studies outlining the change process has been provided by Emery and Thorsrud (1976) in a book describing their projects in Norway. It is probably in Sweden that this approach has had its greatest impact and the number of case studies from the UK is still small. Where there have been successes, as at Richard Baxendale Limited or GKN (Shotton), as well as parts of ICI such as the Grangemouth plant, it is noticeable that it has grown out of an established plant structure of participation. Indeed in each of these three cases there was a well-established consultative system which had developed into some form of works council. This council provided a forum for union-management discussion of a wide range of issues in an integrative, problem-solving manner, closer to the European model. In this kind of context, changes in job design seem to be treated with less suspicion.

Introducing changes in job design

In 1971, Wilkinson, in a review of some of the earlier European cases of job design, concluded that the process whereby the change was introduced was as important as the nature of the actual changes in determining the ultimate success of the exercise. This is not altogether surprising since the process and content of the change may be closely linked; indeed analysis of many of the subsequent cases reinforces this view.

Although job enrichment and autonomous work groups have their roots in different theories and approaches to change, in practice they can be considered together, both having common aims and a common theme: namely, the importance of changes in job design as a means for the extension of shop-floor participation. Whether the outcome of the change takes the form of job enrichment or autonomous work groups, or both, should depend on the change process and the analysis of what is appropriate. This, at least, is the view, heavily influenced by advocates of autonomous work groups, developed by the Work Research Unit (Jessup, 1977), which has also spelt out some of the initial steps that should be considered. Briefly, it argues that the whole change should be highly participative; the first step should be to obtain the approval of senior management and senior shop stewards; then the workforce should be involved and their views obtained, possibly by use of an attitude survey; thereafter a joint steering group, ideally aided by third-party help, should plan progress and work out the details.

There are obvious arguments which can be advanced in favour of a participative approach to change. However, the form and extent of participation may not need to be so rigidly defined. An analysis of cases of change of job design shows that the processes whereby the change is introduced can vary considerably. Sometimes a technological innovation or a change in marketing policy can have repercussions on job content. At other times such changes may arise from attempts to meet customer needs or improve communications. Changes of these kinds can have an almost accidental impact on jobs, sometimes unnoticed by those affected and often not subject to negotiation. In short, while a participative approach to change as a framework within which to design jobs may be considered desirable for a successful outcome, where success is defined in terms of redesigned jobs which provide higher levels of satisfaction and productivity, experience indicates that this has not always been essential.

A participative approach to changes on the shop floor, however desirable, will not, of course, in itself guarantee success, since the complexity of the process requires that many other factors have to be taken into account. Again, an analysis of existing cases suggests that the following issues will often have to be considered:

1 A careful and thorough analysis of the social, technical and information systems will usually be an essential early step.

2 The payment system may need to be altered to meet the requirements of flexible and possibly group work. Traditional job-evaluation schemes may prove limiting, especially when they relate jobs to individuals, and the requirement within an autonomous work group is for flexible group working. This does not discount the possibility of linking pay to job evaluation, but it does point to the need for a more sophisticated scheme, which can take account of group working and which, rather than acting as a limiting factor, encourages initiative.

3 A linked point that must be anticipated is that there may be various 'hygiene' factors inhibiting progress. There may, for example, be understandable anxiety about security, about traditional status differentials and about social and physical working conditions. These should be anticipated and confronted at an early point. One quite likely outcome is that pay increases may be a part of the eventual package. This may be the price for the acceptance of change or it may be linked to anticipated increases in productivity. Normally there will be an expectation that increased responsibility justifies an increase in pay.

4 The repercussions of changes must be taken into account. For example, other production departments, supervisors and customers may be affected.

5 Commitment from senior management rather than just compliance is usually essential, particularly if the change is not to be limited to one small 'experimental' section. Otherwise there is a danger that a change in middle management will bring to an end an apparently successful job-design programme.

6 A long time scale is necessary, and it is not always sensible to see the initial change as the only change. It is likely to throw up a number of problems and issues and, if successful, to raise the desire for further change.

It should be clear, from this brief analysis of some of the forms of shop-floor participation and some of the issues involved in introducing them, that careful analysis is required and that the objectives in seeking to bring about change should be clear. A distinction can be made between the degree of participation permitted by the new system and the amount of participation used in introducing the new arrangements and the two issues can sometimes be kept distinct. However, where one of the goals is to extend shop-floor participation, rather than a prime concern for productivity, then in most cases a participative approach to change would seem to be desirable.

Summary

This chapter has outlined the main forms of shop-floor participation and has highlighted some of the problems and issues
that have to be taken into account in any attempt to introduce
them. Four forms of shop-floor participation were discussed;
opinion surveys, problem-solving groups, briefing groups and
job redesign.

Two approaches to job design, namely job enrichment and
autonomous work groups were examined. It was argued that
although the underlying theories and their practical implications are rather different, in practice the two approaches are
likely to have much in common. The important distinction is
whether to focus on an individual job or a group of jobs.

Another important distinction, which is highlighted by the
contrast between the two approaches to job design, but which
has implications for all forms of participation, is between the
amount of participation permitted by the new system and the
amount of participation involved in introducing it and bringing about change. While a participative approach to change
does not always seem to be essential for a successful outcome,
where a goal of the scheme is to extend participation then it
would seem to be sensible to act participatively from the outset.

More attention was paid to changes in job design than to
other forms of shop-floor participation because it seems to be
the approach most likely to achieve a range of goals. Furthermore it was emphasised that, despite the focus of the national
debate on company-level issues, workers generally seem more
interested in issues directly related to their work. Therefore all
the forms of shop-floor participation deserve attention and
none are mutually exclusive.

Notes

[1] Wall and Clegg in Chapter 3, reviewing the evidence,

conclude that 'the strongest desire is for shop-floor participation'. There is substantial support for this from studies additional to the ones they quote. Apart from academic studies and surveys in specific plants, this view is endorsed by a nationwide survey of workers carried out by the Opinion Research Centre and reported in *The Times*, 14 January 1975, in an article entitled 'What about the Workers?'

[2] Cf. Knight (1976/77).

[3] There are exceptions and some non-union organisations use opinion surveys as a major means of monitoring employee views. The rationale for this is reasonably sound, since in non-union organisations there may be no formal channels whereby workers can communicate their views to management.

[4] For a fuller discussion of the technical problems that can arise in the use of opinion surveys, see Oppenheim (1966).

[5] An illustration of the problems arising as the group gets larger is provided by Ross and Screeton in Chapter 5.

[6] See Eagle and West (1978) for a description of some of the work carried out by the National Ports Council.

[7] See the study referred to in Note 6, as well as the case study described in Chapter 3.

[8] This rationale, and in particular the assumed link between changes in job design, increased motivation and increased productivity, rests on very shaky foundations. Evidence on worker goals, and problems in linking motivation and performance, indicate that quite often higher productivity may not be the outcome. Even where there is higher productivity it cannot always be attributed to the motivating effort of changes in job content. For a fuller discussion see Guest (1976).

[9] For further details of these criticisms see Guest and Fatchett (1974), Chapter 7.

[10] See, for example, the well-known studies at ICI reported by Paul and Robertson (1970).

[11] See a series of articles appearing in the Department of Employment *Gazette* between July and November 1977, entitled 'The Case for Shop-floor Participation'.

[12] See, for example, general points made by Jessup (1977). However, for a fuller detailed review of cases in the UK and world-wide see Taylor (1977a; 1977b).

[13] Probably the best known example of this is to be found at Volvo (Lindholm and Norstedt, 1975). Philips, Olivetti and other organisations have also succeeded in eliminating the traditional assembly line for certain products.

[14] See Emery and Thorsrud (1976).

[15] See Thorsrud (1972) and Emery and Thorsrud (1976).

5 Briefing groups and the development of employee participation

John B. Benson
Personnel Director, Scottish & Newcastle Beer Company
Limited

Background

Scottish & Newcastle Breweries is a company of some 27,000 employees. The company is structured in operating divisions, covering production, the marketing, sales and distribution activities, retail activities in hotels and licensed houses and head office specialist services. In common with all large brewing companies in the UK, the company grew out of amalgamations and mergers of smaller, normally family-controlled businesses. Consequently, the brewing industry traditionally is paternalistic in management style, with for many years a relatively low level of union activity.

However, recognising the changes occurring in society as a whole and the growth of the power and influence of trade unions, particularly at workplace level, Scottish & Newcastle Breweries, in common with many others, was faced with the need to totally review its approach to the management of people and to examine the appropriateness of hitherto accepted styles of management.

In particular the role and influence of the shop steward was growing. Historically the company's industrial relations had been conducted within the framework of an employers' association agreement. This gave an arm's-length quality to industrial relations. Matters arising were dealt with largely by full-time officers and senior company managers from head office. This was unsatisfactory to the lay union representative in that it frustrated his need and desire to influence issues at the level of the work group. It was unsatisfactory as far as the company's long-term interests were concerned because it affected the will and the ability of line-management to influence employee relations locally. Accordingly, it weakened authority and accountability.

While few serious disputes had been experienced, it was obvious that a previously acquiescent work force was increasingly inclined to challenge conventional authority. The first-line supervisory grades were ill-equipped by training and inclination to cope with this development. The growth in size of the total group had weakened the ties of loyalty and identification which had existed within the pre-merger smaller constituent companies. Impetus was provided by a change of leadership at the top of the company.

One aspect of this total review concerned, not surprisingly, the company's approach to communication and the involvement of employees. However, it is vital to recognise that this was only one aspect. The policies which were to be developed on communication and involvement were not viewed in isolation. They constituted only one part of a multi-pronged effort to create change in personnel policies, procedures and practices. Thus, while objectives and policies were being formulated in the area of employee involvement, there was at the same time re-examination of the approaches to management training, payment systems, trade union recognition and procedures, and organisation. It was and remains the company view that no one area of personnel management policy can provide a panacea for the human relations problems which a large organisation inevitably faces. There needs to be a coherent, comprehensive and consistent plan.

Identifying the need

The first steps were taken with an invitation to the Industrial Society to advise and assist the company on better means of communication and explanation to the work force. This intervention of a third party in an area which was sensitive and fraught with difficulties for both existing line-management and the representatives of trade unions was vital in a catalytic way to the achievement of a greater degree of commitment from the parties involved.

This independent assistance plus motivation from the top have been found to be two vital ingredients of any serious attempt at change.

It was obvious that the company experienced communications problems which are fairly typical of large organisations and in particular large industrial organisations, where direct conflicts of interest often inevitably arise. Supervisors believed, with considerable justification, that information from company to work force by-passed them via the shop stewards. Therefore they had abrogated their own responsibility for effective and speedy communication with employees. Not only vertical but lateral communications between functions and departments were poor. Typically, each level in the organisation believed that it communicated well. It had to be those at the next level down who were at fault.

The intention, therefore, was that a more systematic form of communication should be designed to create an atmosphere in which there would be fewer misunderstandings at all levels about company proposals, decisions and actions. It was recognised that not only was there an increasing need for change to be explained and sold to all employees, but also that this was critical to the success of any effective consultative or negotiation process.

In many cases the rise of trade unions and the development of the role of the workplace-based representative had significantly diminished the role of the foreman or supervisor as the principal first-line management contact between the company and its employees. There was a change in the role of the full-time trade union officer, upon whom considerable reliance had historically been placed to win the co-operation of employees at large.

The clear undesirability of paid union officials and shop stewards being the principal advocates and the principal channel of communication of management thinking, planning and decisions was accepted by the company. Not only could they not be expected to communicate in the way in which management themselves would want their views explained, but also their own effectiveness and credibility would be consistently eroded if they were seen to be continually articulating a management view.

The supervisor who, with the increasing power of the trade union and the increasing impact of legislation, was becoming more and more isolated from the management team, had to be helped to regain his position as the natural and effective leader of the work group.

The case for briefing groups

Against the background of these general needs the decision was taken to adopt the briefing-group system, since it was designed to be concerned principally with the spoken and not the written word. It was intended to be much more effective in assisting people to understand what was happening because it provided the oppportunity for question, dialogue and judgement in the face-to-face situation: the opportunity to replace the grapevine, which is rarely charitable in its interpretation of situations or decisions.

The briefing-group system establishes the principle that it is management's role, right and indeed obligation to communicate downwards with its employees as a whole. This is not the natural role of the trade union. It is the trade union's and the workplace representative's role, right and obligation to represent upwards the views of employees and to be the guardians of agreements made.

If employees were to accept the sincerity with which management views were being explained to them, then it was obvious that communication had to take place on a regular pattern in 'peace' as well as 'war' time. Most managements are all too ready to communicate their view of a problem in the period of a crisis. They forget that information communicated only in times of crisis is immediately suspected of being designed only to make propaganda in that one situation and not seen as part of a genuine and continuing attempt to keep people informed.

Another compelling reason for having a disciplined, structured, regular system is that if there is reliance on *ad hoc*, informal contact systems because 'the managers know their own staff', in a time of pressure, when probably the need to communicate is even greater than other occasions, the informal system is all too easily abandoned or forgotten. It is rarely as effective as claimed, in any event.

On the other hand, if there is a formal, drilled approach to which everyone is accustomed and in which everyone knows his role and obligation, then the process can be triggered simply and in a disciplined, calm and naturally accepted way. A structured system can be integrated into the normal pattern of management techniques and activities and after some practice and experience becomes as natural as the use of any other management tool.

How the system operates

In any company the briefing-group system will be organised in a way which reflects the number of levels in the organisation, the number of employees involved and their workplace arrangements. The system is so designed that face-to-face communication takes place between every level in the organisation, starting at the top, and is completed with the briefing at shop-floor or office-floor level.

The briefing is normally conducted by the immediate superior, whether this is the chairman or managing director to his colleagues at board level or the foreman to a group of manual employees in a plant. In practice this means that a brief must begin at the very top of the organisation. There have to be rules on management responsibility and control, briefing procedure, timing and content.

The board of Scottish & Newcastle Breweries has decided to adopt an approach whereby each item of the board minutes is assumed to be available for executive directors' briefing unless it is specifically stated to be otherwise. Briefing therefore begins by executive directors dealing with the most senior level of management immediately below board level. Communication at this level is often assumed in companies to be happening automatically and informally. Frequently it is a very weak link in the chain.

Thereafter the administration and control of the brief belongs to the management line of command as the brief is passed down from level to level. In the early stages of the development of briefing, clear guidelines had to be laid down as to content, procedure and timing if it was to be drilled and effective. In particular, each level of management, including first-line supervisors, needed both to receive a brief and to participate in the creation of the amended brief for the next level down.

Thus a brief may begin at board level covering the broadest policy and information items of sales, investment, financial results, overall company performance, while these items will form only the background to a myriad of other information items — e.g., a department's performance, accidents, training facilities, local sales successes, staff promotions etc, — when that brief has gone through five or six levels of the total company and is being communicated to the work group at the shop or office floor.

Clear rules on the timing of the brief to each level ensure, first, that the structure of briefing is mutually reinforcing and that consistency is achieved. A typical brief would begin in my own department by a personal brief from the managing director immediately after a board meeting, i.e., within twenty-four hours, followed by a brief by me of the senior management team. They in turn hold meetings of their section heads or all of their staff, depending on the size of the department, and so complete the briefing process. This can be timed to occur within hours or to take over a week, depending upon the issues.

Time has to be set aside, of course, particularly for the briefing to work groups at shop-floor level. However, our experience has been that, after initial concern, suitable and natural times and venues have emerged for each work group; e.g., late Friday afternoon for a production location or early on a Monday morning for a retail delivery fleet.

The subject matter has been defined as the information which employees need to know in order to do their jobs more efficiently and effectively as well as details of the decisions and policies which could affect their will to work.

Details of sales performance; employment or promotion opportunities; targets set, achieved or missed, with reasons; discipline problems; new customers; product developments; explanation of the financial results; competitors' activities; accident statistics — are all matters which would normally feature in a brief. The emphasis adopted is of course dependent on the bias of the work group; for example, production targets to maintenance engineers; customer accounts won or lost to both salesmen and delivery men.

Launching the system

To launch briefing in Scottish & Newcastle Breweries Limited, a trial area was chosen — a transport department, in fact. The problems being experienced in that area were fairly typical of industry and of the company as a whole. There was a feeling among supervisors there that they were regularly bypassed and that the most reliable source of information was the shop steward. At the same time, on the trade union side there was criticism amongst the work force that communications between shop stewards and union officials were not as effective as they should have been.

Clearly, agreement had to be reached with the representatives of the appropriate trade unions, where, inevitably, there could have been suspicion of such a management-inspired communication system. It was important to establish that briefing was not a management attempt to undermine the trade union. Indeed in some companies the attempt to have a briefing-group system has been frustrated by the trade unions' opposition to face-to-face communication from first-line management to the organised work group. Therefore in Scottish & Newcastle Breweries the Industrial Society's assistance was sought to obtain commitment from both sides to the mutual benefits of briefing. Some restrictions on *ulta vires* matters were agreed; e.g., the union wished to reserve to itself the right to communicate back to its members improvements in wages and benefits which it had achieved in negotiation.

No particular difficulty was experienced at that time nor indeed has been since then. Experience indicates that most shop stewards welcomed the briefing process or at least accepted it as a natural part of working life. Only on rare occasions was the management right to brief challenged, and then unsuccessfully. Now the process is accepted totally by management, union official, staff representative or shop steward, and employees at large.

Extension from the trial department to other areas of the company followed, welcomed by some and tolerated by others. However, it came to stay.

Monitoring and improving the system

Problems did obviously arise. There was criticism of the relevance of some of the information. An attitude survey conducted as a means of monitoring and evaluation in the early days elicited that, at the lower levels of the organisation, less and less head-office-type information was required. This inquiry also showed that statistical information — e.g., sales and financial information — had to be expressed, not baldly, but in a form and manner which could be accepted and understood.

It was important again to emphasise the criterion that the brief should represent the information that people need to know to do their jobs and which affects their motivation and will to work. Amendments were therefore necessary to the initial approach so that information could be added, subtracted and modified by the relevant level of management as the brief moved down from level to level in the organisation. Greater freedom had to be given to all levels of management in each of the separate and distinct business areas of the company to judge what was of most significance to their particular employees, and less and less were there items which needed to be communicated directly from the top down through all levels to the bottom of the organisation. The supervisor had the opportunity to come into his own as the best judge of relevance, interpretation and response of the group at workplace level.

While, clearly, this was an essential change, it carried with it the obvious danger of loss of control and impetus. Regular monitoring and evaluation by survey, by analysis of feedback and by directors 'walking the job' is necessary. In the case of Scottish & Newcastle Breweries three surveys have been conducted since 1972, each dealing at least in part with attitudes to communication and briefing procedures. Indeed, many of the developments referred to later — e.g., development of a more consultative approach, management training needs, the need for more say in job evaluation, etc. — arose from the monitoring process by survey and by the analysis of feedback from supervisors, written and verbal.

Also, in Scottish & Newcastle Breweries, the chief executive accompanied by a number of senior directors visits each location and operating area of the company once a year. It is possible by this direct contact with the work force to evaluate, by way, admittedly, of an overall impression, the effectiveness of local communication procedures.

Interestingly but perhaps not surprisingly, many managers and supervisors who had claimed that they knew their work groups well and had a natural, easy communication and dialogue with them found the responsibility and the difficulty of quite systematically explaining the management view on issues a much more challenging task than envisaged. A refreshing irony was that many managers who rejected the need for a disciplined approach to the briefing of their subordinates were amongst the most critical of the irregularity, inconsistency or incompleteness of the information flowing to themselves from their superiors. Considerable effort and time was spent on training, making extensive use of closed-circuit television techniques.

Developing participation

At a very early stage there was a significant and consistently expressed criticism that the briefing-group system as being practised, in accordance with the Industrial Society rules, laid too much emphasis on one-way communication.

This was the first pointer to a major reconsideration of communication with employees. It was quickly realised that the involvement of people in greater information and knowledge about the running of the business was a dynamic process. A management policy of 'we will only go so far in employee participation' is not possible. Even if there is no intention to move into a consultative and participative style of management, the effect of giving the opportunity to ask questions, to seek clarification and further information, is to stimulate an organic growth and demand for more formal opportunities of involvement.

Out of one-way downward-flowing communication came the need to develop machinery by which constructive two-way dialogue could take place on matters which were increasingly realised to affect people's working lives.

Hence, as the briefing procedure was extended, after the six-month trial, to the whole of the company, i.e. to all production, distribution and retail activities, there also arose in due course a need to create a series of systems of consultation through representatives. These were required to complement and develop the communications procedures.

Extensive use was made of the Action Centred Leadership programme developed by John Adair and the Industrial Society to assist managers in reorganising their thinking about the elements and activities involved in being a manager (Adair, 1968). The intention of ACL is to teach management that leaders are rarely born and that most individuals can lead successfully, not by charisma, but by the application of trainable techniques and an understanding of individual and team motivation.

At the same time as briefing was becoming the foundation and cornerstone of the company's approach to involvement, other developments were following on, as part of a multi-pronged approach: participative job evaluation, using representatives of the relevant work groups as the majority decision-makers on grades and relativities; experiments in the use of autonomous work groups and consultative committees at important levels of the decision-making hierarchy in the organisation.

One significant development occurred in an area of persistent industrial relations problems and recurring stoppages. Out of the practice of management explanation to all the work group, which in turn stimulated constructive dialogue in face-to-face situations, came first of all a lessening of tensions. With much patience and increasing dialogue, remembering the need to approach such problems from more than one angle, there developed a system of autonomous work groups which has now survived for five years.

The employees who worked in the handling yard of a beer-kegging plant have become involved in purchasing, production planning and personnel decisions through a system of plant committees. In effect there is both consultation and a fair degree of what might be described as delegated decision-making. Not a man-day's work has been lost since the innovation of these dialogues.

The place in participation of briefing groups

A model showing the natural and systematic development of employee participation was gradually emerging through review, monitoring and analysis of the experience being gained. This simple model, which is shown diagrammatically in Figure 5.1, illustrates the 'bottom-up' approach to the development of employee participation.

It is the company's view that a 'bottom-up' approach developing from the work group ensures a more relevant and soundly based representative system of employee participation than that suggested by the legal imposition of worker directors or similar machinery at board level.

Inevitably, consultative or participative arrangements at any level above the tiniest work group must be conducted through the use of representatives. This means that beyond the level of the workplace-based briefing group the organisation is involved in indirect participation and in the interface with the negotiating and collective bargaining machinery.

While this is inevitable, it is desirable and indeed essential that the indirect participative machinery of consultative committees and the like which constitute the 'walls' and the 'roof' of the building of participation is built upon the foundations of the direct involvement of all employees. This is achieved through face-to-face communication with the work group.

Otherwise participation becomes meaningful only for the activist and the representative and, while they tend to be the natural leaders and the opinion-formers, it is essential that both management and union attempt to ensure that participation is as well-informed and representative as it can be made to be. A well-motivated representative is only a small part of the answer to achievement of a motivated and committed work-

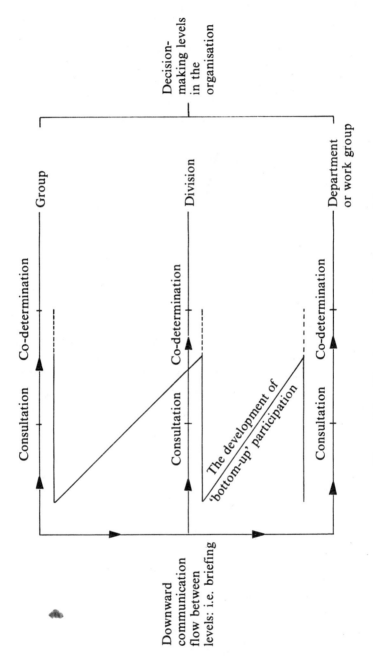

Figure 5.1 *Employee participation model*

force as a whole.

The simple two-dimensional model illustrated in Figure 5.1 shows that participation can be considered as a natural development at each decision-making level; beginning with communication or, as it can be better described, explanation; through consultation; and thence to whatever degree of co-determination can be achieved or is wanted by both parties. This can be through either delegated decision-making or through negotiation or, more probably, a combination of both.

This model suggests that the development of participation is not something which can be achieved by either a unilateral decision or indeed a collective agreement to participate, but that it is a carefully constructed and paced development which requires each level to be tested and operating effectively before the next can fulfil its purpose. Thus true consultation cannot take place at any level before there is a sound system for communicating and explaining to the represented what the representatives are doing and with what issues they are dealing.

A practical example in Scottish & Newcastle Breweries is the case in a transport area of a participative approach to the solution of a major problem. A decision had to be made about changing the location of an existing transport depot. A number of options were open to management. The need to make the move and the feasible options were briefed to all employees so that informed debate could take place amongst the work groups involved concerning the move, the implications of the options and the relative impact of these options on their working lives.

This made it possible to have informed and representative consultation and, if necessary, co-determination through negotiation, upon the implementation of this major change. The result was to achieve a commitment not only from the representatives, but from those who could make the implementation of any decisions difficult or smooth: that is, the work groups as a whole.

It can be seen that the need for the basic explanation system — i.e. the briefing group or its equivalent — becomes more and more vital the further removed from the work group is the level at which decisions are taken and the more indirect the representative, consultative or negotiating process. Effective consultation at divisional or group level is dependent upon machinery by which both management and trade union can in a structured way communicate down through each affected level in the organisation.

As both society's needs and legislation enforce increasing disclosure of information, the need to constantly develop and maintain an efficient structured communication-flow becomes that much greater. Certainly Scottish & Newcastle Breweries' experience, over some seven or eight years, is that as consultation and involvement become greater in quantity and quality, the need is reinforced, not diminished, for an effective briefing policy and procedure.

The other lesson of a number of years' experience is that it takes a very long time to create what, on the face of it, would seem to be a most natural commonsense activity amongst human beings — mutual understanding through mutual explanation.

Summary

Following a review of its management styles and industrial relations the company identified a need for improved communication with and involvement of employees. With Industrial Society advice it was decided to introduce briefing groups in order to create a more systematic and reliable means of communication to employees.

The system was based on the minutes of board meetings to which information of local interest was added at successive briefing levels. Following agreement with the trade union, the system was launched in a trial area and subsequently extended throughout the company.

As a result of monitoring the system's operation it was decided to increase the role of managers and supervisors at all levels in adapting briefs to the needs of their work groups. At the same time the system highlighted the need for two-way communication and led to the development of a range of other methods of participation.

The company's experience, however, has underlined the vital importance of the briefing system in providing the information base for meaningful consultative and representative systems.

6 Introducing autonomous work groups in Philips

Kirsty Ross

Head of Employment Section, Equal Opportunities Commission*

Jeoffrey Screeton

Manager, Quick-Vision Cathode Department, Mullard*

Introduction

Philips Electronic and Associated Industries Limited is a subsidiary of N.V. Philips Gloelampenfabrieken of Eindhoven in the Netherlands and is, for all practical purposes, responsible for the whole of the Philips interests within the UK. Its annual turnover is approximately £500 million and it employs about 48,000 people in a large number of different-sized establishments located in many parts of England and Scotland.

Mullard is wholly owned by Philips Industries and is that part of the business concerned with the manufacture and sale of electronic components, of which the principal are cathode-ray tubes, valves and semi-conductors. The Blackburn plant is the largest in Mullards and currently employs 2,800 people. It is also one of the longest established and has a distinguished history of service to the British electronics industry stretching

* Kirsty Ross and Jeoffrey Screeton are both writing here in a personal capacity.

96

over nearly forty years.

The plant manufactures a range of components including 300 million electrolytic and foil capacitors and about 13 million valves a year. It also manufactures glass and metal components for electron guns, though the guns themselves are assembled at other plants. One of these components is the 'quick-vision' cathode, and it is in the department responsible for this that semi-autonomous work groups have been introduced.

Setting up the department and the project

Philips has a well-established tradition of concern for job design. There have been successful projects in work restructuring in the plants at Hamilton and Haydock and several more in plants in the Netherlands and other parts of Europe.[1] By and large the initiative has been left to managers within individual plants and in this case the desire to do something originated with the engineer who was placed in charge of the department which was to be set up to assemble the new quick-vision heater.

He had seen skilled men given staff status, as a result of which many managers had expected them to behave differently. In his view, changes in behaviour could only realistically be anticipated if there were also changes in the way in which they were treated by management — for example, by demonstrating more trust and providing more responsibility. The opportunity to set up the new department was his first chance to put his ideas into practice and he began to think in general terms of structures other than the traditional pyramid found within the Blackburn plant.

As the technology of the new product unfolded, so too did the complex nature of the end-organisation he envisaged. He accordingly approached the internal consultant for the plant to help and guide him in his efforts to establish a feasible organisation structure for the department. The consultant had experience of job design programmes and had expertise in the areas of personnel and social science. She subscribed to the concepts associated with socio-technical systems theory and in particular the notion of 'joint optimisation', gained by taking account of both the technical and the social requirements.[2] It is probably fair to say that the manager was looking for a set of rules and guidelines to assist him; in the event, of course, these could not be provided and the consultant therefore contributed to the design and analysis of the department until production was well-established.

Initial contact meetings between the departmental manager and the Dutch factory involved in the development of the product took place in December 1973. In March 1974 he had his initial discussions with the consultant and by May 1974 it had been firmly agreed that the project should go ahead. Terms of reference, agreed between the divisional manager, the departmental manager and the consultant were as follows:

1 To arrive at an organisation which can achieve the two-fold objective of producing products on time and of the right quality. To be aware that social trends in industry are dictating the more effective utilisation of labour by allowing each individual to participate fully in meeting departmental objectives.
2 To provide opportunities for personal growth and development of the individuals within the organisation.
3 To endeavour to bridge the gap between engineering and production functions by an open and flexible managerial approach.

Production targets for the first year were established in advance and were not altered as a result of the project. The aim, therefore, was to achieve conventional production goals through a less conventional organisation structure, in the hope that this would increase the satisfaction, involvement and growth of the workers. The third objective was included as an important means of achieving increased satisfaction through the development of semi-autonomous work groups, which would include skilled men.

A number of steps are involved in setting up a new form of work organisation and an error at any stage can lead to failure for the project as a whole. While these steps are much the same for any new department, the chances of something going wrong are probably greater when the process is experimental than when it is based on familiar and well-established procedures.

The first step is to establish the underlying principles and aims. This process, and the contribution made by the departmental manager and the consultant, have already been briefly described. The second step is the detailed planning, of such things as the technology and the systems. In this case many peripheral departments were involved, including materials management, quality engineering, personnel, training and work study. The departmental manager accordingly set up an initial project management team with appropriate members of these departments. This team, influenced by the consultant, considered both the social and the technical requirements right from the earliest planning stage. The result of this analysis is shown in Figure 6.1, which identifies the major or core elements on the production flow-chart and the seven production groups that emerged.

The project management team felt strongly that the technical nature of the work led to the natural formation of these seven groups. At this stage there was little discussion of the degree of autonomy that these groups might achieve. The idea was to develop a loose form of organisation which could later be adapted and strengthened by the group members.

The third step is the transfer of responsibility from the project team to the operational management and the start up of production. By autumn 1974 the production management team together with a nucleus group of three operators and three skilled men were in Holland for technical training. This was a fairly unusual step for the Blackburn plant, which would normally send only instructional staff and not the actual operators for this kind of preliminary training. It was also a depar-

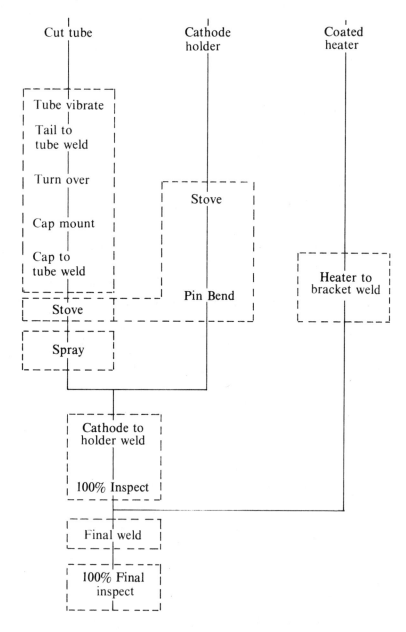

Figure 6.1   *Core flow chart with technological groups*

ture from, for example, the Haydock job-design project and reflected a desire to lay the groundwork carefully and to ensure that the organisational climate within the department was supportive to the kind of structure which had been decided upon. The first eleven people trained — management, skilled men and operators — were intended to form a nucleus which could spread the ideals, which they themselves had helped to evolve, throughout the seven groups.

The fourth step is to move into the production stage, by building up the work force, increasing production and evolving and maintaining the participative group structure. This process is described in the next section.

The new department in operation

In 1975 and early 1976 there was a steady build-up of personnel and of production levels until by March 1976 the intended complement of sixty-five members of the department was achieved. A summary of this development is provided in Table 6.1.

Table 6.1

Growth of production and personnel

1975	Daily production level	Direct operators	Total personnel
January	500	11	15
March	1,200	13	17
May	4,100	27	31
July	4,600	28	32
September	6,800	30	34
November	9,700	39	43
1976			
January	16,000	47	53
March	19,400	58	65

In the early months of 1975, the department was small and highly cohesive. Problems tended to be common to all and developmental problems on machines, for example, were solved by brainstorming sessions of operators, skilled craftsmen and management. Decisions on such things as where cloakrooms and the tea bar were to be located were discussed and thrashed out at general meetings, chaired by the departmental manager and open to all. As production increased, labour and resource planning was seen as something in which all members of the department shared.

By the time the department had grown beyond about thirty people, the value of general meetings declined and workers increasingly looked inward to problems and issues within their groups, rather than outwards to issues in the department and beyond. It was anticipated that groups would ask for meetings between themselves to cope with communication problems, but in the event, and despite strong encouragement from management, this did not happen.

The fully operational department has managed to retain most of the non-hierarchical features for which the departmental manager was aiming. The present structure is outlined in Figure 6.2.

The essential difference between this structure and a traditional one is that a traditional structure would have an additional level of formal unit leader and each leader would be in charge of a larger number of workers than that found in any of the self-contained groups. In other words, one level of supervision has disappeared.

The new production management team consists of the departmental manager, the production foreman, the engineering foreman, the quality specialist, the instructor, the secretary and a work-study engineer who is not a formal member of the department. The skilled group now numbers six, plus a staff apprentice and a student apprentice. There are 7 people in machine group I, 9 in machine group II, 7 in the spray-room group, 9 in the heater to bracket-weld group, 11 in the final-weld group, 7 in final inspection and 4 in the quality-control

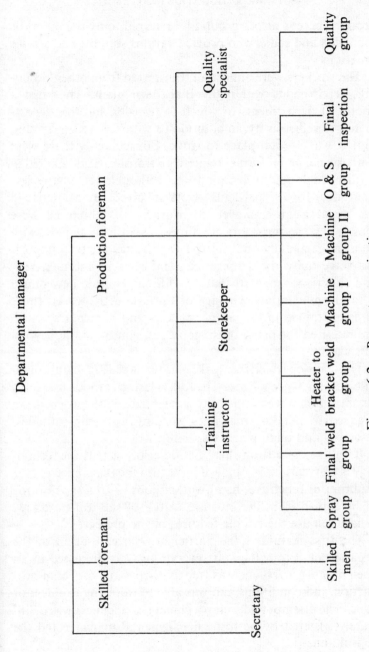

Figure 6.2 *Present organisation*

group. There is also a group of 5 referred to by the others as the 'odds and sods', who provide various support and service functions.

The workers were almost all transferred from other 'declining' departments within the Blackburn plant. They had a choice of departments to which to transfer, but this department offered security, in addition to which word got around that it was a good place to work. Consequently there were both formal and informal requests to transfer. This resulted in a fairly high-quality labour force, although some were less than ideal for the particular work involved. By March 1978 the department employed 81 workers of whom 60 were female.[3] The operators are almost exclusively female, with an average age of about thirty-five. The age factor is important since the work requires excellent eyesight and dexterity, and experience suggests that it is difficult to train newcomers who are much above the age of thirty-two. However, those already trained in the use of tweezers and binoculars, which are required for many of the jobs, can continue well beyond this age.

The tasks on which the workers are engaged are mainly intricate and highly repetitive. The quick-vision cathode measures 10mm x 18mm when it is fully assembled and the workers are engaged in minding machines, welding, spraying cathodes, assembly and quality and inspection work.

It will be clear from this brief description that the technology is conventional — indeed it fits into the Blackburn plant's tradition of repetitive, hand-worked jobs — and the rewards to be gained from the intrinsic nature of the work are few. What then are the unique features of the project?

The first feature is the participative organisation of the department. From the start everything was discussed in an open manner, everyone was free to discuss any aspect of production and conditions and was able to raise any problem or issue. The attempt to develop a climate of openness was deliberately fostered by both the departmental manager and the consultant.

The second feature is that the groups were left to organise everything for themselves. Initially management set the production targets, although subsequently an unsuccessful attempt was made to involve the groups in this. The groups were left to decide how they would achieve these targets and this meant that for example they organised their own job rotation, their holiday days, time off, overtime schedules and 'housekeeping' rotas. They handled contracts with peripheral departments and initiated discussions of factors which created problems for them.

With respect to problems, it soon became clear that some of the existing factory systems are not tailor-made and are not even helpful to the groups. For example the existing paperwork system required the same information to be recorded in different ways on different pieces of paper. It was decided to design and implement a paperwork system more relevant to the needs of the department and the work groups and one which would positively help the groups to develop their autonomy. The help of the administration department was enlisted and a new paperwork system was devised. In essence this means that all the information is now recorded on one piece of paper; this suits the needs of the work groups, the management team and the administration department. In practice it means that information is transmitted more swiftly and the groups are able to react quickly to production programme changes.

Is the project a success?

Management criteria

At the outset, three aims were identified for the project. The first related to quantity and quality of output, the second to opportunities for growth of individuals within the department and the third to some degree of integration of skilled workers and operators.

The most direct production comparison that can be made is with the Philips plant at Sittard in the Netherlands where the same quick-vision cathodes are made. Both quantity and, more particularly, quality figures at Blackburn compare favourably. In addition the Blackburn department went into production, following the trial period, three months sooner than that at Sittard. Part, but only part of this can be attributed to the lessons gained from the experience at the Dutch plant, which had started production two years earlier. Production targets were set by management for the department as it moved into full production. These targets were fairly optimistic and, perhaps as a result of this, they have never really been achieved. Whether this failure has been due to the work group structure within the department is difficult to say. First, full account had not been taken of the time it would take to train workers to reach a satisfactory standard. Second, the workers may not have been committed to the targets. What tended to happen was that certain levels of performance became accepted as norms and stayed as such even when workers had developed more expertise. Third, there was a failure to anticipate a number of serious machine problems. Fourth, some of the maintenance work was rather unsatisfactory, due partly to one or two specific problems with individual personnel.

Although the department failed to achieve what might be regarded as the over-ambitious quantity targets set by management, the quality standards have always been satisfactory. Right from the start, a high quality standard was set, fostered partly by deliberate competition with the Dutch plant making the same product. Judged in comparison with competitors, as opposed to the internal management standards, both quantity and quality of output has been at least as good as, but generally better than, competitors.

Moving on to the second criterion, it can be claimed that the organisation of the work groups did provide the workers with some opportunities for growth and development. Certainly in the early days members of the department formed a close-knit

team in which problems were discussed in an open and constructive manner, although subsequently some of this was
lost. The technology certainly provided a significant constraint, but through the ability to participate in a variety of
departmental and group problem-solving issues workers did
retain opportunities for growth. Some of these opportunities
were used, others, for a variety of reasons, were not. It is worth
noting that the management team regarded the project as a
major development experience for themselves.

The third criterion sought some integration of operators
and skilled men. In the early days this succeeded. For example, when the department was small, management, operators and skilled men met together frequently to resolve problems. The skilled men trained the machine operators and
sometimes operated the machines. Much of this has now been
lost, at least for the time being. One reason for this is that the
AUEW, which has about 400 members throughout the plant,
developed a general policy, as part of its wider bargaining
strategy, which precluded further co-operation of this kind.
Second, management made a possibly inadvertent mistake by
encouraging the craftsmen to go back to their workshop when
they were not required. The effect of this was to loosen their
attachment to the work groups and to strengthen their identity
as a skilled group. As a result, they have evolved as a separate
and identifiable work group on their own. However, there are
hopes that in the future they may again become more integrated into the work groups.

Other criteria might be used to claim that the project is a success. For example, costs were reduced by the fact that fewer
supervisory staff are required than under the conventional
organisation structure, and by the accelerated transition from
pilot-testing to proper production. Despite lack of enthusiasm
from senior management, the organisation of the department
has been maintained and there are plans to expand it considerably, partly because it is able to produce components at a favourable price. The start up of the department went very
smoothly and the work force seem satisfied. Only five people

have left the department, an exceptionally low level for the plant; absenteeism levels are reasonably low and there are no industrial relations or worker problems except those which apply to the plant as a whole. Perhaps it is fairest to claim that in several respects the project can be viewed as a success, while in all others it is at least as good as the more conventional approach to the organisation of work.

Worker Criteria

No formal monitoring of worker reactions to the project has been conducted. Observation and individual reactions suggest, however, that satisfaction is fairly high. Evidence for this includes the requests to transfer to the department and the low level of labour turnover. The project does seem to have provided workers with some opportunities for growth, though the significance of this is hard to assess. Finally it is worth noting that, while the project provides workers with job security and opportunities for social interaction, it has had no impact on the levels of pay.

Consultant's criteria

From the consultant's viewpoint the project is a success in that the start up of the department went smoothly and the organisation structure works well. However, the groups are less self-sufficient than was hoped and management is still required to sort out inter-group problems. Another criterion on which the results so far might be viewed as a little disappointing is that the project has yet to expand beyond the boundaries of the department.

Some issues arising from the project

Although this project can be judged a success according to certain criteria, it was obviously not without its problems. Some of these problems were inherent in the specific project but others have more general implications and highlight issues which must be taken into account in any attempt to introduce this kind of participation:

1 Problems inherent in participation from the bottom up

Within the Blackburn plant the departmental manager was given a reasonably free hand to organise his department as he wished. However, for this particular project he had support neither from his immediate boss nor from the group of top management within the plant. From their point of view there was no need to introduce a less hierarchical structure and they were suspicious of any attempt to give workers more information and participation. This lack of support was one of the reasons why the project failed to spread more widely through the plant and raises some questions about the value of participation which starts from the bottom and lacks top-management commitment.

If dissemination had been a crucial objective, then top management support would have been important from the start. On the other hand this might have meant that the project might never have got under way; as a result the consultant felt that it was best to keep the project at a relatively low profile.

2 Problems inherent in the participative process

A major objective of the project was to develop an open, participative climate within the department. Yet the workers came from other parts of the Blackburn plant and had an established set of expectations about their role. Within the quick-vision cathode department, boundaries were initially left deliberately unclear. At first this held some attractions for the workers, but they fairly soon realised that participation held its own dangers. For example, an open discussion could backfire by laying responsibility for certain failures at the feet of workers. Perhaps because of this, workers refused to set their own targets; they defined target-setting as outside their boundary of responsibility and left management to fix targets instead.

They refused, after a certain point, to institute intergroup participation unless it had direct repercussions; therefore management had to decide whether, for various reasons, a worker had to be temporarily transferred from one group to another, but the group decided who should be transferred. The groups became reluctant to make many positive suggestions; on the other hand they did point out problems, such as poor layout of benches, which inhibited social interaction. In short, the management aim of providing opportunities for growth through open boundaries was used by workers, with predetermined expectations, to limit their own sphere of responsibility. The groups decided how much they wanted to participate and did not go as far as management would have wished. This highlights the importance of worker expectations and the difficulty of radically altering established patterns of behaviour and established worker/management relations.

3 Problems inherent in the wider social system

This project could only be developed to the limits of the departmental manager's area of responsibility. Top management imposed a constraint; so, too, did the unions. Although the unions were not directly involved, the GMWU convener, representing the operators, was strongly supportive, having already worked with the consultant on similar projects. To the AUEW this was something new and they were suspicious; coupled with this, their plant bargaining strategy militated against co-operation on the project. These constraints must be part of the analysis of the social system and in this context they both limited and helped to encapsulate the project within the one department.

4 Problems inherent in the payment system

A central problem in the failure to obtain worker commitment was the poor relation between effort, performance and reward. When the workers asked what was in it for them, the answer was — not very much. Pay was not linked to production levels and therefore there was no financial incentive to increase output. Instead pay was based on a job-evaluation scheme which placed a premium on physical effort rather than responsibility. Therefore, where workers participated and in so doing exercised more responsibility, they received no financial reward. An inability to offer financial rewards in return for the outcomes of participation seems likely to constrain the effectiveness of a project in this kind of production context.

5 Problems inherent in the technology

The largely predetermined technology imposed severe limits on what could be done. Ideally the kind of work carried on in the department will eventually be automated out. When this happens, the requirement will be for alert machine-minders. On the other hand, the project does indicate that even with highly repetitive short-cycle work, there is scope for introducing some degree of shop-floor participation.

Conclusions

This chapter has outlined the steps involved in the introduction of semi-autonomous work groups in a department assembling quick-vision cathodes. It has highlighted the successes and the failures and has identified some of the limiting factors.

At present it is possible to detect some changes in attitudes at the Blackburn plant. Among senior management there is a growing concern for participation, stimulated partly by the current national debate. As a result they may perhaps begin to look more favourably on the kind of initiative we have described. Where the project itself has failed to provide a pressure for further change, the national debate may succeed in generating some sort of interest and action.

Summary

In 1973 plans were developed to manufacture quick-vision cathode heaters at the Mullard plant in Blackburn. The departmental manager wanted to use the opportunity of setting up a new operation to try out certain ideas on organisation and job design. To help in this, he involved an internal consultant, who subscribed to the principles of 'socio-technical' design.

Together they set three objectives for the department: to achieve quality and quantity targets; to provide opportunities for personal growth; and to bridge the gap between engineering and production. Through careful planning, extensive preparation, including training of staff and group problem-solving and a gradual build up of activities, the department was successfully launched. By March 1978 it employed eighty-one workers.

The department operated seven semi-autonomous work groups along stages in the production process, which retained the conventional technology with its repetitive work-cycle. Participation occurred through open discussion of all aspects of production and conditions and through the control given to the groups to organise everything for themselves.

The results show that quality and quantity of output was excellent, but not everyone used the opportunity to participate and the engineers failed to integrate into the groups. However, satisfaction appears to be high and labour turnover is low.

The project highlights a number of problems in introducing shop-floor participation. For example, participation from the bottom up makes dissemination difficult; it is difficult to gauge where workers will draw the line in participating in management issues; and the wider plant industrial relations system, the payment system and the predetermined technology all represent significant constraints.

Notes

[1] See Blake and Ross (1976).

[2] For a fuller discussion of these concepts, see Chapter 4.

[3] The numbers had been increased by the setting up of an evening shift. The workers on this shift are organised along group lines and operate successfully within the structure.

7 Team organisation in a construction firm

David Searle
Managing Director, Morgan & Grundy Limited

The company

In May 1972 I took over a company that was at that time engaged in the manufacture of metal laboratory furniture and fume cupboards. It soon became apparent that we were not actually marketing the skills we had, since we spoke of ourselves as 'furniture manufacturers'. As a result of this marketing policy we found ourselves, in the majority of cases, being used as such, and in these circumstances were in direct competition with a considerable number of other companies. The fundamental image of the company was therefore changed to that of being 'laboratory makers': that is, we started to sell on the grounds that we would design and build a laboratory, if necessary, from the foundations up. We would of course as a result of this utilise furniture and fume cupboards of our own manufacture but would also use the products and services of many other companies. This philosophy enabled us to expand at a significant rate and at the same time to rationalise our products, since, whereas in the past we were very happy to manufacture special items to others' designs, in those cases where we were the design authority we were able to reduce the number of specials to a minimum.

In 1973, as a result of this policy, we purchased another company engaged in the manufacture of PVC fans and extraction systems, and in the installation of mechanical services.

In November 1974 it was decided that we should also take under our wing another group company that was engaged in the manufacture of wooden laboratory furniture and we then had the problem of putting the two furniture companies together, since, by so doing, considerable economies could be achieved. This move was implemented, for it was already apparent that there was going to be a further down-turn in the UK economy.

The reason for change

As the original company had grown, it had become increasingly apparent that many problems were emerging in terms of worker-involvement, lines of demarcation, etc. The merger of the two companies, with an effective doubling of some of the departmental sizes, only served to highlight these problems and make a problem that was progressively growing within the original company explode into a size where something needed doing urgently.

We had up to this moment a traditional structure as in Figure 7.1 and problems occurred in and between the sales/estimating/contracting/installation departments. So far as the company was concerned, the symptoms of breakdown were:

(a) a decrease in performance so far as the ultimate customer was concerned;
(b) a decrease in the profitability of contracts;
(c) a decrease in the availability of information regarding the state of a contract;
(d) an increase in demarcation and friction between functions;
(e) an increase in the turnover of the more important skilled staff.

All the foregoing were recognised as being caused by people feeling not to be involved or responsible for a contract, cou-

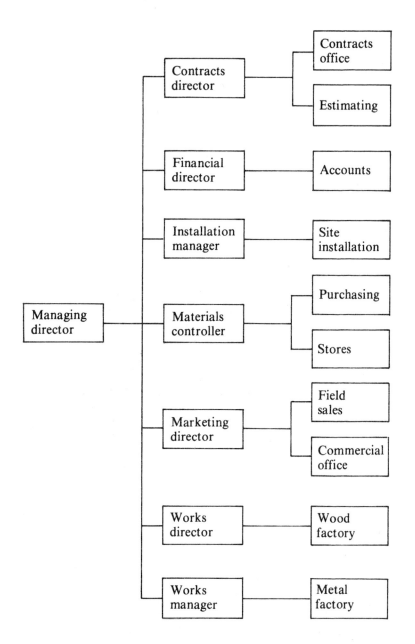

Figure 7.1   *Old organisation*

pled with such a large number of contracts in progress (some 400) that at no time was anyone in a position to feel that they knew the detailed state of any particular contract.

The traditional method of operation

At this point it is appropriate to look at the company organisation immediately after the merger and the method by which we conducted our business.

The method of operation was as shown in Figure 7.2 and began with our receiving an inquiry which resulted in a sales engineer visiting the client, discussing his needs, and undertaking to present him with a proposal involving both a laboratory design and a price.

The sales engineer would post into the office a sketch of his interpretation of the customer's needs (Interface 1) and this sketch would be passed to the contracts department for the preparation of the necessary drawing, which in turn would be passed to the estimating department for the preparation of an estimate. The completed estimate would be passed to the Commercial office (Interface 2) for turning into a proposal, which would then be forwarded to the Sales engineer for presentation to the client.

In the event of this proposal being accepted without any alterations, the order would then be received by the commercial office, which would process it and pass it to the contracts office (Interface 3), which in turn would prepare the necessary layout drawings, bills of quantities, orders on sub-contractors, etc., calling on the commercial office typists for any clerical facilities required.

After raising all the necessary contract paperwork, the contracts office would hand over the contract to the manufacturing units/purchasing office (Interface 4), who in due course would hand over to the installation department (Interface 5), which would be responsible for ensuring that all the necessary materials were available, agreeing with the client a site avail-

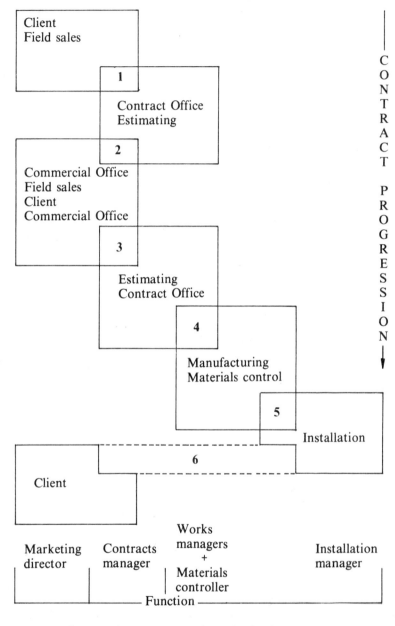

Figure 7.2 *Traditional method of operation*

ability date and installation and commissioning the laboratory.

There was in such an organisation, as can be seen, a whole
series of interfaces at which the responsibility for a contract
changed hands, with all the usual symptoms of persons or
departments on each side of the interface arguing as to
whether or not a certain matter was 'their responsibility' and
often resolving their difficulties by making the problem the
responsibility of some earlier interface in the chain. At the
same time, no person at the level of those who were actually
doing the work felt responsible for, nor could feel responsible
for, the profitability or otherwise of a contract, and hence, in
the long term, for the profitability or otherwise of the company.

Any sales engineer could have his drawing prepared by any
contract engineer who in turn would pass it to any one of
several estimators and, in the event of an order resulting from
this proposal, the contract might be allocated to another contract engineer and be installed by any one of many installation
engineers, in each case depending upon the workload of particular individuals within the departments.

This interface problem became apparent at all levels, and
there are many examples that could be quoted as warning
signs, but a few will suffice to given an indication:

(a) any attempt by management to question the orders
    received figure was quickly countered by a reply of the
    form, 'If I could only have the estimates done properly
    and on time, then I could get out the orders';

(b) any attempt to question the poor performance of the esti-
    mating department was countered by, 'If only the sales
    engineer would send in all the details and stop specifying
    special furniture, then we could provide the necessary
    estimates';

(c) on receipt of the order, the contract engineers would
    complain bitterly about the lack of information con-
    tained within the estimate, the fact that it was impracti-

cal to install due to building structural problems, and while the 'special' was quite a good idea, it could not possibly be engineered, whereas one of our standard pieces of equipment would have met 95 per cent of the customer's needs;

(d) the installation manager would complain that insufficient time had been allocated for installation, which in turn was the fault of the contract engineer for not being more careful with his design, the estimator for not allowing more time in the estimate and the sales engineer for not foreseeing the difficulties and highlighting them at the outset.

Hence the need for change.

Financial disadvantages of the traditional structure

It is interesting to look at some of the ways in which the original structure militated against profitability:

1 The sales engineer was interested only in obtaining an order, since this involved him in receiving a commission. To make sure of this he would obviously, at all times, be tempted to negotiate the minimum price.

This had particular dangers where quotations involved such things as installation work and 'specials', where it was very easy to underquote.

2 The contract engineer would process a contract as quickly as possible, again in order to obtain his commission, yet at the same time be interested in maintaining a substantial level of overtime payments. In processing the order he would have no particular incentive to effect any cost savings if they affected his rate of output, or if this involved him in extra effort.

3 The estimator would not consider in any depth the unknown elements of a contract and would if necessary take risks, often on the wrong side. At the same time there

was no incentive for him to turn estimates round quickly, but a large incentive to maintain his level of overtime payments.

4 Installation engineers were not interested in completing a job rapidly or at a minimum cost, but only in maintaining a maximum level of overtime.

These are only some of the disadvantages — many more could be mentioned.

Principles of change

This analysis of the problems of the organisation showed that it was necessary to:

(a) destroy interfaces wherever possible;
(b) give authority and responsibility over as wide a field of activities as possible;
(c) increase job interest and involvement;
(d) increase financial involvement;
(e) if possible provide incentives and a financial reward based on performance.

The team concept

After considerable thought, I decided that a team concept would meet parameters (a), (b) and (c) above and that, with such a concept, it should be possible to devise a suitable incentive scheme to meet (d) and (e). The principle laid down for this concept was that, from the receipt of an inquiry from a client and until that client was handed over a completed laboratory built to his satisfaction, the business should be handled by a group of persons with total responsibility and authority for that contract, and they should be rewarded or penalised on the basis of the financial success or failure of that contract. As an ideal concept, this has not been achieved in total, but it has been in large part, and has produced many of the benefits anticipated.

The teams

On the basis of the foregoing, it was necessary for each team to have within it a person or persons from each of the departments that were previously involved in the processing of a contract. That is:

(a) a sales engineer;
(b) a member of the commercial office;
(c) contract engineers;
(d) an estimator;
(e) installation engineers.

It had already been accepted that it was impracticable to split the manufacturing units and/or stores into team components, therefore there was no attempt to give each team any element of these facilities. This was not a serious weakness since traditionally the interface between production and the other functions had created the least of the problems. The number of people included in each of the new teams was typically nine. The country was already divided into geographical regions for sales purposes and it was decided to continue in this manner, making each team responsible for all the contracts within a certain region. Each of the vacancies previously listed was therefore filled as follows:

(a) the sales engineer covering the region concerned;
(b) a secretary from the commercial office;
(c) two contract engineers from the contracts office;
(d) an estimator or a contract engineer from the contracts office;
(e) three installation engineers from the installation department.

At this point in time it was decided to make the sales engineer responsible for his own estimating, thereby eliminating one of the interface problems, and the position of estimator was changed to that of project co-ordinator. This person was intended to act as the central co-ordinator within the team for all contracts; that is, his or her duties would involve progressing materials from the manufacturing units and purchasing, and co-ordinating the installation engineers to ensure that at all times there was parity between materials availability, installation engineers and site availability. The management organisation then became as shown in Figure 7.3 and it will be noted that the only person it was possible to put at 'the top of the tree' was the client, whilst those persons in line-management positions were now in a position where their duties consisted of:

(a) laying down fundamental policies for their function;
(b) offering the benefit of their experience as and when required;
(c) most important, having free time to consider the future rather than the present.

Conditions of employment

Prior to the team concept, the conditions of employment for each of the persons concerned were as follows:

(a) the sales engineer was on staff conditions; that is, he received an annual salary with no overtime, was paid sick pay and also commission based on the value of the orders he received;
(b) like the sales engineer, the contract engineer was on staff conditions, except that he received overtime payment plus a commission payable at the time he completed all the parts lists, etc., for any particular contract;
(c) the estimator was on staff conditions with overtime but no commission;
(d) the typist was on the same conditions as the estimator;
(e) installation engineers were on hourly paid conditions (no sick pay, etc.) and received overtime but no commission.

For any team concept to work, it was felt that all members of the team must have the same conditions of employment and the same motivation, and it was therefore decided to raise them all to a common standard; that is, make them all staff on

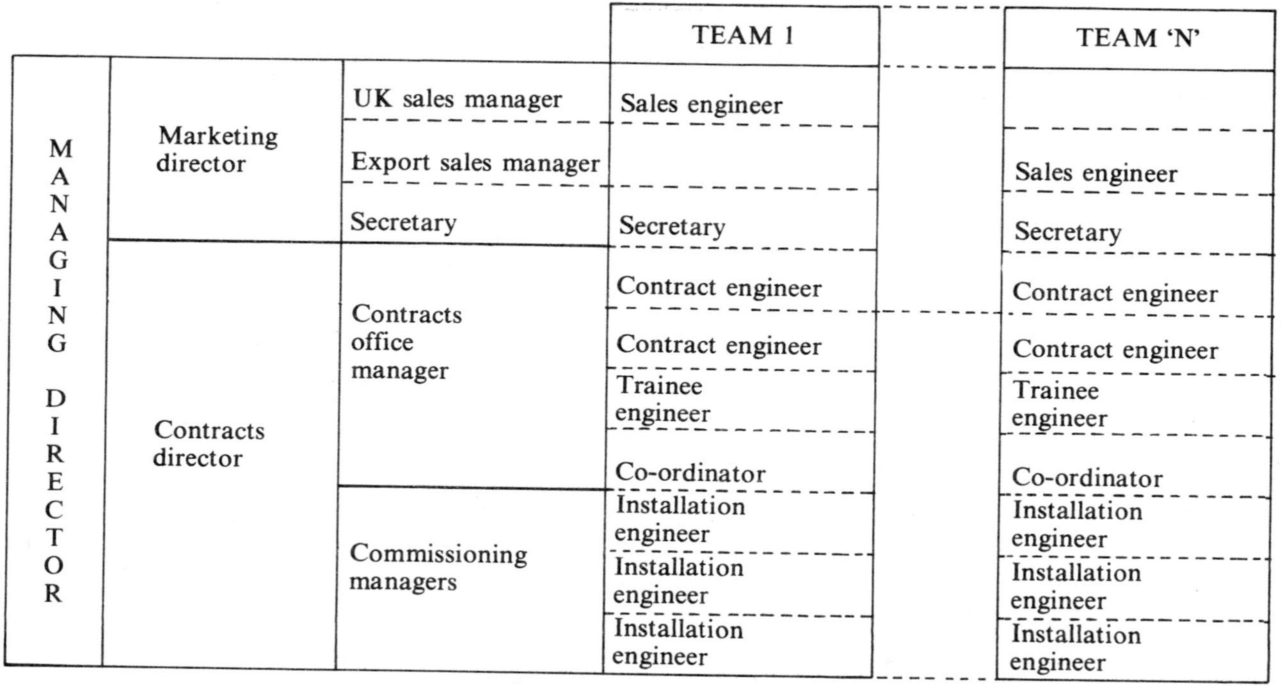

MANAGING DIRECTOR		TEAM 1	TEAM 'N'
Marketing director	UK sales manager	Sales engineer	Sales engineer
	Export sales manager		
	Secretary	Secretary	Secretary
Contracts director	Contracts office manager	Contract engineer	Contract engineer
		Contract engineer	Contract engineer
		Trainee engineer	Trainee engineer
	Commissioning managers	Co-ordinator	Co-ordinator
		Installation engineer	Installation engineer
		Installation engineer	Installation engineer
		Installation engineer	Installation engineer

Figure 7.3 *New organisation*

a basic salary with no overtime, but with a common bonus scheme ideally directly related to the profitability of a contract.

These changes in conditions had to be negotiated carefully with the various grades of persons being introduced in to the teams.

Financial incentive

To make the concept truly effective it was decided that a system of financial incentives should be introduced and that each contract should be judged independently on the basis of any excess contribution it made: that is, any contribution in excess of that required by the company. This excess would be divided on the basis of 40 per cent to the team and 60 per cent to the company and within the team it would be divided equally amongst the members with the exception of the typist, who would receive a half-share.

At the same time, since the two sales managers, the marketing director's secretary, the contracts office manager and the commissioning managers, although engaged in an advisory capacity, were expected to assist the teams in every manner possible, it was decided that each of them should in turn receive a bonus payable on the integrated total of all the teams.

As a large part of the business was involved in quoting and estimating such things as installation time, the sales engineer could influence this bonus, whilst, at the same time, the contract engineer could influence it by clever design and the installation engineers by efficient installation. Thus all those who previously had no reason to improve a contract's profitability, now had a financial incentive to do so.

It can of course be argued that with such a system it was possible for the sales engineer to become greedy and price the company out of the market place. However, during the introduction of the concept, it was made quite clear to all concerned that, first, they had to consider in their own interests the long-term prosperity of the business and in this context it was more important to be efficient than to raise prices. At the same time it was arranged for the company contribution formula to be varied in the light of the volume of business at any one time so that with a decreasing volume of business all the existing contracts would be prejudiced and the distribution of bonus reduced by an increase in the overhead recovery rates. To give the system impact it was also decided that bonus would be paid monthly on the basis of the contracts completed during the previous month.

Quality assurance

The system as envisaged was seen to have one inherent defect, and this was that the teams could progressively lower the company's standards of laboratory building and at the same time fail to satisfy the ultimate client's needs. With this in mind, the two senior installation managers who previously controlled the installation engineers of the two companies, were appointed commissioning managers. Their duty was to visit a site at such a time as the team asked for a final inspection and to accept or reject it. In the event of their accepting it, they would officially take the client around the installation and 'hand over' to him. As a result of this 'hand-over' the commissioning manager could write to the client confirming that hand-over had taken place and a copy of this letter was to be used as an instruction to the quantity surveyors to raise the final invoice. This final invoice in turn was to be used by the accounts department to pull the contract cost cards and include them in that team's completions for the month. This hand-over had the additional advantage of establishing a clearly defined date from which:

(a) settlement of the account was due;
(b) the warranty period commenced;
(c) settlement of any retentions fell due.

Introduction of the concept

Having determined the concept, it then became necessary to:

(a) sell it to those involved;
(b) establish the necessary control systems;
(c) educate the members of the teams as to how the new concept would work.

Selling the concept

Since the conditions of employment of all the various categories of staff were going to be changed to a greater or lesser degree, it was necessary to convince them that these changes offered them significant advantages, bearing in mind that people were going to lose overtime payments, etc.

Two things made this possible, the first being, I believe, that people wanted to get rid of all the existing problems of interface disputes, etc., and could see that perhaps there would be more personal involvement in a contract and, at the same time, less friction. Second, they also realised that by getting down to doing the job in a methodical manner, savings could be effected, and as a result they could envisage significant bonuses being paid. Perhaps it was at this moment that the bonus payment had its most significant effect, since I am not sure that without it the changes could have been effected so easily, if at all.

Meetings were held by the management with all those concerned *en masse* and then with individual groups of personnel, to sort out any particular problems envisaged. At the same time it was pointed out that there would be a three-month trial period at the end of which the situation would be reviewed and any necessary changes introduced.

Systems

In order that the teams might measure their own performance on both completed contracts and those still in progress, it was established that a monthly print-out be prepared giving contract costs for each team. This system had to be sophisticated enough to enable them to evaluate the effectiveness of their individual and corporate actions. These changes involved a considerable initial effort in system design, and then, as the teams became more effective and asked for ever more information, further changes had to be made since the momentum could only be maintained if it was seen that management was serious in its intent to provide whatever was considered to be reasonable in the interest of the team performing more proficiently.

Education

It was necessary to discuss the concept in depth with all those involved. Meetings were held with all of these people together and separately, in teams, to explain all the ramifications the system could have, the manner in which they personally and jointly could affect performance, the interpretation of the computer print-out, etc.

The three-month trial period was also arranged, during which time everything operated as in the eventual concept but no conditions of employment were permanently changed, nor was any bonus payable. This period was intended to be used to establish that the concept would work to the benefit of all those involved and at the same time to establish that the systems were fully understood and fully operational.

Unfortunately, insofar as the system of evaluation was concerned, this exercise did not prove particularly successful and it appeared that, since no real money was actually involved, people did not take the interest that was anticipated in the computer print-outs. Nevertheless, it did enable the groups to come together as teams to start to understand one another in this new environment.

Purposely no team leader was nominated since it was felt that this person should emerge as the operation got under way.

Initial problems

Many problems emerged, most of them small and of such a nature that a small change overcame them. However, one or two significant ones which were not fully anticipated are of interest.

The first and most serious of these was the personality problem. We had put together groups of people with traditionally different backgrounds and attitudes, and often incompatible personalities. We had put them together on the basis of an amalgam for each team of, as we saw it, the necessary skills required and the strengths of those involved. Problems arose immediately, and for some considerable period it was necessary for management to become very involved with each of the teams concerned in order to help them overcome their differences. In certain cases it was necessary to transfer people between teams, but this was an exception rather than a rule, and, in general, management was involved in talking-through the problems with the persons concerned.

The second difficulty was the question of leadership within the individual teams. For the first three months after the trial period, the teams operated without managers. It soon became evident, however, that there was a need for a person whom a client could talk to about his job and who could determine priorities between as many as forty contracts. In certain teams a clear leader emerged very rapidly and was appointed manager, but in others this did not happen, and management decided to intervene and promote one of the team members to the position of team manager. This was, as should have been expected, a singular failure, and we should have realised that if such a person did not emerge automatically, then in fact it indicated that the team did not have within it the necessary capability. This problem was overcome eventually only by employing people of sufficiently high calibre to work within the teams.

The other significant problem was that of educating the members of the team to understand in depth the results and cost implications of their actions and the manner in which these actions affected the print-out.

Operation of teams

The atmosphere within the teams is relaxed and yet purposeful. The whole team feels and acts as a unit as regards satisfying the client's needs. Teams interview and take on their own personnel. Weak members of a team can be 'squeezed out' by the other members of the team. When necessary, decisions are taken on an *ad hoc* basis by independent members of the team and accepted as binding on the rest.

All sales quotations are checked by the team before they are submitted to the client, and if necessary are reasoned through by discussions between the salesman and other team members. For contracts with a large installation element, the installation engineers are involved in the estimation of the installation cost. On large contracts, one of the engineers will be involved with the salesman and client before the quotation is prepared to ensure a total understanding of all the ramifications of the job.

Depending on the work load at any time, salesmen will act as contract engineers and contract engineers as salesmen or installation engineers. Clients with repeat business establish a close relationship with all members of the team and have been known to object when we have had cause to make changes.

Conclusions

There can be no doubt, looking back over three years, that the original aims have been met and that many of the old problems have disappeared. People are more involved and, we believe, happier in their working environment. The system has been advantageous to the employees, the company and the client. The profitability of the contracts has improved, our sales have increased dramatically, we have a far better relationship with our clients and we are keeping our better staff.

There can, however, be little doubt that the management totally underestimated the degree of effort required on their part to make the system effective. This work has been extremely rewarding and all those concerned feel a sense of excitement and satisfaction when they see the advantages the concept has produced.

Summary

The company, engaged in the design, supply and installation of laboratories, was concerned about decreasing performance and profitability, accompanied by increasing internal friction, demarcation and loss of important staff. The organisation consisted of four separate functions involved in different stages of each contract, with many of the problems arising at the interfaces between functions. The existing reward systems did not favour action designed to increase efficiency or profitability, and it was not possible to hold anyone responsible for individual contracts.

To overcome these problems the company, except for the manufacturing operations, was reorganised into a number of teams, each team containing all the commercial, estimating, engineering and installation skills required to deal with contracts from start to finish. Each team was made fully responsible for all the contracts in its region, from initial client contact and quotation to completion of installation, and was given a share of profits on completed contracts.

The chapter describes the implementation and operation of the system as well as the supporting changes in control and reward systems and in the functions of senior management. It also describes the problems encountered during the introduction of the new system and how they were overcome. Following introduction of the team concept the company has increased both its sales and its profitability, as well as the personal involvement of employees.

Part III
Participation at plant level

Participation at plant level in the UK has a longer if less exciting history than most other forms, in the shape of 'joint consultation' — usually, in the past, confined to issues of secondary importance. In recent times, however, there has been a complementary increase in the real influence of the work force at local level through the growth of plant-bargaining, and the two approaches are now apparently beginning to merge in an increasing number of cases.

In this section we look specifically at these developments, with Chapter 8 providing a general review of the growth of local and productivity bargaining, and the enhanced role of works councils. Though the approach to significant forms of plant-level participation may be from the bottom up, as at Scottish & Newcastle Breweries (Chapter 5) or from the top down as at Cadbury Schweppes (Chapter 11), it is of particular interest to follow developments at a single site over a period of time, and Chapter 9 provides a case history of participative change at one ICI plant which shows how plant-level participation can provide the means of integrating the framework of a national agreement with a grass-roots involvement in joint problem-solving, and create a single forum out of elements of joint consultation and collective bargaining.

8 Plant-level participation

David Guest

Lecturer in Personnel Management, London School of Economics and Political Science

This section of the book is concerned with forms of participation which are designed to deal with issues arising at the plant level [1] in organisations. Implicitly, this assumes that the plant is part of a larger organisation. Indeed the form that plant-level participation takes is likely to be influenced by what already exists at other levels as well as by historical trends such as the move towards more localised collective bargaining; and in practice all the forms of participation found at plant level, with the possible exception of certain types of works council, can also be found at other levels in the organisation. The important and distinguishing feature, therefore, is the concern with plant-level issues.

Any organisation has some degree of choice over the level at which certain decisions are made and countervailing pressure will often exist favouring both centralisation and decentralisation. For example, consistent pressures over a number of years favoured the development of collective bargaining at company and plant, as opposed to the national level.[2] Many production decisions are likely to be most appropriately dealt with at plant level, although factors such as size, complexity and standardisation of operation across units will all influence this. The increasing use of computers and associated information and control systems has usually extended the flexibility and choice of level of decision-making. The content of plant-level participation is therefore likely to vary considerably from one organisation to another.

The most widespread forms of plant-level participation in the UK are collective bargaining and joint consultation, although recently there has been a growing interest in works councils. The remainder of this chapter will explore the nature of these three forms of participation and examine some of the issues raised by them. Before embarking on this, it is important to recognise that plant-level participation can also include individual forms such as briefing groups. The case of Scottish & Newcastle Breweries, described in Chapter 5, is an example of the use of briefing groups at a variety of levels. Plant-level participation may also take the form of suggestion schemes or attitude surveys, both of which were mentioned in Chapter 4 and will not be discussed again here.

Collective bargaining

The analysis of the meaning of participation in Chapter 2 utilised control as the crucial variable. Defining participation in terms of control over management decisions inevitably embraces collective bargaining and indeed the trade union movement constantly refers to collective bargaining as the major form of participation. To those employers who view participation as a means of creating involvement and commitment to organisational goals, the inclusion of collective bargaining, which they may see as a form of confrontation rather than collaboration, will appear strange. Yet it deserves consideration for several reasons: first, within our definition, it does constitute a form of participation; second, the unions view it as such; third, it has historically emerged as the major formal system of worker-management interaction on a wide range of issues; and, finally, because it provides an important part of the organisational and cultural context in which other forms of participation might develop. This last point will be considered first in more detail.

Collective bargaining as context

In many organisations collective bargaining is well established at both company and plant level. Where this is the case, the available evidence (see for example Parker, 1977) indicates that both management and shop stewards are reasonably satisfied with the opportunities that it provides for interaction and negotiation.

For trade unions, collective bargaining represents the chief form of participation and they are emphatic that one of their primary goals is an extension of its scope and coverage. Any other form of participation which might appear to offer an alternative or a counter to collective bargaining or which encroaches upon its sphere of control is therefore likely to be opposed. On the other hand, proposals which build on or extend collective bargaining are more likely to receive union support.

The reasons why the union movement gives priority to collective bargaining are partly historical, partly a reflection of the fact that it deals with the key topics of terms and conditions of employment, including pay, and partly because it provides the essential base on which union power is built. Crucially, it has provided workers, through the union, with an opportunity to exert collective control over decisions affecting them where other approaches have failed to do this so effectively.

For these reasons, the TUC has argued that all participation should take place through a single union channel of representation. Forms of participation such as autonomous work groups or works councils, which may appear to be approaches not under direct union control, therefore tend to be opposed or, at best, treated with considerable suspicion. Labour Party policy and the majority report of the Bullock Committee have both been heavily influenced by the arguments of the TUC. Thus the Bullock Report quotes, and builds into its own proposals, the TUC statement that 'collective bargaining is and will continue to be the central method of joint regulation in industry and the public services' (TUC, 1974, p. 7).

Developments in participation through collective bargaining

The Donovan Report (1968) identified the growth of plant-level collective bargaining as one of the most important changes in the post-1945 industrial relations scene. It added that the piecemeal and chaotic development of informal plant-level procedures was partly to blame for many of the industrial relations problems found in the UK in the 1960s.

The Donovan diagnosis probably overstated both the growth and the influence of plant-level bargaining. Much of the public sector still has centralised bargaining and in the private sector many of the developments have occurred at company rather than, or in addition to, plant level. In private industry, therefore, the significant point was more the diminishing role of industry-wide bargaining. What the debate surrounding the Donovan Report did succeed in doing was to focus considerable attention on collective bargaining at plant level.

Retrospective analysis (see Gennard and Roberts, 1970; Guest and Fatchett, 1974) has pointed to a number of factors influencing the growth of company and more particularly plant bargaining. Three seem to have been particularly important. The first was the economic factor of virtually full employment for most of the 1950s and the first half of the 1960s, resulting in increased local union power and competition for labour among local employers, pushing up wages and moving away from the national guidelines. Partly linked to this, a second influence was the growth of the shop steward movement and a recognition by management that to manage effectively they had to gain the co-operation of the work force partly through the shop stewards. The third factor was the growing concern for and emphasis on productivity. Productivity bargaining inevitably required negotiation at the local level and became particularly significant because it helped to extend the scope of collective bargaining to cover issues such as manning, training, job evaluation and work allocation, topics which had often previously been viewed as areas of managerial prerogative.

Surveys over the last ten years suggest that the growth of plant-level bargaining has continued (see Parker 1974, 1977). More recently this trend has been consolidated by legislation such as the Employment Protection Act, 1975, and to a lesser extent the Health and Safety at Work Act, 1974. Both pieces of legislation extend the access to information of shop stewards and will in many cases extend the areas of joint regulation. Recent pay policy has rekindled an interest in self-financing productivity deals, so that an industry such as mining, which for many years has had centralised wage negotiations, has now added an element of pit bargaining.

Two counter-trends to the growth of plant bargaining may be noted. One is the persistent attempt to operate a national wages policy, which effectively limits the scope of 'free' collective bargaining. The other is an attempt by many large organisations to unify and simplify their negotiating systems to provide more central control. While such moves may limit the scope for local negotiation over wages, the scope of plant bargaining may extend instead to cover other topics.

The implication of the growth in trade union membership, the impact of recent legislation and the extension of the scope of local bargaining is that collective bargaining constitutes a major form of indirect participation which management must take into account in any action it proposes.

Management and collective bargaining

Despite opposition by some managers to any encroachment into areas of management control at plant level, one of the interesting features of the growth of plant bargaining is that much of it has been initiated by management in an attempt to compete for labour or raise productivity. Furthermore the brief review of shop-floor schemes in Chapter 4 indicates that the chance of success of job enrichment or autonomous work groups, which are usually management initiatives, is increased when the worker representatives are involved and a pay increase is provided. In short, a considerable number of managers have seen benefits in initiating an extension of the scope of plant-level bargaining. Coupled with the fact that the great majority of both managers and shop stewards are satisfied with their relations at this level, the evidence suggests that it may be in management's interest to look far more closely at the potential of extending this form of participation.

One of the main reasons for opposition from the CBI and many management organisations to an extension of collective bargaining is its potentially divisive nature. It is to be expected that on a number of issues the goals of employer and employee will diverge. Where collective bargaining, as a result of historical tradition and the current industrial relations climate, becomes a forum for confrontation, management in particular, but possibly also the work force, may seek an opportunity to develop an alternative form of participation where a wider range of issues can be considered in a more open and less conflict-ridden way.

This raises the more fundamental question of whether forms of joint regulation other than collective bargaining can and should be developed at plant level. It is in this context that a works council, along the lines of those developed in West Germany where worker representatives have co-determination rights on a number of issues, deserves consideration. Before turning to the nature and scope of works councils, and accepting the central role of collective bargaining, it is important to take into account the process of joint consultation and the reasons why it is widely regarded as relatively unsuccessful.

Joint consultation

Joint consultation is a formal system of communication and discussion between management and worker representatives. These representatives will often, but not always, be shop stewards. The aims of joint consultation seem to have been to provide a channel of two-way communication and in particular to inform workers of management plans and policies and seek worker opinions on these and related matters. Whatever the outcome of these discussions, management retains the right to take the decisions about the topics under discussion. Therefore one attraction of this approach for management is that it involves no loss of control. This is not to deny that worker representatives may influence management decisions. Furthermore, simply by communicating information, management is providing a potentially powerful source of control. Nevertheless, some analyses suggest that, while some of the information is concerned with production issues, much is either historical or essentially trivial.

The growth of joint consultation particularly in the public sector can be traced back to the setting up of Whitley Councils, soon after the 1914-18 war. The heyday of joint consultation, however, was in the late 1940s and early 1950s when the success of the joint production committees during the 1939-45 war was channelled into consultation committees throughout much of industry. A survey conducted in the late 1940s (NIIP, 1952) showed that 73 per cent of the sample of 751 firms had some sort of joint consultation. However, by the end of the 1960s, another survey (Clarke, Fatchett and Roberts, 1972) indicated that the proportion of organisations still maintaining joint consultation machinery had fallen to 32 per cent.

The decline of joint consultation parallels the growth of plant bargaining. The reasons for the decline can be attributed to the fact that it has tended to deal with non-contentious issues which, although of interest to some workers, were marginal compared with the topics covered by plant bargaining. Even for those non-contentious kinds of issue, management has often preferred to communicate direct with the work force, thereby by-passing the joint consultation system. Since, in addition, consultation gave no control over decision-taking to the worker representatives, it is not surprising that with the advent of plant bargaining, and more particularly productivity bargaining, it began to fall by the wayside.

Although the decline in joint consultation seems to be continuing, it has persisted in a number of contexts and may even be going through something of a minor revival. There are, of course, the circumstances which have been described, in which it limps along without fulfilling any very useful purpose; but there are also situations where it can make a contribution. These include the following:

1 Organisations where collective bargaining remains largely centralised. In parts of the public sector and in a number of medium and large companies, much of the pay bargaining is centralised and plant bargaining is relatively underdeveloped. There are therefore still useful issues for discussion through consultation.

2 In large organisations lack of communication on a range of issues often produces a felt need for greater contact. Consultation can help to fill at least part of this need. In addition the growing concern for adequate disclosure of information has led some organisations to revive their consultation systems for this purpose.

3 There are some companies and nationalised industries where the traditions of joint consultation are strong. The company ethic and often the enthusiasm of a number of key individuals has meant that joint consultation, often somewhat adapted, has survived in an effective form.

4 Sometimes the spirit and aims of joint consultation have survived in an amended form, typically as some type of works council. Despite trade union antagonism at the national level, there is some evidence of growth in this area as management seeks to develop its own ideas and also to counter union plans to extend collective bargaining.

Traditional pure forms of joint consultation probably have a limited future. As the Bullock Report observes:

> It has been customary to draw a distinction between consultation on the one hand and negotiation or collective bargaining on the other, but in practice the distinction is blurred and there has been a gradual trend in recent years

towards the fusion of consultative and negotiating machinery. The purely consultative system, where it is clearly
understood that, however much influence those consulted may have, any decisions taken are those of management, is becoming less common. Consultation is being
developed to the point where those consulted acquire a de
facto power of veto over certain actions of management
[pp. 42-3].

The implication of this statement is that new systems are evolving out of joint consultation. Although they involve joint decision-making and a power of veto, they need not take on the
form and values associated with traditional collective bargaining. Some form of works council may therefore hold considerable attractions for management.

Works councils

In a number of European countries, most notable among
them probably being West Germany, a works council has a
clearly defined meaning. In the UK, however, the term has
been used very loosely to refer to a variety of plant-level activities ranging from traditional joint consultation and information meetings at one extreme to joint regulation of a range of
activities at the other. Typically, the works council will involve
some merging of consultation and bargaining and will therefore involve a greater or lesser degree of shared decision-making and joint regulation. This trend in the UK seems to be
paralleled in those other European countries where works
councils have traditionally been largely consultative and
where there appears to have been a recent growth in the shop
steward movement.

Evidence to the Bullock Committee demonstrated the variety of forms of plant committee which have developed in
recent years. One review of the company evidence to the Committee (Drinkwater, 1976) identified at least ten titles to

denote plant-level variants on works councils. Many of the systems behind these titles seemed to represent attempts to develop beyond traditional joint consultation. The value of such systems for management is that they attempt to deal in a constructive manner with a range of issues, mainly in the areas of production and personnel, which might otherwise provide the subject matter for potentially divisive bargaining. They also provide a forum for the discussion of management plans, policies and performance, information on which is now more widely communicated to the work force. Another impetus comes from recent legislation and in particular from the Health and Safety at Work Act, 1974, which provides for joint safety committees, with union control over the appointment of worker representatives The subject matter of these committees and the powers vested in them suggest that they do not fall neatly into either of the traditional categories of joint consultation or negotiation.

Works councils and their variants are based on certain ideological assumptions and in particular on the belief in the mutual benefit to be gained by both employers and employees from increased efficiency of operation. Arguing the case for parity representation on company boards, the TUC, in its evidence to the Bullock Committee, implicitly accepted this viewpoint by referring to the 'essentially joint interest of labour and capital in the enterprise' (TUC, 1976, p. 44). Of course not everyone on either side of industry would accept this integrative view and the engineering unions, for example, are strongly opposed to any actions which will perpetuate the existing capitalist system of ownership and control.

The contrasting conflict-based distributive ideology, which implies, on the union side, the goal of a truly socialist state, including some form of worker control in industry, would lead to a more exclusive focus on collective bargaining. Where such views are dominant, and also where workers, rightly or wrongly, are highly suspicious of management's motives, attempts to introduce works councils are likely to be opposed and management would be wise to consider whether a different strategy would be more sensible. Where management decides that it would like to proceed with the introduction of a works council, it must be ready to face a number of possible union objections. One issue, which was raised earlier, is the demand for single-channel representation. This may be overcome by accepting election or appointment through the trade unions, thereby at the same time encouraging non-union members to join a union. There are sufficient examples of successful schemes to suggest that the existence of two systems of plant-level participation side by side need not present serious problems. A linked objection, again raised earlier, is that the new scheme may erode the union power exerted through collective bargaining. Again, there is no reason why this need be so, particularly if shop stewards participate in both schemes and can therefore see when there is a danger of issues being discussed in the wrong context.

Perhaps one of the best-known examples of a works council, where collective bargaining and consultation have been combined and where many of the issues raised here have been thought through and resolved, has operated successfully for many years at the Glacier Metal Company (see Brown, 1971; Jaques 1951).

Whatever criticisms may be voiced at national level, trade unionists within companies are often fairly open to innovations. The growing number of works councils, and the varying forms that they take, suggests that they may be more widely developed in the future. Whether their development makes sense depends on the existing culture and industrial relations climate. In some organisations, where collective bargaining works well, it may be more sensible to extend it. At the other extreme, where it is highly divisive, alternatives may be opposed and rendered impractical. Between these two points, there may sometimes be a case for developing a new form of plant and company-level participation along the lines of a works council.

Summary

Three forms of plant-level participation have been discussed, namely collective bargaining, joint consultation and works councils.

Collective bargaining has developed at plant level during the last twenty-five years in response to a variety of pressures including full employment in the 1950s, the growth in the number and influence of shop stewards and productivity bargaining. It is important to the discussion of participation for several reasons: first, as the preferred form of participation for the unions, it provides an important element of the context in which any new forms may be developed; second, it provides the means through which other forms of participation may have to be negotiated; third, it provides a forum for management-worker interaction with which both sides are satisfied.

Joint consultation has operated at plant level for many years, but since its heyday in the late 1940s has gone into decline. This can be attributed partly to the non-contentious, often historical issues with which it has dealt and its growing insignificance in comparison with collective bargaining at plant level. There are, however, some organisations where it has continued to flourish and it may be showing signs of a small revival.

Where there is a revival in consultation it may often appear in the form of a works council and in this context works councils have been criticised by the unions. Nevertheless, where they provide opportunities for joint regulation, as in West Germany, works councils may provide a valuable forum for the discussion of issues which fall outside the conventional scope of collective bargaining. Whether it is more sensible to build on existing collective bargaining or to develop works councils depends very much on the historical and cultural factors within the plant.

Notes

[1] It is worth emphasising that the concept of 'plant' is in itself problematic. For example one site may contain several plants and within one plant there may be a number of operating units. There may, therefore, be a number of layers at which participation can occur between the shop-floor and company levels.

[2] Gennard and Roberts (1970), for example, identified a range of factors of which near full-employment and a critical shortage of certain categories of labour were among the most important.

9 Developing participation in a chemical works

Geoffrey Richards

Works Manager, ICI Grangemouth

Introduction

The Works at Grangemouth with which this case study is concerned is part of the Organics Division of ICI. It employs nearly 2,000 people and has been in operation since 1920. The works is engaged in the manufacture of several hundred fine chemicals (dyestuffs, pigments, pharmaceuticals, agricultural chemicals), mostly in small-scale, multiproduct, batch units accommodated in thirteen principal manufacturing buildings. Services (steam, electricity) are generated on site and maintenance and minor capital work is carried out by the works engineering department.

Formal joint consultation with hourly-paid employees was introduced in 1929. It operated at three levels: viz., company, division and works. The 'Works Council' comprised equal numbers of management and employee representatives and its function was essentially advisory. The main topics dealt with were safety, welfare (canteens, changing accommodation, protective clothing, etc.) and company schemes, such as long-service awards, pensions and employee profit-sharing, which were not the subject of negotiations with trade unions.

Formal joint consultation with staff, along similar lines, did not start until 1963.

Parallel with the consultation arrangements, negotiating procedures, including procedures for handling disputes, had been agreed with unions representing hourly-paid employees in 1937. Similar arrangements for staff have been agreed during the past few years. The agreement required negotiations at local and intermediate level under the chairmanship of the works manager. In the event of agreement not being reached, a headquarters conference between the company and the national officers of the union involved was required at which the local people acted only as advisors. Although the detailed arrangements have been subsequently modified, the existing negotiating agreement is the same in principle.

The position prior to 1965

During the postwar period, a seller's market existed, enabling a considerable expansion of the business to take place by major capital investment. By 1953, however, worldwide competition had become intensive and the profitability of the business declined. To cope with this, three main strategies were evolved to improve productivity; namely:

(a) manufactures were concentrated into fewer production units;
(b) method study was used extensively to improve work methods and organisation;
(c) incentive schemes based on work measurement were extended.

Incentive schemes of this type were not new to the works. The first such scheme for process operators had been introduced in the early 1930s. However, no such scheme existed in the engineering department and attempts by management to introduce such schemes were fiercely resisted by the craft unions on the grounds that they were divisive and contrary to their principles that all their members should be treated alike. The consequences of this were serious because:

1 The craftsmen earned significantly less than other craftsmen in the company who had accepted incentive schemes. To increase their earnings, they frequently used industrial action to gain other benefits (e.g. working conditions payments) and the union/management relationship deteriorated into one of confrontation.

2 The low profitability of the business made it impossible to make a case for major capital investment to replace plants which were now becoming technically obsolescent.

By 1964 the whole future of the works was being questioned.

1965-67: Application of incentives in engineering department

Fortunately, a significant expansion of world trade occurred in 1964, resulting in higher sales and some improvement in profitability. This afforded a breathing space for management to try a different strategy than confrontation. The initial steps were difficult in that communication with shop stewards and employees was poor and attitudes on all sides were rigid.

The first step was to modify managerial attitudes. Many managers had operated in a win/lose environment for so long that 'winning' had become an objective in itself. It was necessary to rethink what management objectives really were; i.e., to make the business viable, ensure continuity and pave the way for possible expansion. Managers had to recognise, too, the realities of the power situation which prevented the imposition of their solutions and hence called for a different managerial style.

The next step was to use the negotiating machinery, whenever industrial action occurred, to explore with shop stewards the thinking behind their actions and also management's thinking. As a result of these discussions, management made every effort to change its stance where this could be justified and this led gradually to a climate in which people were more willing to explore issues, even though a great deal of mutual mistrust remained.

It now became possible to examine with shop stewards their fears and objections to incentives. They were given some training in rating and work measurement to remove the 'mystique' and then the management discussed why it believed that it was important to the works that the engineeing department should operate an incentive scheme.

Eventually, it was agreed to give incentives a try provided application was supervised by a management/union group. In the event, the application went through reasonably smoothly, thus achieving a number of objectives:

1 It improved the efficiency of engineering department.
2 It improved the trust between unions and management.
3 It reduced the lack of confidence by top management in the site as one suitable for major capital investment.
4 It established three important elements of a change programme;

(a) there must be at least a minimum level of mutual trust;
(b) there must be some understanding of the changes proposed and the need for them;
(c) jointly agreed actions, jointly monitored, produce a higher degree of commitment than change brought about by management edict.

1967: The need for further change

Despite the improvements in the engineering department and the sanctioning of a major capital project, much of the business was still far from satisfactory and further improvement was essential. Now that some degree of rapport had been established with the shop stewards, it seemed sensible to find out whether further change was possible — particularly as experience elsewhere suggested that failure to keep moving would lead to exploitation of the incentive scheme and the forming of new entrenched positions by unions and management.

During the period 1965-67 the company had been experimenting, by agreement with the signatory unions, with ways of improving the payment structure and improving productivity to pay for such changes. The so-called 'Manpower Utilisation and Payment Structure Agreement' (MUPS) covered experimentation on a limited number of sites, but by 1967 it had been agreed that discussion of the thinking behind this agreement could be held at any site. (For details of MUPS, see Roeber, 1975.) Local management saw this as the ideal basis for the discussion of further change following incentives application.

1967-69: Manpower utilisation and payment structure agreement

The first step was to hold two weekend seminars at a local hotel, involving the shop stewards, local union officials and senior managers. Although such seminars are commonplace today, the idea was new to the people concerned and was viewed with considerable suspicion. The presence of the officials helped to allay fears and local management ran a programme which they had designed. The core of the programme was a detailed examination of the MUPS agreement, but included short sessions on macro-economics, the state of the business, theories of motivation and job evaluation (which was new to craftsmen but not general workers). Also included was a syndicate exercise in which shop stewards and management representatives were asked to consider what they would like to see changed in the works. The basic idea was to try to get both groups to level with each other about their objectives whilst examining any ideas put forward in the light of business realities as management perceived them — which it became obvious were different from the perceptions of the shop stewards. A secondary objective was to assist the shop stewards and union officials to understand the payment structure (annual salaries based on job evaluation) proposed in the agreement.

Everyone found the seminars stimulating but the shop stewards now had a problem. Their members were demanding to know what had gone on at the seminars — was it an attempt by management to seduce them? But the shop stewards did not feel sufficiently confident to put over to their members all that had been discussed. A solution was found in management conducting a shortened version of the seminar for all employees in the presence of shop stewards, who could and often did support management in their attempts to arouse interest in further change. It took nearly a year to cover all the hourly-paid employees, taking up more management effort than could really be spared. The lesson learned here was that, in initiating and carrying through a major change programme, additional resources are required if other activities are not to suffer.

Management now suggested to the shop stewards that they should explore together what changes might be mutually acceptable without any commitment to implement the changes. The objective was to find out whether the improvements in productivity which could be agreed would pay for the increased wages contained in the MUPS agreement and the costs of implementing such improvements and still produce some improvement in the profitability of the business. This was agreed to on the understanding that there was no commitment to implement change.

Initially, the senior managers met all shop stewards in a totally unstructured series of meetings with a view to establishing a mechanism for proceeding. This was found to be non-productive, so the possibility of a small working party was put forward. Initially, this caused difficulties because each union insisted on being represented and the larger unions wanted proportional representation. This could only be achieved by using the total group. The breakthrough came when the larger unions agreed to forgo proportional representation provided:

(a) they had some increase in representation compared with the smaller unions; and

(b) there was a balance between craft unions and the general worker union.

This group was still larger than ideal (18, including 3 senior managers) but was the best possible. It was christened the Central Administration Group (CAG) and was to guide and co-ordinate proceedings for the next three years as well as acting as the focal point for communications.

Development of management thinking

While all this had been going on, senior managers had been studying the problems involved in changing the style of management — already seen as crucial to the success of a change programme. Seminars were attended where the ideas of Maslow, MacGregor, Herzberg, Argyris, Schein, Beck-hardt and others were looked at. The senior management group examined its own behaviour and made efforts to change it, ably assisted by I. Mangham. The group also attended two one-week sessions with Scientific Methods Inc. (based on the Managerial Grid Organisation Development ideas of Blake and Mouton) — part of which was repeated for all staff down to supervisor level. Visits were paid to other sites where experimentation was already taking place.

Early in this process, it was decided to experiment with Management by Objectives with a view to involving staff more in thinking-through change processes and understanding the need for a different management style. Later emerged three main concepts; namely:

(a) job enrichment aimed at improving motivation by producing jobs which were more challenging;

(b) job reorganisation aimed at creating self-contained, work-oriented groups to the extent that economic considerations allowed;

(c) a more open style of management aimed at escaping the traditional paternalistic style and developing in the language of Transactional Analysis — an 'adult/adult' relationship between all employees.

Joint planning for job reorganisation

This thinking was displayed to the CAG and, after much discussion, it was decided to experiment with the ideas of job enrichment and job reorganisation in part of one of the manufacturing departments. The area selected was that where success was thought to be most likely — the value of early success and the difficulties of early failure having been learned from experience on other sites.

All the people involved in the selected area — managers, supervisors, process operators and craftsmen — were introduced to the concepts, their purpose, the sort of changes which might be entailed and so on, and then the total group was left to develop its own ideas for change. This the participants did with tremendous enthusiasm and, in a surprisingly short time, produced proposals which they were very keen to implement.

These proposals produced a dilemma for the CAG. To implement them meant abandoning incentives, whereas the company and unions nationally were insisting that change should not be carried out piecemeal but on a site basis when the whole change programme had been approved. The CAG, on the other hand, needed to know whether the proposals now before it were workable. In the event, it was agreed to pay an upstanding wage based on average earnings to everyone involved in the experiment. A trial proved highly successful, increased outputs being achieved without incentives whilst the feeling of achievement led to considerable satisfaction amongst those involved.

The main changes which were worked out were the following:

1 The process work was reorganised. The existing arrangements had been worked out by classical work-study methods during the period when incentive schemes based on work measurement were in operation. In general, this meant that a process worker usually carried out parts of several processes which were located near one another — usually on one floor of a manufacturing building. By reor-

ganising the work, it became possible for each process worker to operate one or more complete processes. Although this necessitated his going up and downstairs to a greater extent, it was found to be more satisfying to do a complete job.

2 The process workers were structured into three grades:

(a) a basic grade for people in training;
(b) a senior operator grade for experienced people able to operate a substantial number of processes; such people could be used flexibly and economically;
(c) a process group leader who, besides being capable of doing the work of a senior operator, could carry out a range of activities previously carried out by a supervisor or by a specialist tester.

3 Broad planning, previously carried out centrally, was devolved to departmental level. The detailed planning which is required on each shift because of changing work patterns and absence of process workers was now undertaken by the whole shift, whereas previously the supervisor had performed this task on his own.

4 These changes allowed a reduction in the number of supervisors and also a change in the pattern of their work. More time could be devoted to the technical development aspects of their job.

5 Maintenance workers, both shift and day men, had previously formed part of the engineering department. As many as was economically feasible now became part of each production unit and were integrated into the production team. This change was designed to (a) improve motivation, since the maintenance workers could now see more clearly their contribution to the efficiency of production; (b) facilitate the determination of priorities and such activities as plant hand-over and safety systems; (c) facilitate the implementation of agreed work-sharing whereby process workers could carry out certain activities, previously reserved to engineering workers, when the latter

were not available. The engineering department still retained its responsibility for maintaining engineering standards across the works, for controlling resources which could not economically be decentralised and for carrying out major engineering development work.

1969-70: Weekly staff agreement

The MUPS agreement was by now out-of-date and during the latter part of 1968 and early 1969 a new agreement was negotiated at national level. The new agreement, known as the Weekly Staff Agreement (WSA) (see Roeber, 1975), was signed on 10 June 1969 and, while similar to MUPS in many respects, differed in that:

(a) the money offered in return for change was increased, although still in the form of an annual salary;
(b) the principle of the 'closed shop' was accepted;
(c) the principle of no enforced redundancy arising from the agreement was introduced explicitly;
(d) the craft unions insisted on building constraints into the work-sharing area;
(e) the need for continuing change was spelt out; i.e. this was not to be a one-off productivity deal.

The signing of this new agreement led to increasing pressures from employees to extend the limited experiment to all other manufacturing areas and this was done relatively quickly and along similar lines to those described for the trial area. The restructuring of engineering resources and increasing work-sharing in the craft area and between craftsmen and general workers was much more difficult and took much longer than in the manufacturing areas, much to the annoyance of the process workers. By 1970, however, an overall acceptable package had been worked out, although it fell short of management hopes, particularly in the area of work-sharing. Two problem areas remained:

1 There were minor difficulties in changing from the old payment structure to the WSA payment structure. These difficulties were resolved by compromise.
2 One small group, the total works membership of one union, declined to make any significant change. In the end, this failure was accepted by everyone as preferable to not proceeding with the rest of the change programme, but it led to strained relationships for a long time afterwards.

Effect on staff

The changes worked out with hourly-paid employees (now to become staff, paid an annual salary weekly) had naturally had significant effect on the job of some monthly-paid staff. It had always been intended that the change programme should ultimately embrace all employees but government policy at the time made it essential to separate out — often in a rather artificial way — the change programme as it affected montly-paid staff in order that they could receive extra remuneration to which they were entitled. Unlike WSA, this change programme (called Staff Development Programme — SDP) was not negotiated with unions but worked out directly with the monthly-paid staff, few of whom were members of unions at this time. The changes were similar to those involving weekly-paid staff, and included organisational changes bringing together the work of related specialists, the decentralisation of engineering and other services to manufacturing areas, and the introduction of matrix organisation to certain areas.

1970-72: Implementation of WSA and SDP

The total change programme having been agreed locally and nationally by the company and the unions, implementation continued under the guidance of the CAG. At first, numbers of small problems had to be ironed out; but morale was high, for the proposals appeared to work satisfactorily and further recognition of increased confidence in the site by the company came in the form of a second major capital investment in 1969 and a third in 1971. Gradually, the work of the CAG diminished and problems tended to be sorted out informally or at the works council. The small work groups, which had worked out the changes in their own areas, continued in operation.

1973: Unionisation of formal joint consultation

In early 1973, the company and unions nationally agreed to a new formal system of joint consultation, similar in structure to the old three-tier works council system but different in concept in a number of important ways; namely:

(a) all representatives at works level (now called the Works Committee) and higher-level committees were to be shop stewards;
(b) management representation was much reduced — at works level from 1:1 to 1:4;
(c) a fourth level of consultation — at departmental level — was introduced;
(d) constraints on subject matter for consultation were very much reduced.

The new agreement allowed the works committee to take over the functions of the CAG. It also permitted (by local agreement) the workgroups, which had worked out the WSA proposals, to be informally linked to the formal consultation system.

1973-77: Further development

(a) Consultation/negotiation dilemma

While consultation and negotiation are the subject of separate formal agreements, in practice some elements of negotiation appear in the formal consultation process and some elements of joint problem-solving appear in the formal negotiating process. There have thus arisen dilemmas for shop stewards and managers about how best to resolve some problems and within which official framework. By mutual agreement, initial attempts are usually made to resolve problems locally, utilising any help which can be obtained. By using a problem-solving approach the best possible but acceptable solution is sought rather than negotiating some deal which satisfies nobody. Only in the event of failure is the official negotiating procedure used — although the unions and management retain the right to use the negotiating machinery at any time. It requires experience and goodwill on the part of all concerned to make the best use of the means available for resolving problems.

(b) Communications

In any method of employee participation, communications play a vital role. Whilst unions and management have developed their own systems of communications over the years, the need to agree on how to handle items of concern to all parties has been found to be critical. Initially it was agreed to use a system based on that used to communicate information from the works committee. At the end of each meeting, time is set aside to decide what items need to be communicated. The wording of the communication is then worked out between the secretary (a member of management) and the two senior shop stewards. The main channel of communication is then via management members of the works committee and the management line to the work groups. A supporting channel of communication is via the shop steward on the works committee to all shop stewards. Figure 9.1 represents this diagrammatically. Upward communication took place by the reverse process.

It became clear that the system did not work very well and a small management/shop steward group carried out an investi-

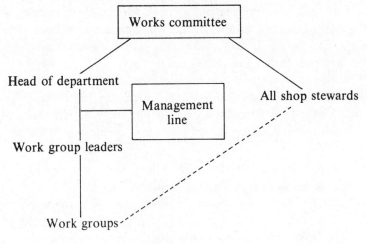

Figure 9.1

gation using a questionnaire technique. This showed that there were losses in the management line and that some work groups did not understand the communication — sometimes did not even receive the communication. These problems were soon shown to be due to lack of enthusiasm and lack of skill on the part of some managers.

Recent work, carried out in conjunction with Messrs Jackson, MacFarlane and Ostell (1976, 1977) of the University of Stirling, and again using a questionnaire technique, has shown that, despite much effort being put into improving communications, there are still problems. The main improvements that have been tried out are that

(a) one management member of the works committee communicates direct to workgroup leaders,[1] thus obviating the loss in the management line and speeding up the whole communication process;

(b) the same management member is available to the meeting of all shop stewards to clarify any points which are not well understood;

(c) work group leaders have received training in the skills of communicating.

The system works reasonably well for simple communications from works committee, e.g. about canteen prices or holidays, and only falls down where the skills/commitment of the work group leader are inadequate.

With more complex communications, e.g. business information or communications involving a number of related elements, other problems have become apparent. A pilot study of a business information communication revealed the following facts:

1 That because of holidays, sickness, etc., not every individual actually received the information.

2 That the subject matter, involving much business information and an underlying message about the need to improve manpower productivity, was only remembered when the information was seen to be of direct relevance to the listener.

   A second study, based on the Works Annual Plan but idenfifying the relevant plan for each work group, gave better results but showed the following key areas for further improvement:

3 Better feedback loops from the shop floor to the works committee. These require development, to pick up responses to communications.

4 Further improvement in the leadership of the work groups. The groups tend to require action from other people before considering what they can do themselves to effect improvements.

5 Information retention. This is still inadequate, although it is much better where people have been involved in working out consequential action plans. A system is needed for retaining information where it can be readily referred to.

Two other important points emerged:

6 That the process of validation by questionnaire techniques was becoming counter-productive. People objected to the extra work involved in the validation process and this sometimes detracted from their enthusiasm for the prime task.

7 That this type of communication exercise involving complex information and requiring face-to-face discussion to
develop understanding can be used only sparingly
because of the effort involved. It is most appropriate
where the information is complex and action was
required. Other types of communication need to be used
when the information is simple or does not require
action.

Communication systems for monthly-paid staff, whilst different in detail are similar in principle and pose the same problems.

(c) Use of working parties

Where problems to be resolved are complex, the works
committee and other committees are too large for effective
problem-solving and would absorb too much effort. Two
types of sub-group or working parties have, therefore, been
evolved to look at problems and recommend solutions:

(a) where problems are arising frequently — e.g., over canteens, changing accommodation etc. — a standing sub-
group meets regularly and reports to the full works committee;

(b) where one-off problems arise, an *ad hoc* sub-group is
formed to look into the problem and recommend a solution to the full works committee. The sub-group is then
disbanded.

Examples of one-off problems, which have been handled in
this way, include:

(a) review of the Working Conditions Payment Scheme;
(b) review of the effectiveness of communications;
(c) legislation of various kinds e.g., the Health and Safety at
Work Act;
(d) redeployment during a serious downturn in business,
aimed at minimising losses and avoiding layoffs.

This type of problem-solving works reasonably well; difficulties which have to be looked out for include the following:

1 The sub-group needs a clear definition of its role, the problem, the constraints within which a solution has to be found, and the time-scale on which recommendations are required.
2 When the time-scale is long, interim reports are necessary, however brief, so that people know that the problem has not been quietly shelved.
3 When sub-groups report back to the main committee, there is a tendency to repeat the whole discussion of the sub-group. There has to be some commitment to accept the recommendations of the sub-group unless there are outstanding reasons for doing otherwise.

(d) Implementation of agreed decisions

Traditionally, decisions once arrived at, are implemented by management. This is still the most usual practice but alternatives have been tried with some success:

1 During the 1975 recession, demand for products reduced by one-third for a period of eight months. It was decided that no one was to be laid off but that every effort should be made to redeploy people to minimise the cost of this decision. An *ad hoc* working party with a senior manager leading the working party was set up to resolve what action was necessary. Atypically, this group was empowered to go ahead and implement its decisions without reference back to the works committee. In practice, it formed two sub-groups to handle the engineering and general worker redeployment problems separately. This modification of the usual process produced action faster and with a minimum of difficulties.
2 Payments for abnormal working conditions are, by national agreement, restricted to an agreed level which is periodically renegotiated. Because of the diverse activities within the company, each site is left to work out an

equitable scheme within this framework. The original schemes were worked out by the CAG and implemented by a shop steward/management team. This worked very well for several years but eventually dissatisfaction arose with one or two of the answers. A sub-group of the works committee, distinct from the group operating the scheme, was formed to handle problems where the validity of the scheme was being challenged. The works committee, however, retains overall control and acts as the appeal body on the odd occasion when this is necessary. There still remains the possibility of referring difficult issues to the negotiating procedures if all else fails.

3 The company provides each works with a sum of money each year (known as the Benevolence Grant) which is available for helping employees who get into financial difficulties. Often, the individuals can be counselled to help themselves, but sometimes money is required either as a loan or as an *ex gratia* payment to resolve difficulties. The guidelines for operating this scheme have been established by works committee, but implementation is carried out by a small group comprising shop stewards and the welfare officer. The only check kept on the system is to ensure that the group operates within the framework of the scheme.

4 Some problems involve both weekly- and monthly-paid staff and joint groups have been used successfully to resolve problems. Indeed, the three referred to above involved monthly-paid staff representatives nominated by the staff committee. This is particularly important if decisions, to be implemented other than by management, affect both weekly- and monthly-paid staff.

5 Sometimes, decisions can be arrived at by works and staff committees which become difficult to implement because small groups are in disagreement. Typical of this sort of problem was a decision to change the shift system. A sub-group investigated the alternatives and made recommendations for change. It soon became clear, however, that

employees were not unanimous in their views. To test where opinion lay, a ballot was held which showed that, in the major union involved, there was a majority in favour of change. But management was unwilling to accept more than one shift system for reasons which it declared, and it was clear that employees were divided in their views between three systems. Two systems had already been tried out in various parts of the works, but the system recommended by the sub-group had not. It was agreed to hold a trial of the third system — it being understood that ultimately the choice of a single system would be necessary. Over a period of a year, acceptance of one system of shifts was achieved, with the exception of a very small group where the management reasons for a single-shift system were much less relevant. This group remains on a different shift system.

Problems of availability of effort

1 The success of the site has resulted in major capital investment leading to the employment of large numbers of contractors. This produces very real difficulties because

   (a) contractors' ways of working are different from those in the works;
   (b) payment systems are different;
   (c) similar work is performed by members of different unions.

For some years, it has been custom and practice to tell employees about these contracts and whilst they were few in number the management effort involved was acceptable.

As the number of contractors has grown, employees have demanded more and more details of the contracts before agreeing to them. Ideally, management would like to agree the framework within which contracts would be handled and keep shop stewards informed on a regular basis of the contracts in operation. Some progress towards such an approach has been made, but such are the suspicions and attitudes towards contractors by employees, and such are the difficulties of ensuring that contractors (particularly sub-contractors) do what they say they will do, that more management effort than can be afforded is still tied up in resolving problems in this area.

2   The extension of joint consultation recently by the formation of 'Business and Investment Groups' at national and divisional levels is also putting a strain on the system because of the amount of information available. We now have to resolve the problem of how to contain an expanding field of involvement within the limitations imposed by the availability of management effort. This would seem to be possible only if (a) existing systems can be made more efficient, (b) less effort-consuming ways of doing things become acceptable for the non-critical issues. The first is a matter of skills-training; the second is a matter of mutual trust.

The present

The accelerated programme of change has been going on for ten years and it is fair to ask whether it has been a success. It is not possible to answer in a quantitative fashion because one cannot quantify what would have happened had the change programme not started or had some other change programme been implemented.

It is possible to say that, over the ten years, the following changes have taken place:

1   The profitability of the business has improved from being unsatisfactory to a position where virtually all is satisfactory or can be made so on a short time-scale.

2 The confidence in the site is now such that continuing major capital investment has occurred over ten years and is planned to continue.

3 The rate of improvement of output *per capita* has doubled and a further 50 per cent improvement is planned over the next two to three years.

4 Numbers employed are slightly higher than they were ten years ago.

At worst, then, the change programme has not been harmful, and comparison with other sites would suggest that it has been successful. That is not to say that anyone is completely satisfied. The work of the people from Stirling University referred to earlier has highlighted the possibilities for further improvement in the existing systems, particularly

(a) in bringing the effectiveness of communications in all work groups up to the level of the best;

(b) in developing the further involvement of work groups in bringing about improvements in their own areas.

External factors continue to play a major role in impeding change. The most important are:

1 Massive government legislation, which diverts management effort away from an evolving change programme and necessitates modifications to the programme which are not always appropriate. Some of it also makes a joint approach more difficult by concentrating on 'rights' rather than on ways of evolving solutions satisfactory to all concerned.

2 Wage control has made it impossible to link reward to the improvements achieved and instead has distorted wage relationships and thus created internal tensions. Whether this improves in future remains to be seen.

3 Inter- and intra-union disputes still arise — often the result of external circumstances that we cannot control and find it difficult to influence.

The future

Such are the uncertainties of the future, that forecasting precisely where we are going is virtually impossible. Future legislation in the area of industrial democracy may, indeed, necessitate some change in direction. But some general areas for improvement seem to be essential — whatever the forms of participation which develop:

1 Better communications systems, tailored to the needs of any given situation, will be required.
2 More and better training — particularly for line managers, supervisors and shop stewards — will be essential.
3 Clearer definition of roles will be an increasing problem. Already the difficulties of the supervisor have become apparent as his traditional role has started to change, while that of the shop steward has also changed significantly. Major changes in technology are also changing the jobs which people perform. And last, but by no means least, the unionisation of managers to senior levels is raising issues of how to perform more than one role and how to reconcile such roles.
4 Further development of the work group concept aimed at improving efficiency and job satisfaction in a participatory way.
5 Continuing education for all employees in business economics so that they understand the basis on which decisions are made.

There seems little doubt that further experimentation and development in the whole area of participation is essential and that such experimentation requires validation in ways that are not counter-productive. In the past, participation has often been seen to be unhelpful at best, impossible at worst. It has sometimes been seen as a soft option or as management abandoning its responsibilities. Experience has shown that this is not the reality. Participation can be made to work — although it is certainly not a panacea for all problems in industry.

Indeed, it has its problems, not the least of which is the amount of management effort required to make it work. And it certainly is not a soft option. Participatory management calls for more effort and requires new skills — but it can be very rewarding to the manager who is interested in developing new concepts of management. It can also be very rewarding to the shop steward and union official, who are able to play a more constructive role in looking after the interests of their members.

Above all, it offers a basis for bringing about change in a planned way when it is becoming apparent that the future success of the business — and hence the ability of everyone to meet their objectives — depends on the ability to change quickly and effectively in a rapidly changing world.

Summary

This chapter described the development of participation in a single works over the period of the last thirteen years. A change programme started in 1965 against a background of established negotiating procedures and a joint consultation system with limited terms of reference.

The first stage in building up mutual trust led to the acceptance of an incentive scheme for craftsmen which had before been strongly resisted.

Further developments took place within the framework of two major company-wide agreements (MUPS and WSA), with the holding of seminars with union representatives and shop-floor workers, followed by the setting-up of a union/management working party which agreed on an experiment in participative job reorganisation. The success of this experiment in one manufacturing area, where changes were jointly worked out by managers, supervisors, process workers and craftsmen, led to similar jointly agreed changes throughout the works with more responsibility being delegated to individual operators and work groups.

Further developments have included an extension of the role of the works council, the development of a system of joint working parties to produce proposals on specific issues and problem areas and sometimes to implement them, and improvements in the communication systems. Experience has shown that availability of management time and effort is one of the major limiting factors in the development of participation.

The chapter concluded with an attempt to assess the success of the change programme and some views on its future development.

Note

[1] Work group leaders are formally appointed leaders of work groups. In the case of process work groups, they are the plant managers (next senior manager above the supervisors) who work on days and can co-ordinate the separate discussions with the four shifts who cannot readily be brought together. Where all the people in a work group are on day work, the work group leader is usually the supervisor.

Part IV
Participation at Company Level

Employee participation in companies can mean both financial participation and participation in management. While theoretically the two aspects are linked, there is rarely a very strong practical connection, and the bulk of this book is concerned with ways of increasing employees' share in decision-making. But while none of the cases described is primarily concerned with the financial aspects of participation, at least two of them (Chapters 7 and 9) contain a strong financial element, and the overview of company-level participation which opens this section reviews current practice in this area.

The two main approaches to company-wide participation in management decisions are through company councils and employee directors. Chapter 11 describes one of the better-known recent examples of a company council structure, illustrating both the advantages and the limitations of this form of participation, which is favoured by many employers. Representative examples of employee director systems are harder to find, as is clear from the review of this area in Chapter 10, and for the present the main source of experience of board-level participation in the UK, albeit at divisional level, remains the British Steel Corporation, whose experience, discussed in Chapter 11, provides an important pointer to some of the major implications and problems of this approach. Among the issues it highlights are the importance of clear aims and widespread commitment, and the difficulties which can face employee directors without an unequivocal power-base in the trade union movement, all of them questions which will be discussed more generally in our last section.

10 Participation at company level

David Guest
Lecturer in Personnel Management, London School of Economics and Political Science

Introduction

The primary focus and concern of the current debate on participation has undoubtedly been the possibility of developments at company level. The two most widely discussed proposals are that worker representatives might sit on the boards of companies and that workers might share in company profits. There has been a great deal of discussion about both these aspects of company-level participation but, particularly with respect to worker representatives on company boards, relatively little action in the UK.

Before examining in a little more detail these two approaches, which are, in effect, unique to the company level, it is important to recognise that other forms of participation also occur at this level. In most organisations there will be some form of company-wide collective bargaining and an increasing number of organisations are introducing something like a company council which provides a forum for discussion of plans and policies. This is illustrated by the next chapter which outlines the development of a multi-tier structure with a company council at its highest level. Even the subject matter of briefing groups and opinion surveys may deal with issues that are essentially matters for board-level decision. However, it is the relative inability of these more conventional forms of participation to influence some of the important board decisions that has led some union leaders to advocate worker representatives on the board.

Worker representatives on company boards

While the initial interest in the idea of workers on company boards arose partly as a result of activities within the EEC, the chief impetus has been the change in policy of the TUC and several important trade unions. This, in turn, has influenced Labour Party thinking. Yet it would be wrong to discount the importance of developments in other European countries, since the general trend would seem to be towards extending and consolidating the role of worker representatives on boards. The draft Fifth Directive of the EEC, which seeks to introduce some system of board representation throughout the Community, continues to be the subject of widespread disagreement and therefore some way away from ratification, but the underlying principle still attracts considerable support.

More recently the prospect of legislation in the UK has become a real possibility. The Labour Government's White Paper[1], in rejecting the more extreme proposals of the Bullock Committee, and encouraging further debate, has sought a middle ground which need not result in total rejection should there be a change to a Conservative Government. Briefly, what the White Paper proposes is that, as a first step, all companies employing more than 500 people should have a Joint Representative Committee which would have a right to information and consultation on the company's strategic planning. This committee may request the introduction of one-third of worker representatives on a supervisory board. Where this request is opposed by the employers, there will be a statutory obligation to introduce such a board. There is flexibility over the option of whether worker representatives should sit on a unitary single board or a supervisory board and a considerable time lag is built-in before statutory imposition comes into force. The role of non-union members and inter-union allocation of places on a board is left unclear, but the overall aim of providing a flexible and essentially voluntary approach to the extension of company-level participation comes across strongly.

It will be some considerable time before the White Paper is translated into legislation, and a change of Government may delay legislation even longer. But with all political parties now favouring an extension of participation, the White Paper offers managements a number of choices. For example, should they now take steps to develop joint representative committees? In practice, the recent steps taken by several companies to set up company councils (including the experience of Cadbury/Schweppes described in Chapter 11), come close to meeting this goal. Should companies take positive steps to prepare for and indeed encourage worker representation on company boards? And if so, should this be on existing boards or through the setting up of supervisory boards?

The experience of worker representation on boards, which takes different forms in different countries, has generally aroused the opposition of sections of management. But in West Germany, Holland and the Scandinavian countries, it has not been the disaster that was predicted in some quarters. It can, of course, be argued that the situation in the UK is different because of the divisive nature of industrial relations; and, whatever their motives, industrialists seem to be united in opposition to the imposition of worker representatives on the boards of companies.

There are so few examples of worker representatives on the boards of companies in the UK that it is extremely difficult to discuss the practical experience of introducing this form of participation. Yet a small but slowly increasing group of organisations have decided that this is a step worth taking. They include companies in the public sector such as the British Steel Corporation, the Post Office and Harland & Wolff. More recently both British Shipbuilders and British Aerospace are reported to be considering steps in the same direction. In the private sector firms like Bonsor Engineering and Bristol Ship Repairers have introduced worker directors.

In no case has a supervisory board, along West German lines, been introduced; instead a single-tier, as favoured by the majority report of the Bullock Committee, seems to have been considered appropriate. The aims behind these initiatives are not always easy to discern, although a general belief in the value of participation seems to be important, implying almost an ideological commitment. Government pressure has been a factor in the more recent cases in the public sector. In the private sector a belief in participation seems to be coupled with a belief in the value of the two-way communication that can take place in the boardroom and the additional dimension to decision-making and policy development that the contribution of worker representatives can provide. These aims are based on the assumption that the worker representatives remain very much in the minority. The Post Office scheme, where there is parity representation, provides an interesting exception and an attempt to develop a scheme based on more widely accepted criteria.

The present limited experience suggests that two prerequisites for the voluntary introduction of worker representatives onto company boards have been commitment on the part of the chief executive and support or at least no outright opposition from the trade unions. The process of setting up the scheme is likely to require extensive consultation and planning, since a wide range of decisions have to be taken on such issues as the number of representatives, how and when they are selected or appointed, who is eligible and whom they represent. An initial problem is to decide who takes these decisions and these and many other issues are raised in Chapter 12 in which Ken Jones outlines the steps involved in the introduction of worker directors in what is the best-known and most firmly established scheme at the British Steel Corporation.

While many of the fears of industrialists about the harmful consequences of having worker representatives on boards may prove to be unfounded, anxiety about bringing collective bargaining into the boardroom plus fear that their control will be diluted, makes it improbable that many company boards will choose to extend participation in this way. Indeed, unless there is some ideological commitment, they are more likely to feel that any objectives that they may have which are associated with participation can be better met through other forms, such as works and company councils. In addition it is worth emphasising that the Code of Practice on Disclosure of Information is now part of the Employment Protection Act and many companies have been giving attention to the way in which information can most sensibly be communicated to and discussed with the work force.

Financial participation and economic democracy

While there has been vocal disagreement about the value of worker representatives on company boards, there has been a rather quieter but more positive debate on the possibility of some form of profit-sharing. It is worth emphasising again that this debate is by no means confined to the UK since most countries in Europe as well as the USA already have examples of some form of financial participation and in many cases there are plans to extend it. In this context, the government's consultative proposals[1] are simply the first steps along an already well-trodden path.

Companies have long sought to link pay, performance, productivity and involvement. To achieve this they have introduced a number of schemes varying from piecework, through productivity bargaining and financial rewards for suggestions to profit-sharing and even common ownership. Many companies in the UK already have various kinds of profit-sharing scheme and there is an extensive literature on the subject.[2]

Management may have several objectives when considering the introduction of some form of financial participation. Clarification of these objectives may make the choice of approach more straightforward. As with other forms of participation, several approaches are available and these must be considered in relation to the objectives, the context and what is feasible.

At least seven objectives of financial participation can be identified. These can be listed as follows:

1 *To get the financial reward system right*
Some companies may want to use profit-sharing in an attempt to remove inequities in their payment structure. This is a dangerous reason for introducing profit-sharing and it may be more sensible to try to alter the structure. However, in the context of pay policy, the Department of Employment has acknowledged that profit-sharing may constitute a self-financing productivity deal.

2 *To introduce economic participation as an end in itself*
This partly ideological objective ranges from, on the one hand, a desire to increase the proportion of the adult population in the UK who own shares from its present low level of less than 5 per cent[3] to, on the other hand, an attempt to redistribute wealth through the creation of a capital fund. The general idea of a capital fund is that each year a small proportion of a company's shares should be transferred to a central fund, until eventually a point is reached where effective control passes to representatives of the work force and the community at large. This is almost the only approach the unions favour and also reflects the policy of the unions and the centre-left parties in Denmark and Sweden. (Meidner, 1978).

3 *As part of a general policy to extend participation*
Representatives of all sides of industry have argued that those who share in the creation of wealth should also share the rewards. While this may be partly accomplished through the normal payment system, an additional kind of commitment on both sides may be implied by profit-sharing.

4 *To increase involvement*
The hope is that workers who own a share, however

small, in a company, may become more involved in its success. At the same time they may become more aware of
the need to create wealth and generate profits. By looking
at company goals from a point of view other than that of
an employee, those goals might begin to take on a new
meaning.

5 *To raise productivity*
Profit-sharing might create a greater awareness of how
wealth is created and thereby help to increase the concern
for productivity and cost-effectiveness. Value-added
schemes may appear particularly attractive where this is
the goal.

6 *To reward service to the company*
Profit-sharing might be offered as a reward for a given
length of service.

7 *To encourage savings*
Individual companies may wish to encourage employees
to save and invest. Various PAYE linked schemes already
exist, but some employers may wish to offer some kind of
deferred profit-sharing scheme as an additional reward.
In West Germany, legislation known as the '624 Law'
exists whereby agreements can be reached which require
a company to invest 624 Marks per annum (£165)[4] for
each worker in some sort of savings scheme. Workers typically choose a savings bank or building society rather
than shares in their own company.

Having established the objectives, the next step is to ascertain what sort of schemes are available. Clearly some of the
objectives listed above might more appropriately be met
through an incentive payment scheme or a conventional self-
financed productivity bargain. Leaving these aside the basic
alternatives are either a cash payment or a distribution of
shares. The cash payment, in particular, would normally be
linked to the level of profits. A variety of more or less complicated schemes exist for deciding how much cash should be distributed and increasing attention is being given to value-added

schemes.[5] The government has encouraged the use of added value as a means of explaining company reports[6] and a number of companies such as Marks & Spencer and Kalamazoo have already moved in this direction. A recent survey indicated that the most common kind of cash scheme involves a once a year payout, usually based on pre-tax profit figures.[7] Some companies have a profits threshold: in other words they will only make a payment if profits are above a specified level.

There are several kinds of share-scheme:

1 *A straight bonus in the form of shares instead of cash*
These shares, usually offered at the current market price may be cashed straight away and one of the concerns that has been expressed is that this could have a negative impact on the Stock Exchange share value. Sometimes there may be a choice of cash or shares, with tax incentives to accept and retain shares for a certain period of time. This is the basis of the most favoured plan in the current Liberal Party-inspired government proposals. Marks & Spencer, who only offer shares, also offer strong incentives to retain the shares. ICI, which has one of the best-known profit-sharing schemes, finds that approximately 60 per cent of workers sell their shares almost immediately and the evidence suggests that most workers view the shares as a pay bonus rather than an investment or a stake in the company.

2 *A deferred share scheme*
A number of companies, of whom Habitat and Bulmers are two of the best-known, have introduced schemes whereby shares are placed in a trust for a number of years and then gradually made available. This constitutes a kind of enforced saving which also rewards long-service employees. A trust of this type will require 'trustees' and in the case of Bulmers half are employee representatives while at Habitat one of the three trustees is an employee.

3 *Shareholding trusts*
A few companies have established trusts into which

shares for employees are placed. Individual employees will normally have no control over these shares but will receive, as a cash payment, the dividend income. Usually the trust will have started as a gift and again a joint set of trustees will usually be required.

4 *Common ownership*

At companies like John Lewis, Scott Bader and Kalamazoo, the shares, once privately owned, have been placed in a trust for the workers. The workers are not, however, free to dispose of the shares and although they may have some control over the appointment of trustees and of senior management, in the case of both John Lewis and Scott Bader the family which originally owned the shares still retains a dominating influence over the management of the enterprise. Workers, as nominal shareholders, will normally receive an annual 'dividend'.

One context in which workers effectively control all aspects of the enterprise is in a workers' co-operative. A few of these exist in this country, the best-known probably being at Meriden (Coates, 1976). Each worker will have one share and that will entitle him to a vote at general meetings: however, co-operatives, while very interesting forms of participation, have not generally been successful enough to indulge in profit-sharing other than through wages.

Any company which decides to introduce some form of financial participation has a number of decisions to make during the planning of the scheme and the process of implementation. It has to decide, for example, whether to include everyone, full-time and part-time, or only a limited number of perhaps longer-service employees, and whether to have an immediate payment or a deferred scheme. These decisions should be related, where possible, to the objectives of the scheme.

In addition, the following issues need to be taken into account when setting up a scheme of financial participation: (a) the attitudes of the unions; (b) the case of multi-plant companies; (c) the proportion of shares to be distributed; (d) the question of back-up policies.

(a) Union attitudes

A number of unions have been quite willing to support schemes of financial participation on a company-by-company basis, but the official union attitude, reflected in TUC statements, is fairly hostile. They view profit sharing primarily as a form of window dressing which provides an appearance of participation without any real control over management decisions. This accepts the reality that private shareholders have no effective power unless they own a very large proportion of shares. A second argument is that share-ownership adds to the risk of employment by putting all of a worker's eggs in one basket. If the company collapsed, as in the often-cited case of Rolls-Royce, both employment and savings could be lost. A further argument is that the degree of profit-sharing normally envisaged does nothing to reduce the inequitable distribution of wealth in society.

Further arguments are sometimes raised against profit-sharing. One is that it unfairly punishes those who, often through no fault of their own, work in unprofitable organisations. Linked to this, it is difficult to apply to the public service sector, although some of the American utilities have developed schemes which partially disprove this.

Worker attitudes may help to offset union opposition where this does exit. One survey, under the auspices of the CBI, found that in 1976, 86 per cent of workers surveyed thought that giving workers a share in the profits would help to improve productivity.[8] Some recently introduced schemes, where the take-up is voluntary, show large proportions of the workforce opting to buy shares.[9]

(b) Multi-plant companies

In some companies, certain sections may be markedly more profitable than others and the question then arises whether or not there should be a differential sharing of profit. Most companies decide that there should not, thereby removing part of the incentive. But the objectives of the scheme may not be concerned with profit-sharing as an incentive to higher productivity. In any case, in most schemes the link between effort, performance and reward will be tenuous at best. The exception to this may be value-added schemes which pay a bonus more frequently than once a year.

(c) The proportion of shares to be distributed

A concern of some industrialists is that profit-sharing will lead to dilution of the total stock of shares to the point where too great a proportion is owned by workers. One decision that has to be taken, which will have an influence on this, is how often a distribution of shares as part of a profit-sharing exercise will occur. Another decision is what proportion of shares should be allocated to profit-sharing. Various systems have been devised for calculating what is optimal, but one calculation suggests that it should not exceed an eventual total of 25 per cent of all shares.[10] A limitation of this sort need not apply where the aim is to develop a central capital fund.

(d) Back-up policies

Whatever the objectives of profit-sharing may be, they may not be immediately obvious to the work force. Neither may the criteria by which workers qualify for the scheme. There is likely, therefore, to be a requirement for back-up information and possibly training. If, for example, the objectives are linked to long service or productivity, then policy on the consequences of leaving the company or low plant-productivity must be developed and communicated.

It will be clear from this brief introduction that there is a wide range of choices, and many important issues need to be resolved in any attempt to introduce financial participation. At present it is a fairly fashionable topic, supported by the major political parties and increasingly being introduced by a range of organisations. Typically, the kind of organisation that has introduced profit-sharing has a history of successful profit-generation and a wider interest in participation. Yet it must be remembered that, however laudable the objectives may be, most schemes are far removed from the day-to-day concerns of shop-floor workers and consequently their impact on behaviour, though extremely difficult to ascertain, seems likely to be minimal. Furthermore they do not in themselves provide any participation in decision-making.

Summary

There are two forms of participation particularly associated with the level of the company, namely worker directors and most forms of profit-sharing. In addition company councils, usually linked to works councils, have been developed recently in a number of organisations.

Despite the proposals of the Bullock Committee, and the Government White Paper, there is little evidence as yet of any strong desire for worker representation on company boards and only a very small group of organisations have taken active steps in this direction. Usually this has been the result of a government initiative or some sort of ideological commitment on the part of the chief executive. In almost all cases, worker representatives are in a minority. Recent developments at the Post Office provide one interesting exception to most of these points.

Seven objectives for financial participation were identified. The main forms of financial participation are either a cash payment or a distribution of shares. There are several kinds of share scheme, the more important ones being the straight share bonus, the deferred share scheme, shareholding trusts and common ownership. The only approach favoured by UK unions and the one advocated by centre-left governments in Scandinavia is a capital ownership fund whereby wealth is gradually transferred to representatives of the work force.

With a certain degree of political support and no cohesive union opposition, a further development of conventional profit-sharing schemes seems likely.

Notes

[1] *Industrial Democracy*, London, HMSO, Cmnd, 7231, 1978.

[2] See for example Bell (1973) Copeman (1974) and extensive journal articles, for reviews of progress (IDS, Study 160, 1977: *Industrial Relations Review and Report*, no. 165, 1977).

[3] According to research by Professor E. Victor Morgan of Reading University, reported in *The Times*, 4 October, 1977, p.21, an estimated 3.8 per cent of the UK population aged 16+ personally own shares. The same article cites research by Professor Phillip Blumberg of the University of Connecticut estimating that in the USA the figure is nearer 25 per cent.

[4] This figure has recently been raised considerably.

[5] See for example Wren (1975).

[6] See the government Green Paper *The Future of Company Reports*, Cmnd 6888, London, HMSO, 29 July 1977.

[7] IDS, Study 160 (1977).

[8] Cited in *Industrial Relations Review and Report*, no. 165, 1977.

[9] For information on take-up of schemes at Racal, BICC and BOC International, see *European Industrial Relations Review*, no. 35, November 1976.

[10] See Copeman (1974). Other estimates, however, suggest that between 5 and 10 per cent is the maximum share capital that can be allotted to profit-sharing in any ten-year period. The amount depends partly upon the kind of scheme being operated and on the goals and concerns of those involved. See, e.g., *Financial Times*, 13 February 1978, p. 16.

11 Multi-level participation at Cadbury Schweppes

Derek Williams
Personnel Director, Drinks Division, Cadbury Schweppes
Limited

Introduction

It is most unlikely that any company is going to decide on one
fine morning, that, as a discrete action, it is going to introduce
a company wide system of participation into its decision-making processes. Most major companies already have fairly
extensive activities which relate the contribution of their
employees to the company's aims and objectives. These may
include consultation, communication, training, personnel policies and practices, trade union recognition and collective bargaining arrangements.

In considering how to increase the effectiveness of employee
involvement in the company's aims and objectives each company must know or ask itself what its values, objectives and
visions are regarding its treatment of individuals and the type
of company it wants to be. This examination, for a business
enterprise, should be about how to create a greater degree of
mutual trust, satisfaction and effectiveness to achieve shared
commercial objectives, rather than vague generalisations
about democratic rights. No enterprise has ever done its
employees any favours by failing democratically: people want
to work for a successful organisation. They have more concern for this than they are often given credit for.

A clear philosophical and thinking base for participation which has been talked through in the company is more important than any formal structure which may ultimately emerge. In Cadbury Schweppes I believe this philosophical base does exist firmly. Prior to the merger of the two companies, both enterprises had a long history of joint consultation and well-developed personnel practices. This background was conducive to further planned and agreed participation developments aimed at consolidating past practices between the two partners and creating the same type of opportunity at the new, higher, composite level created by the merger.

Extending participation

In 1973 the main board identified the need for an extension of involvement by employees in the operation of the business. The principal reasons were:

(a) the growth of the company in size, diversity of interests and complexity of organisation;

(b) the change in the general social climate, particularly the challenge to all forms of imposed authority;

(c) the genuine belief that employees have a contribution to make towards better decisions;

(d) the influence of Britain's closer contact with other European systems of management and particularly of the EEC's draft Fifth Directive on company practice; and

(e) the growth and direction of British legislation affecting employment.

In April and September 1973 the Chairman of Cadbury Schweppes, then Lord Watkinson, invited about twenty employee representatives from all parts of the company in the UK to meet the main board and to discuss the company's financial results for 1972 and the first half of 1973, on the days when these were released to the press, and to discuss also the overall state of the business and other matters of general interest.

At the second meeting the Chairman asked the employee representatives if they would like to meet the main board on a regular and formal basis and they welcomed the suggestion.

A joint working party, including two representatives from each of the major divisions and from the central service function, together with an appropriate management team, was set up to consider how the suggestion could be implemented. The objectives of this working party were to make proposals, as a basis for discussion, through the established joint consultative machinery, on

(a) the future development of mutual understanding in the wide ranging and complex issues facing the main board, and

(b) a representative structure for employee contact with the main board,

within the overall context of a flexible approach which would allow for developments based on experience.

Following over two months of detailed discussion through all existing consultative channels within the company, the report and structure recommended by the working party were accepted and subsequently agreed without alteration by the main board. Wherever possible the implementation of the agreed recommendations at site and divisional level was based upon existing practices and traditions, ard in particular on the existing joint-consultation schemes.

The system

The resulting system of representation has basically three tiers, with local variations depending upon size and geographical organisation. The three tiers complement the organisational levels of the UK group. Therefore joint consultative committees or councils on factory and office sites and in sales and distribution functions provide for discussion with site or functional management, divisional councils with divisional boards of management, and the UK group conference with the UK region's board.

Site councils discuss essentially local items, including:

(a) production, distribution or sales needs, changes and output;
(b) financial performance and results;
(c) capital investment in plant and machinery;
(d) labour requirements and changes;
(e) training, safety and welfare and many other local items.

Divisional councils and the UK group conference discuss relevant broader issues, including:

(a) financial performance;
(b) plans for product, plant and production development or rationalisation; social and environmental policies; and
(c) any items referred up to them by mutual agreement from other councils.

The aim of the councils and of the system as a whole is to increase the degree of employee involvement in the decisions that can affect them by enabling these to be fully discussed, but it is clearly stated that, finally, decisions have to be taken by managers. Delegates understand this, and in fact often make the point that it is management's job to take decisions — they wish to have the opportunity to understand the information on which decisions are based and to express their views before the decision is taken.

There are minor variations on the general pattern in the drinks division as a result of its wide geographical spread, and in the small divisions where there is a direct link from joint consultative committees to the UK group conference.

The UK group conference and divisional councils are generally composed of up to thirty-five to forty employee representatives, elected by site and functional councils, who meet the directors and senior managers concerned.

All categories of employee are represented within this structure. The objectives of the election procedures upwards through the structure are to ensure representation of all employees' interests at the appropriate decision-making level and to provide the opportunity for joint consultative committees or councils and divisional councils to balance those interests as far as possible.

Site council members are elected by all members at a particular site in elections which are held separately from trade union elections, though in many cases the representatives are also shop stewards as most sites are almost totally unionised. Subsequently, each council elects a member from its own members to go forward to the next council level. The constituencies for a factory site might include:

(a) production employees;
(b) warehouse employees;
(c) quality control employees;
(d) clerical employees;
(e) trunker employees;
(f) supervisors;
(g) management.

Site councils have typically between eight and twelve members and are chaired by a senior manager, usually the manager of the site or function. They meet in company time at about six-weekly intervals — more frequently than under the old joint consultation system.

Each council is run according to an agenda and the minutes are made available at all appropriate sites. These councils also provide the opportunity for inviting elected representation on working parties, committees or panels. They can also create the opportunity for more frequent dialogue with smaller groups of members between council meetings.

Learning to use the system

At both the introduction of the current arrangements and during their development a considerable degree of attention has been given to training. Initially this was in the form of courses for managers and council members on the subject of participation aims and structure. As the system has developed the training concentration has been on wider commercial knowledge for representatives and on exploring operating participation skills for managers. The latter took the form of a series of two-day workshops with groups of managers, staged in conjunction with the industrial training board. Exercises and team tasks given to each of the workshop groups involved them in trying to make use of the knowledge and talents of their own team, and members were encouraged to analyse the process of participation, and its difficulties, within their own group.

Perhaps even more important, however, has been the gaining of practical operating experience by frequent contact on items of major business importance within the new structure. This practical experience has come about through the interaction between senior divisional management and each division's UK group conference delegates. This is a number of about five to seven representatives according to the division's size. Similarly, at the UK group level group directors meet regularly on specific issues with a UK liaison group of representatives. These are drawn one from each major division. This system of more frequent and informal meetings with a smaller body of representatives can service the main council structure in a very effective way.

In summary, therefore, the current arrangements are broadly a three-tier system of councils reflecting Cadbury Schweppes' UK regional structure, supported by working parties and divisional and regional liaison groups of a smaller number. The development of training activity is along the lines of (a) raising management skill in managing by participation (this has included Board members), (b) increasing the representatives' capacity to participate by wider commercial training, and (c) trying to cement both by increasing practical experience of involvement in a live way on significant business issues.

Evaluation of our experience

Probably the three questions which we are most often asked, and which we ask ourselves, are:

1 What are the difficulties of operating in this way?
2 Is participation a help or a hindrance?
3 What have the management and work force got out of it?

It has not been untypical of our experience to find the question of what we mean by participation being asked repeatedly over several years. This quest for definition tended often to pull the process into introspective phases, particularly in the early stages. Something close to a working definition only really emerges if, as stated earlier, a company has its value-system, vision and objectives in mind and examines its progress against these in the light of practical experience.

Basically, it is now clearly accepted that the management has the job of managing and the accountability for taking the final decisions. During this process, representatives and management seek to create opportunities to secure a greater degree of involvement by those who will be affected before final decisions are taken. This is relevant involvement in the decision-making process.

Difficulties

One of the first difficulties lies in the manner of presenting issues for discussion. One cannot approach representatives with vague statements and hope for any positive result. Instead there will be comments such as 'What have you called us in for if you don't know what you want or what you want to do?', or 'Clearly management hasn't done its homework yet'.

We now tend to start from one of two positions. Either management identifies and tables certain problems, such as business performance, financial position or market changes, or alternatively the management may go in with a problem and a specific proposal on the way to handle it. For example, to meet a certain market position may require investment in one place while creating the need for closure elsewhere.

Too firm a proposition can of course be met with the reaction 'It's a *fait accompli*', or 'You are just trying to brainwash us to your way of thinking'. Wherever possible we have found that the most productive type of involvement comes from a clear definition of the problems or objectives followed by a joint examination and discussion of the range of options open for action. Whilst this is ideal it is not always possible and in a dynamic market situation quick decisions cannot always be avoided.

One of the other difficulties that emerges has to do with the capacity of representatives (who themselves can be a changing group because of the elected nature of their position) to cope with the complexities of the issues, the nature of the risk-taking situations and the fact that management thought, planning and targeting comes from a vast multiplicity of sources. In particular, a small group of representatives cannot be expected to cope with the sheer number of decisions made or with the product of the total management structure. One cannot complement the management structure with a parallel structure of involvement because having a shadow management is not feasible, and neither is it wanted. Therefore there is a need for skill in identifying and presenting the involvement opportunities and for mutual trust that these are on relevant issues both where participation is possible and where a valid contribution can be made. The choice of issues for participation is guided by the attempt to ensure involvement in three areas — the business situation, the company's financial performance, and the effect of the company's development, growth or contraction on the people concerned. These are also the areas which were agreed to be important by the original working party.

Nevertheless, many decision-making processes may finally lead to a dead halt with no action taken. In the meantime one can have raised anxieties or expectations to no ultimate avail and probably left out and partly alienated some section of management on the way. Probably the most difficult situation to handle is the one where a proposed course of action, in which representatives have been involved, is intended in all good faith but rests implicitly or explicitly on certain assumptions, say about costs, earnings or the market-place, whose importance may not have been sufficiently appreciated in the early discussions. For example, proposals to redevelop an old factory may be discussed, assuming certain levels of customer demand and development cost. Where one or more of the main assumptions or conditions changes it can often invalidate the proposed and discussed course of action. When this happens, and it is the daily experience of managers, representatives can find themselves in a very difficult situation with their members, to whom they may have reported back on the original basis. They may also feel let down by the company and some loss of trust may follow.

Another major difficulty for representatives occurs when they are involved in a decision-making process which adversely affects their members, such as a redundancy situation, and then subsequently have to represent their members in their role of trade union stewards and defend them against the consequences. This can be done with great skill and understanding by representatives, but sometimes awareness of it can lead to a defensive posture at the outset of the involvement.

When this kind of situation arises, the original problem giving rise to a possible closure or redundancy is discussed very fully in the participation system. We find that this makes an important contribution to a full understanding of the situation in any subsequent trade union negotiations and reduces the level of conflict. The representatives, in both the participation structure and the trade union negotiations, make it quite clear that they are there to represent their members' interest and to negotiate the best possible terms if need be. At the same time the representatives who have been in the participation system and take part in the trade union meetings are able to give their officials a much better briefing, and perhaps a better view of the attitudes and viewpoint of the workers affected.

From the management standpoint a real difficulty arises

when some representatives have been involved in an issue before the whole of the management chain. This can lead to disaffection and alienation when representatives have more information than a manager, and exhibit the fact in a way that embarrasses him in front of other employees. For this and other reasons Cadbury Schweppes includes elected representatives of management in the participation structure, but even this is not the complete answer.

Help or hindrance?

The second question was 'Is it a help or a hindrance?'. One important problem that has to be admitted is the time that the involvement process can take up. This can become particularly acute for line managers, who still have deadlines to meet and workloads to cope with after any formal or informal participation. But while decisions which seemed clear and simple, such as the transfer of a product from one division to another, have been delayed by lengthy discussions, there have been other cases where participation has changed the course of action envisaged, resulting, as in a decision concerning the appointment of health and safety advisers, in a new solution acceptable to both parties which worked well.

There are a number of reasons why we believe participation has been a help, not a hindrance. The public examination and debate to which decisions are exposed increases the sharpness of decision-making, and employees have greater faith in decisions if they feel that their representatives have had the opportunity to put their views.

In addition I feel that participation has had a direct impact on what I see as the main contributory factors to successful performance. In a competitive industrial society a company must seek continually to improve its performance in such terms as volumes, margins, earnings, returns on assets, customer satisfaction, technical and product superiority, and so on. To achieve this performance improvement internally a company needs clear targets, identification with these, a collective energy to pursue them, the skill to achieve them and the will to go for them.

The five ingredients of target, identity, energy, skill and will are ingredients in all successful performance, individual or collective. Participation can become a natural means of involving many employees, in a variety of ways, in improving the quality of these five ingredients.

At the UK level there has been employee involvement in target-setting. The company has identified what it regards as necessary targets and performance criteria related to the performance of competitors, and has discussed them in great detail with representatives, resulting in the recognition of the necessity of these targets. At a divisional level we have recently gone through a budgetary exercise and identified, with representatives, the need to make a stated substantial reduction in fixed costs. This led to the representatives holding further meetings and coming back to us with an enormous number of suggestions which would contribute to the reduction in fixed costs.

The energy generated by participation has been shown as clearly in discussion of other concrete issues — our sales practices, whether we have got enough salesmen to match the competition, whether we have got too many people in central positions, the shape of our organisation and whether we are properly geared to meet the market situation.

As delegates get more involved in the managing or decision-making process, they share the excitement of identifying the problems and establishing targets, they become motivated to solve the business problems and beat the competition, and develop their own skills and capacity to participate and contribute.

Thus participation is a help, not a hindrance, because it is an energy system which gives those employees who really want it the opportunity to identify with the direction in which their companies need to go and help them get there. Who would have thought ten years ago that by today we would have representatives of all types and levels of employees and trade unions sitting regularly together in one room with their managers and directors to discuss business targets, objectives and achievements, with both the knowledge and the commitment to contribute. In any other field of endeavour this would have been called a technological breakthrough.

What we have gained

The third question was, 'What have we got out of it?' This is hard to quantify because we are dealing with a style of managing and a quality of relationship. It is not possible to put a value on these but the question is asked by many managers and representatives. And there are demonstrable results. We find that these are noticed particularly by newcomers to the company or by visitors who stay for a short period. They discover a wide-ranging energy and willingness to engage with managers in real problems and the identification of real targets. There are, and have been, special contributions at specially difficult times. The level of dialogue and debate can be thoughtful, literate and numerate, and usually very commercially oriented. There is a developing understanding of the realities of economic life and generally speaking a more thoughtful approach to the personnel implications of possible decision courses. Both management and work force representatives are finding more ways of accommodating to each other's major objectives, and this must be real progress.

There are some perceived drawbacks too. No one wants to make unwarranted claims for the system. It takes time, a great deal sometimes, it raises expectations and it creates frustrations. There can be costs, and the system may not automatically lessen more traditional industrial relations pressures. On balance, however, we perceive the gains as far outweighing the drawbacks; and is there really any other way?

Conclusion

In conclusion, it seems to me that progress in participation is based on as much conscious thought and evaluation as other important business matters. This attention begins with the Chairman and Managing Director. Effective participation cannot just arise or evolve of its own volition. Now our representatives and managers add considerably to this conscious evaluation and development process.

In the drinks division (Schweppes) we have found it more helpful to think operationally rather than conceptually about participation. This means asking how we can do it and getting practical experience on key issues rather than engaging in too much argument about definitions. We are a business institution and not an ideological or political one. As such we seek to manage our employee relations in a way which gives considerably enhanced opportunity for work force representatives to contribute to the way in which the organisation makes its decisions.

The system is not without its frustrations, but our aims and beliefs in seeking this greater degree of involvement are to increase the satisfaction and interest in working for our company, to secure wider but relevant contributions to better decisions and to create understanding and support for the company's priorities, targets and longer-term aims.

Summary

In 1973 the board of Cadbury Schweppes decided on an extension of employee involvement in the operation of the business. A three-tier council structure, corresponding to the main organisational levels and based on the previous joint consultation systems of the two companies, was set up on the recommendations of a working party, which included representatives from the main parts of the company and management. The issues discussed in these councils range from local operational questions to company performance, targets and plans, but final responsibility for taking decisions rests with management.

The introduction of the structure was helped by training for both managers and representatives.

Difficulties encountered in the operation of the system included:

(a) the presentation of issues — whether to state problems or solutions;

(b) the choice of issues, to ensure involvement in matters of concern but to which representatives can contribute;

(c) the problems caused when changed circumstances lead to changes in decisions previously discussed;

(d) separating participation from subsequent negotiation on adverse issues;

(e) the time taken up and the demands made on managers.

These problems were seen to be outweighed by the ability of the system to generate energy and commitment leading to improved organisational performance. Participation has also resulted in greater clarity in management decision-making, improved understanding of issues by representatives, and employee contributions to the quality of the decisions made.

12 The process of change in the worker director scheme in the British Steel Corporation

Ken Jones

Senior Personnel Manager in the British Steel Corporation 1967-76

The worker-director scheme in the BSC has now been operating for ten years. In that time, it has been commented upon in numerous articles, books, radio and television programmes and has been the subject of one major academic study, Brannen, Batstone, Fatchett and White's *The Worker-Directors — a Sociology of Participation* (1976), and a book, *Worker Directors Speak* (1977),[1] by the worker-directors themselves. Consequently, this chapter is not an attempt to review the history of the scheme, nor to give firm answers to such imponderable questions as, 'What benefits did BSC employees/the trade unions/management gain from the scheme?' Instead, the emphasis will be on the process by which the scheme was introduced, revised and, hopefully, made more effective, and on the lessons that can be learned from it for the future development in the UK of board-level employee representation.

Origin of the scheme

It was the organising committee of the British (at that time called the National) Steel Corporation which took the initiative and made the proposal regarding the worker-director experiment to the TUC in April 1967. The Iron and Steel Act did not require the Corporation to have worker-directors, nor was any political pressure brought to bear on the Corporation to make these proposals. However, there was at that time a growing interest in the UK in the subject of 'industrial democracy', and the National Craftsmen's Co-ordinating Committee for the Iron and Steel Industry had made proposals for employee representation at board level.

An initial experimental scheme was discussed in detail with the TUC Economic Committee. Such eminent trade union leaders as Frank Cousins, Jack Jones, Vic Feather, Len Murray, John Boyd, Danny McGarvey, Dai Davies, and Joe O'Hagan were involved in discussions over a period of several months. The TUC representatives expressed strong reservations about the initial proposals, in particular over the fact that worker directors would be expected to resign their trade union positions. Nevertheless the discussions led to a jointly agreed experimental scheme.

In formulating its proposals the organising committee had been guided by the view that the worker-directors should not be placed in the situation of being regarded as formal representatives of the employees — that was the function of the unions and their officers. The scheme should try to minimise the problems of divided loyalties for the worker directors by insisting that they resign any trade union positions they held, and it should minimise the anticipated resentment and personal conflicts which might occur between worker-directors and the management who would normally supervise them. The aim of the scheme was to develop a situation in which worker directors as individuals could bring to their group boards their personal knowledge and experience of the industry, and act as a voice, reflecting shop-floor views at the group board discussions.

The agreed scheme did not include any precise definition of the role of the employee directors but was limited to the following points:

1 Up to three employee directors would be appointed to each group board.[2]
2 Appointees would work at their normal jobs when not undertaking their directorial role.
3 The appointments would be made by the Chairman of the Corporation from a short-list of names provided by the TUC from employees of the British Steel Corporation.
4 Part-time trade union officers could be appointed but they would be expected to resign their trade union positions.
5 Employee directors would serve on the group boards responsible for the works in which they were employed. (The original proposal of the organising committee suggested that employee directors should not serve on their own boards, but the proposal was amended as a result of the discussions with the trade unions.)
6 The employee directors would be appointed for three years and would receive a salary of £1,000 per annum plus compensation for any loss of normal earnings.
7 The scheme was to be regarded as experimental and reviewed in consultation with the TUC.

The scheme was formally supported by both the main board of the Corporation and the trade union officials representing employees in the new Corporation at national level. However, trade union involvement in the development of the initial scheme was minimal.

Within the BSC, the Chairman of the corporation, Lord Melchett, and the Board Member for Personnel and Social Policy, Ron Smith, and such individual part-time members as Peter Parker and Stan Harris, were strongly committed. Lord Melchett, although politically a Conservative, had a deeply held personal belief in the need to involve representatives of the BSC employees in the decision-making processes through collective bargaining, joint consultation and employee directors. But the problem was seeing that the spirit of the agreement was transferred to the group boards which would be chaired and manned by men who, in the main, were not over-enthusiastic about the experiment. When the confidential research report on the experimental scheme was submitted to the BSC and the Trade Union Steel Industry Consultative Committee of the TUC (the Steel Committee) in September 1971, it showed that at the outset only about 7 per cent of the original group directors supported the scheme and 47 per cent were positively against it, or, put in a more colourful way, 'We know very well 70 per cent — more than that — were dead against us when we went into the first board meetings. A few favoured worker directors because they thought it was a good thing. Others because they had to.'[3]

Development of the scheme

The employee directors attended their first group board meeting in April 1968. The first major change to the experiment came about with the agreement in late 1969 between the BSC and the Steel Committee to the first job description for the worker directors, which had its origins in the dissatisfaction of the worker-directors themselves with their unclear role and with the attitude of BSC management and the trade unions towards them. When the worker directors met Lord Melchett, Ron Smith and myself early in 1969, they let us know in no uncertain terms of this unease.

It can be summed up in the word 'rejection' — rejection by management and many of the employees. But what was an even bitterer pill to swallow was that of their rejection by the unions, for all of them had been nominated by the unions, the great majority of them had held important local union offices for many years, and over half of them had also served their unions at national level. The fact was that the early months coincided with a very bitter period in the relationship between the Steel Committee and the BSC over the subject of white-collar union recognition, and the worker-directors were either caught, almost inevitably, in the cross-fire or dismissed by the unions as being completely irrelevant to this crucial issue.

When the worker directors met Lord Melchett, they asked if they could meet together for up to a week in order to try and pool their experiences and reach a consensus among themselves about the nature of their problems and how these might be resolved. The outcome of the meeting was the presentation to Ron Smith of a brief document outlining the worker directors' views which, amongst other things, stated, 'We soon realised that if our contribution was to be confined to attending board meetings, monthly or bi-monthly, then it would be impossible to justify our appointment as employee directors.' Also, there was a clearly felt need for a job description which would legitimise their position, outline their rights to be more involved in the policy-formulation process, and open up again the possibility of an official relationship with the trade unions.

During the next nine months a series of meetings took place on the subject of the job description, between the Corporation and the worker directors, the Corporation and the Steel Committee, and within the Corporation, at a time when the old geographical groups, based on the original private companies, were being broken up and re-formed into new product divisions.

Within the Corporation, the process of reaching an acceptance of the need for development of the experimental scheme largely consisted of Ron Smith convincing the Chairman of its existing inadequacies, based on observation, informal discussions with the worker directors and generally critical trade union and press comments; a discussion of these misgivings with the existing group chairmen and, more importantly, the new managing directors-designate of the new product divisions. The new managing directors were also made aware of how much importance the Chairman attached to ensuring that the experimental scheme was developed according to the spirit, as well as the letter of the new job description. It should not be assumed that all the managing directors-designate were enthusiasts for the scheme. The discussions certainly revealed that some of them were worried about increasing the involvement of the worker directors in the policy-formulation process. But others had already had enough experience of the worker-directors to be convinced that the Corporation could benefit from making greater use of their talents. At the very least, as sounding boards of shop-floor opinion, they could facilitate communications upwards and on occasions, downwards. Also, the Chairman, who had selected and appointed them, was a supporter of the scheme.

During the discussions, considerable concern was expressed about the danger of the role of worker directors in the future getting mixed up with that of the executive directors and management. Lord Melchett and Ron Smith, and the great majority of the worker directors were at one with the future divisional managing directors on this issue. Although one or two of the worker directors saw little merit in their continuing to perform their normal jobs, the overwhelming view of the rest was that, if removed from their working environment, this would undermine their already battered credibility with the shop floor. Consequently, the debates centred on how much time should be allowed. It eventually came to be accepted that there should be approximately a 50-50 division between functioning as a part-time director and carrying out the normal job as employee. In practice, this varied greatly, according to the type of job and degree of involvement in, for example, the sub-committees and working parties on which all the individual worker directors eventually found themselves serving.

The issue which caused most misgivings amongst divisional managing directors was the question raised by the worker directors as to whether the corporation was prepared to remove its objection to their holding trade union positions. The worker directors themselves had not been unanimous on this matter, but they agreed that the case should be presented to Ron Smith for the Corporation's lifting the ban. Smith eventually agreed that there would be an advantage in the worker directors' holding 'non-negotiating positions', which would give them a status once more in the unions and both make it easier for them to reflect union views at the board, and also provide them with the framework of a report-back mechanism. Melchett was also convinced of the validity of these arguments, and eventually he and Ron Smith succeeded in convincing the divisional managing directors to support this possible development. By the end of July, Melchett, Ron Smith and the divisional managing directors formally met the worker directors to discuss a second draft of the job description and their future role in the new product divisions.

A meeting was held between the worker directors and the Steel Committee in September not specifically to discuss the job description, but to review a whole series of matters related to the Corporation and the role of the worker directors. The chairman of the Steel Committee was still deeply sceptical about the worker-director concept in general, and the BSC scheme in particular. This was the first meeting between the worker-directors and the Steel Committee in over eighteen months, and the atmosphere of resentment on one side, and suspicion on the other, was not conducive to a productive meeting. When the worker directors mentioned to the Steel Committee that they were pressing for the right to hold non-negotiating union offices again, the Steel Committee expressed so little interest that the worker directors withdrew their request to Melchett.

The final stage in this adaptation of the original experimental scheme occurred formally at a consultative meeting between the BSC and the Steel Committee in December 1969. The Steel Committee had been presented with the second draft of the job description at a consultative meeting following the July meeting between Melchett and the worker directors, and it had been discussed in the Steel Committee as well as in some, if not all, the constituent unions. Whilst agreeing that it marked a positive development, the Committee had reservations about the clause regarding the power of the divisional managing directors to decide which sub-committees, etc., the worker directors should participate in. These reservations were very similar to ones expressed by the worker directors earlier, but no changes had been made when they had put them forward. It was agreed prior to the formal meeting that the clause should be rephrased so that it was clear that the managing directors would consult first with the worker directors before deciding whether they should participate on such committees. More importantly, Melchett made it clear that he expected the managing directors to involve the worker directors in policy formulation at divisional level far more than they had previously. Consequently, at the formal consultative meeting in December 1969, agreement was quickly reached on the revised job description, and the reallocation of the worker directors to the new product divisions.

In spite of the new agreement, the meeting between the worker directors and the Steel Committee, and subsequent correspondence between the Steel Committee and the BSC, demonstrated quite clearly that, whatever the job description said, there would be little open encouragement from the Steel Committee with regard to developing greater co-operation between the worker directors and the unions at national or local level. Consequently, the worker-directors were to enter a very dangerous period. They were to become more closely involved with management and obtain a better understanding of the reasons for management thinking, whilst remaining, in the main, rather distant from the formal union system. However, some of the worker directors were able to exploit very effectively the clause in the job description which said that they could attend 'by invitation, other trade union meetings as observers within their division', and attend 'their own trade union's meetings within the division'. The Steel Committee certainly did not positively encourage such involvement, but neither did they oppose it. The result was that, within a year, some of the worker-directors began to attend joint meetings not only of the part-time officers of their own unions, but of other unions — something virtually unheard of in the steel industry.

Evaluation and review

The worker director experiment was originally intended to last for three years (April 1968 - April 1971). This was extended to four years, primarily because of the change in the role of the worker directors resulting from the change in job description and the reorganisation of the Corporation. The Corporation and the Steel Committee agreed that the formal evaluation of the experiment should, therefore, not take place until the autumn/winter of 1971.

Both the Steel Committee and the BSC were initially to make their own assessments of the experiment. They were also to have made available to them the two-year independent research report. This was, consequently, the first occasion when the trade unions, the BSC, the worker directors and a group of informed outsiders could bring their influence to bear on the process of assessing and possibly modifying the scheme.

The full research report was submitted on 30 September 1971. Its basic conclusion was that the employee-director scheme, although not causing any harm, did not really contribute anything to the development of efficiency or employee-involvement in the BSC. This assessment did not come as a shock to those who had been closely involved with the research team, but it did cause some concern amongst a number of the most senior people in the Corporation. Although there was considerable disagreement with this general conclusion, there was far broader acceptance of many of the report's detailed criticisms, in particular the damage done to the scheme by insisting that the employee directors resign their trade union position.

The worker directors themselves were probably more upset by the report than anyone. They felt that they had been extremely open with the researchers and had helped them to make whatever contacts they desired at local level. But the researchers, in the eyes of the worker directors, had seemed unable to appreciate their difficulties or the more subtle and less obvious ways they brought their influence to bear upon the BSC management and the trade unions. Yet, the worker directors accepted that the report had considerable value: 'They certainly helped to pinpoint failings in the system and failings in the role of employee director which we were performing. It's a pity they didn't highlight the good points of the role as well.'[4]

The research report showed that there was now a majority of individual board members at divisional level who supported the worker-director concept, whereas in the early days only about 10 per cent supported the idea. Furthermore, the concept was supported by the majority of full-time trade union officers, about 70 per cent of ordinary employees and approximately 85 per cent of the trade union activists at local level.

When Lord Melchett met the divisional managing directors, the first question considered was whether or not the scheme should be continued, and each individual managing director had to express his personal view. Of the six managing directors present, two certainly had doubts about the value of the worker directors as late as 1969, but the meeting was unanimous that the experimental stage should be terminated and the worker directors made a permanent part of the structure of the Corporation. The group was equally unanimous about the need for change, and, in particular for ways of strengthening the relationship between the worker-directors and the trade unions. The two methods considered appropriate to achieve this were to involve the trade unions more closely in the selection process and to allow worker directors to stand for election again to certain non-negotiating union positions. It was anticipated that, on this occasion, the trade unions would wish to play a considerably more active part than before in deciding the future of the worker directors.

The eventual BSC paper, 'The Future of Employee Directors', which was prepared after lengthy discussions with the worker directors, affirmed the Corporation's belief that the worker directors should continue to be appointed, but that the scheme needed to be modified, in such aspects as the method of appointment and the employee directors' relationship with the unions.

The subsequent joint BSC/Steel Committee meeting soon agreed that the worker-director scheme should continue as 'both sides clearly saw the institution of employee directors as supplementing the major functions of negotiation and trade union-based consultation' and the discussions concentrated on the methods of appointment and the links with the trade unions. The members of the Steel Committee were united in wanting a more radical approach to both selection and the question of trade union office than the Corporation was prepared, at first, to accept. The initial negotiating stance of the Steel Committee was to leave the entire selection procedure in the hands of the trade unions (this could have included direct election from the shop floor to the board).

The Corporation's view was that the local union organisations, the trade union side of the joint consultative committees and, finally, the Steel Committee should be involved in providing a short-list for the Chairman of the Corporation to select from — basically, the system used in the 1968 appointments, except that there would be a greater involvement of ordinary members and local activists at the plant level. The union side quickly abandoned the idea of direct election and accepted the arguments for involving the Chairman. Lord Melchett then suggested that it might be feasible to think of a joint trade union-management final selection committee, which would suggest to him a number of nominees, possibly in order of preference, for appointment.

It was agreed that this might be a suitable compromise, and after internal discussions within the BSC, with line and functional management, and with the worker directors, and discussions in the constituent unions, the selection procedure agreed allowed each individual union to use whatever method of internal selection of names it felt was appropriate for forwarding names to the Steel Committee (including the possibility of direct elections within individual unions). The Steel Committee would then vet the nominees, largely to try to get an adequate balance between the unions, before submitting a list to the joint selection committee, which would be responsible for providing a final short-list for the Chairman to consider.

However, the Chairman made it clear that he had no desire to choose between various nominees so long as the selection committee was unanimous in its views. Instead he would be prepared simply to see one nominee for each position. But the final power of appointment should rest with him.

When the next major selection took place, the Chairman appointed eight new worker-directors, whom the joint selection committee had unanimously recommended. In two cases, however, the selection committee were unanimous in asking the Chairman to see three nominees for each of the positions and then to exercise his own powers of appointment.

Consensus was reached on this issue comparatively easily because everybody involved in the negotiations accepted the unsatisfactory nature of the original procedure and the importance of ensuring that the trade unions were fully involved, and seen to be so, in any future appointments procedures.

The question of the holding of union office produced a considerable degree of inter- and intra-organisational tension. The Corporation admitted that it had been mistaken in insisting that the worker directors should resign their trade-union positions and was prepared to accept that they should be eligible to stand for election for non-negotiating positions. The unions were united in opposing this limitation and argued that the ordinary shop steward or branch official would not be negotiating at departmental level about the type of issue which might be discussed at divisional board level. Consequently, there was no danger of role conflict.

A further set of informal discussions, both within the BSC and with the unions, resulted in the simple statement that 'links with the unions are to be strengthened and employee directors are to be given the right to hold union office'. The new job description made it clear that the worker director was entitled to hold 'appropriate part-time trade union office, when requested by the local membership of his trade union'.

Since that time, the majority of worker directors have held trade union offices varying from local committee men to union convenors to president of the union. Some of the individuals have been involved in negotiating at plant, divisional and national level. The much-feared role conflict did not seem to inhibit the worker directors and other part-time and full-time union officials, while the ordinary membership seemed to understand that worker directors could not be rigidly mandated, even though they were also union officials, nor could they report everything they knew to their membership. Undoubtedly, the holding of union office increased in certain ways the difficulty of the role, but the advantages outweighed the disadvantages. However, it needs to be noted that the executive council of one of the prominent unions in the industry refused to allow its worker directors to stand for selection, and in one case where the local membership selected a worker director, he was forced to resign.

Later developments

The period from 1968 to 1973 saw a gradual development in the significance and effectiveness of the worker director scheme. At the same time there was an increasing involvement by the national trade unions in determining the structure and conditions of the scheme. From what was basically a top-management-determined experiment, it moved into the situation of becoming a management/trade union scheme. The way was thus opened for further significant developments to take place at local level in response to the perceived needs of the unions, management and the worker-directors themselves. For instance worker directors, without any formal approval of the head office management, began to sit on works management committees and a whole series of other influential bodies which previously had been the prerogative of management.

One of the critical issues for employee representatives in any organisation is the process by which they communicate with and relate to the individuals they represent. Once they were holding trade union office again, the worker directors found that they were often invited to address meetings of the workers' side of the joint consultative committees and other types of joint trade union meetings. Nevertheless, in conjunction with the trade unions, they often had to develop forums which were almost outside the normal trade union machinery:

> I call a regular meeting with all the union officials. An ITSC man may chair it, and an AUEW man be the secretary, and we invite the union officials representing all the branches to have discussions on whatever happens to be relevant at the time.[5]

Although in certain industries, such as motor-car manufacture and other types of engineering, it is now usual for there to be joint shop stewards committees and even company-wide shop steward combine committees, there is no such tradition in the steel industry; consequently the worker directors have had to develop their own system of reporting back and seeking the views of their fellow trade unionists.

From 1973 to 1976 there was minimal progress at national level in spite of a number of attempts to stimulate action. In December 1974 a BSC working party, which included representatives of the worker directors, unanimously recommended the further development of a variety of participative methods which included an increase in the number of worker directors at divisional level and their formal introduction at main board level.[6]

On several occasions during 1975 the report of the working party was discussed in the BSC but the only outcome was the proposal by the Chairman, Sir Monty Finniston, to the Secretary of State for Industry that he should appoint approximately three worker directors to the main board. For whatever reason, Finniston's proposal was not supported by the Secretary of State and no action was taken.

The proposals for strengthening the worker director scheme at divisional and works level fared no better. The process of obtaining a consensus in the Corporation proved to be very difficult, and the suggested modifications to the scheme were watered down until eventually in early 1976 the Corporation made a modest proposal to the Steel Committee for an increase of three worker directors at divisional level whereas the working party considered that another 10 to 12 were required. Not surprisingly the Steel Committee rejected this offer partly because it was considered inadequate but also because the Bullock Committee was now sitting, with terms of reference which made fairly radical recommendations a distinct possibility. In the words of one of the worker directors, the BSC proposals to the Steel Committee were 'too little and too late'.

The new Chairman of the Corporation, Sir Charles Villiers, who assumed office in mid-1976, soon made several public statements favouring the extension of various types of employee-participation schemes in the Corporation. These developments were, however, to be within the overall context of a Steel Contract between 'the industrial and staff grades working in the BSC on the one hand, and the directors and managers of BSC on the other, through their respective representatives'. (Letter from Sir Charles Villiers to the chairman of the Steel Committee, 14th August 1976). The contract provided the basis for negotiation on an inter-locking network of employee participatory bodies from departmental to main board level and other improvements in employment conditions, in return for a trade union commitment to support a whole series of policies designed to improve the efficiency with which the BSC manpower was used — this included support for the works closure programme and relaxation of demarcation barriers.

The initial reaction of the Steel Committtee was somewhat muted. However, the worker directors responded by suggesting to the Chairman in October 1976 the establishment of a trade union/management/worker director working party to consider in detail the employee-participation aspects of the steel contract proposals.

1977 was a year of deepening financial crisis for the BSC and also a year of acrimonious national debate about the recommendations of the Bullock Committee. At the same time a major reorganisation of the Steel Committee was slowly taking place and until this was completed it was difficult to reach national agreement with the trade unions on any issues, let alone such an important matter as the steel contract.

In spite of these formidable obstacles the Corporation and the reconstructed, more representative, Steel Committee, agreed in September 1977 to participate in a joint union/management working party on the issues of industrial democracy in the BSC. After approximately six months a report was produced which recommended a considerable increase in employee involvement, through the medium of the trade unions, in all levels of decision making from shop-floor to the main board. With regard to the Corporation board, the working party adopted the view of the main union in the industry (which had also been advocated by the existing worker directors in their manifesto included in *Worker Directors Speak*), that approximately one-third of the board should consist of lay union representatives. But before these proposals could be discussed between the BSC and the Steel Committee, indeed even before the working-party report could be debated inside the individual unions, the Secretary of State asked the trade unions to nominate six members for seats on the main board.

The new participation plan was discussed at a meeting of representatives of all the Steel Committee unions and top BSC management at a two-day conference in early July. The result was that the executive committees of the individual unions gave an undertaking that they would come to a final view in the near future.

Consequently, approximately eleven years after the Organising Committee of the BSC made proposals to the TUC regarding the establishment of an employee-participation scheme which included collective bargaining, joint consultation and divisional employee directors, there will be in existence a system which effectively integrates the whole spectrum of representative employee-participation methods from shop-floor to the main board. However, it is ironical that, because of the precipitate action of the Secretary of State for Industry, some of the largest unions in the industry have felt compelled to react very quickly to the request for nominations. This has, in most cases, meant a selection process which has consisted of making nominations and completing the selection in executive council meetings — a process which seems strangely at odds with one of the basic principles of industrial democracy!

The contribution of the worker directors

The question is often asked, 'What practical contribution have the BSC worker directors made to the running of the Corporation?' It was felt by BSC top management that the worker directors had made three important contributions to discussions at the divisional boards:

1 They were often able to represent viewpoints different from those of the professional directors at the board meetings, because although, like most of the other directors, they had a deep knowledge of certain aspects of the steel industry, based upon an average experience of twenty years in the industry, they saw the problems in a different light because of different work, educational and social experiences. In the words of one of the managing directors, 'The worker directors often seem to challenge the unspoken assumption of many of us on the board and this I find to be valuable and so do many of my colleagues.'

2 The worker directors proved to be a very independent and valuable source of criticism within the boards. Every other member of a divisional board was not only formally responsible to the chairman of that board but he also knew that his chairman was responsible for formally assessing his performance, and could have an impact

upon his future within the Corporation. The worker directors had been nominated by the trade unions and had been appointed, initially, by the chairman of the corporation. Later their appointments were dependent upon the joint management-trade union selection committee. As they gained confidence they were more prepared not only to question the views of other directors, but also to challenge the chairmen of the boards.

3 The third factor in the contribution of the worker directors was that they represented a 'gut feeling' with regard to the views of the shop floor. However good the personnel director, however effective the joint consultation and negotiating machinery, issues came up at board meetings which were unforeseen and which had a very real effect upon the workforce. In such a situation, it was extremely valuable to have an individual member of the board who was closely in touch with the shop floor and who, on a basis of real understanding of the shop floor and contact with the representative trade union system, could attempt to assess the possible reactions to particular proposals. It was accepted by the executive management members of the boards that these were 'off-the-cuff' opinions, and the individual worker directors could well, at a later stage, wearing their trade union hats, come back and challenge the views of the board.

From the point of view of the trade unions and the workforce, it is difficult to be so precise about the advantages. Certainly, there is some evidence to suggest that ordinary employees gained a measure of satisfaction from knowing that there was somebody on the divisional boards who had the same sort of work experience as themselves, came from a similar background, lived in similar conditions and, therefore, should have some appreciation of the way they felt about matters.[7] This may be one of the reasons why approximately 70 per cent of the employees were in favour of the concept of workers on the board.

The trade unions, at national level, for the first few years of the scheme, saw very little advantage in it. When it was amended so that the individual worker directors could also hold any trade union office and they saw that worker directors were, indeed, capable of regaining the offices they had once held, they began to realise that there were certain possible advantages to the trade unions when taken in conjunction with the development of the joint consultation and collective bargaining systems within the corporation. What was happening was that opinions which reflected trade union feeling and aspirations were brought to bear upon the thinking of the management when that thinking was at a very malleable stage. However good the consultative and collective bargaining system may be, by the time management get to the situation in which they are consulting, they have already taken views about a particular situation. By being involved in working parties and advisory committees, at divisional and works level, worker directors were able to bring the viewpoint of the ordinary employee to bear at a very early stage in the decision-making process.

Worker directors have now been involved in over forty different types of working parties, sub-committees and advisory committees at national, divisional or works level. Most of these were concerned with the personnel function but particularly significant was the way in which worker directors showed that they could contribute to planning committees and cost committees at works and divisional levels. Even more importantly, worker directors, without any formal plan by the head office of the Corporation and the Steel Committee, became involved with the works-level management committees. This very heavy involvement of the worker directors in the support structure to the divisional committees was largely the result of their own insistence plus support from a small number of individuals from the head office of the Corporation. It demonstrated their determination to locate the place where ideas are originated:

When you only attended the divisional management committee you sometimes felt you were just rubber stamping because the decision to put in planning forms and so on came from the groups. So we asked to go to the group management committee and found that the group had its own planning committee and that we were actually rubber stamping that. So we moved to the planning committee within the group to get to the source of decision making.[8]

It was in these working parties, sub-committees and advisory committees at the various levels that the worker directors probably made their major contributions. In the committee structure they were less inhibited than in formal divisional meetings, and management was more prepared to listen to their views because thinking was at a more flexible stage and many more options were still open. The degree of acceptance they achieved in these committees may be judged from the fact that on several occasions worker directors were asked to chair certain sub-committees not only of management, but also joint committees of management and the trade unions. Their involvement at this level also gave the worker directors valuable information and understanding which they were able then to make use of in their role as union officials, either at local or national level.

It could be argued that the contribution of worker directors at local level and in the committee structure is far more valuable than at divisional or national level. There may be some justification in this view, but at the same time it would be quite wrong to conclude that, there is no need therefore, for worker directors at national level. The national level is the final keystone in the arch of participation and it rests upon a supporting structure at plant, group and divisional levels. Also, it would be erroneous to suppose that a support structure has to exist before anything at higher levels can be attempted. The case of the BSC demonstrates that one of the quickest ways of getting effective new forms of worker participation at local level is through having a system functioning at divisional level to support developments at lower levels.

Finally, it must be made clear that, in the words of one of the worker directors, 'people who think involvement at board level alone is participation, don't know what they are talking about'. If it is to be effective, employee participation in management should consist of the whole spectrum of participation, including joint consultation, works councils, collective bargaining, job restructuring at the workshop level and worker directors, and the various types of participation need to be integrated with one another.

One danger is that, unless introduced and developed skilfully, board-level participation could become yet another bureaucratic device inhibiting instead of stimulating business development. A further danger is that traditional conflictual bargaining attitudes on the part of management and unions could be transferred to a new arena — the boardroom — thereby ensuring that the locus of decision-taking in the organisation shifts to somewhere else.

The BSC worker directors have consistently argued, both within and without the Corporation, that the most effective way of minimising these risks is for management and unions jointly to develop a flexible, integrated participation scheme from shop-floor to board room, tailored to meet the situation of the particular organisation and the aspirations of its employees and management. In holding these views the BSC worker directors were not unique but they were the only people in this country whose opinions were based upon practical experience and in recent years industrialists, national trade unionists and politicians on the Left and the Right have publicly acknowledged how valuable they found the worker directors' experience to be in coming to their views on the subject of board-level employee representation.

The path trodden by the BSC worker directors, and the difficulties they encountered, will in a few years' time be faced by many other worker directors in the public and private sector and perhaps they will take some encouragement from the way the BSC worker directors overcame prejudice, indifference and hostility on the part of many managers and fellow trade unionists and not only survived but made a major contribution to developing the initial tentative scheme.

Summary

The British Steel Corporation's experiment of including employee directors on its group boards was initiated by the organising committee of the Corporation and agreed with the TUC but received little trade union support in its early stages. The need to clarify the role of the new worker directors quickly became apparent, and, following nine months' discussions initiated by the worker directors, a job description was agreed, which extended their scope to participation in sub-committees and other decision-making bodies, emphasised their links with the trade unions and their dual role as directors and employees working in their normal jobs.

An independent review of the experiment after three and a half years concluded that the initial requirement that worker directors should relinquish their trade union offices had done much to reduce the scheme's effectiveness, but that the concept of the scheme was supported by a majority of employees, and by trade union activists as well as directors. It was decided to make the scheme permanent, while revising the job description, increasing the trade union role in the selection of candidates and restoring the worker directors' right to hold trade union offices. From 1972-76 the main impetus for the further development of the concept came from the local level, and, in spite of attempts to strengthen the scheme at divisional level and to introduce it at national level, no progress was made until mid-1978.

The major contributions of the worker directors are seen to include the ability to bring a different viewpoint to board discussions, providing a more independent source of criticism representative of shop-floor views. The ability to get employee and trade union views heard before possible decisions are firmly formulated, particularly at the level of sub-committees and working parties, is highly valued. The BSC experience points to the importance of having means for participation at all levels of the enterprise, not merely on the board, and of management and trade unions jointly working out a system which fits the conditions of the organisation.

Notes

[1] Listed in the bibliography under Bank and Jones (1977).

[2] The four group boards set up initially each consisted of between seven and eleven full-time members, two to three external part-time members and three employee directors.

[3] *Worker Directors Speak*, p. 24.

[4] *Worker Directors Speak*, p. 66.

[5] *Worker Directors Speak*, p. 46.

[6] In 1970 one member of the original group of employee directors was invited to join the main board of BSC as a non-executive director, but ceased to work at his previous job.

[7] This may have been of particular importance in a period of contraction in the steel industry. For a description of the employee directors' response to this situation see *Worker Directors Speak*, Chapter 11.

[8] *Worker Directors Speak*, p. 44.

Part V
Implementing Participation

The case histories in the preceding sections deal with specific forms of participation and how they have been implemented. In this last section we take a more general perspective in an attempt to explore the implications of moving towards greater employee participation in the management of organisations.

The first two chapters focus on the different concerns raised by participation for management and trade unions. Chapter 13 examines the implications for the managerial role, both of the effect that employee participation might have on managerial accountability, and of the part that management needs to play in the introduction of new systems and structures. Chapter 14 reviews the range of different attitudes to participation which exist within the trade union movement and the prevailing views of the trade union role in the process. While these views may appear unwelcome and even unreasonable to some managers, they have to be taken into account in any initiatives which management wish to take. In this chapter Denis Gregory also provides a contrasting perspective to some of the earlier chapters, presenting a somewhat more critical view of developments like the worker director scheme in British Steel and some of the forms of shop-floor and plant-level participation described in earlier chapters.

The next two chapters look more closely at the problems of implementation. Chapter 15 looks at the implementation of participation as a problem of organisational change, and, drawing on a wider range of experience of change strategies, tries to outline the major strategic choices and the factors that have to be considered in making them. Chapter 16 supplements this approach by emphasising the importance of training in the implementation process and reviewing both the thinking and the experiences arising from a particular training assignment. While this example of a training application was obviously geared to a particular participation system, and thus cannot be regarded as a model for other companies, it provides a useful insight into the problems of training for participation, a subject on which very little information is available at present.

The final chapter attempts to look into the future by identifying the main pressures which will shape the development of employee participation in the UK and the directions which this development can be expected to take.

13 Implications for management

Kenneth Knight

Director, Management Programme, Brunel Institute of Organisation and Social Studies, Brunel University

Introduction

Whether participation is defined as involvement in decision-making or sharing control, it seems to encroach on an area — decision and control — which is usually regarded as central to the job of management. Yet the survey quoted in Chapter 3 found less than a third of managers opposing participation as an 'unwarranted intrusion upon managerial prerogatives' (p. 43), and, reviewing the experiences described in this book, we do not get the impression of a radical change in the nature and responsibilities of management. Rather, these accounts indicate a shift along a spectrum of managerial attitudes and behaviour — from autocratic to participative — which is probably not confined to organisations consciously seeking to increase employee participation. What these accounts do show, however, is that participation involves managers in a number of new tasks.

The aim of this chapter is therefore to try and give answers to two questions. First, it asks whether employee participation, in any of its forms, constitutes so radical a departure from existing relationships as to invalidate accepted conceptions of management's function and accountability. In second place it tries to identify the special roles which managers are called upon to play in the development of the various approaches to participation.

Is participation incompatible with management?

As we have seen, any definition of participation must involve some sharing of control over areas of decision-making. Yet the concept of management seems to rest on a view of the manager as sole accountable decision-maker. How far can management go in sharing this responsibility and still remain management?

Informing and consulting

The left-hand end of the participation continuum (Chapter 2, Figure 2.1) should not give much trouble. Where participation is limited to information-giving and consultation, management's power to manage and to take decisions seems not to be in question. There have, of course, been some doubts and misgivings about the effects of wholesale disclosure of information. It is sometimes felt that such disclosure limits management's freedom of action by giving valuable ammunition to the 'opposition'.

Such misgivings may be based on a view of necessary conflict between management and workers, akin to the capital-labour conflict postulated by Marxists. An individual manager might, of course, object that, whether necessary or not, such conflict does in fact exist in his own enterprise and that his managerial task of, for instance, maximising return on investment, is made impossible if he has to open his books to the trade unions. Where a union deliberately sets out to use information *against* employers this argument may be valid, but reported examples of this are rare. On the contrary, many managers now believe that the increase in mutual trust which can result from sharing information with employees is a powerful factor in improving the organisation's performance — a view which is exemplified by a number of the contributors to this book.

Joint decision-making

The question of whether participation is compatible with management accountability has more force, however, when we move along the continuum to forms of participation, such as a certain types of works council[1], the extension of collective bargaining to 'strategic' issues and joint control through 50-50 supervisory or management boards. On the face of it these represent a real encroachment on management's 'right to manage'.

The analysis of managerial authority made by Wilfred Brown (1971) and Elliott Jaques (1976) is useful in clarifying this issue. These writers point out that at every level in the management hierarchy, managers, and indeed all types of employees, take decisions as part of their normal work, within a more or less clearly defined area of discretion. This area of discretion is bounded, explicitly or implicitly[2], by decisions and policies made at higher levels of the organisation. In the case of directors and even the chief executive their decisions are limited by policies determined corporately by the board.

The introduction of a representative system of employee participation may appear to blur this situation in the absence of clear definition, but it does not really alter it. What it does is to provide an opportunity for employees, through their representatives, to share in the making of 'policy' decisions. These in turn, create the prescribed limits within which the individual manager, as previously, uses his discretion in taking the executive or operational decisions which are part of his job. Indeed the participation of employees in agreeing policies is sometimes seen as strengthening managers' authority to take decisions within their area of discretion.

A special situation may arise where, as a matter of agreed policy, certain decisions are taken jointly by a senior or middle manager, such as a factory manager, with a representative body such as a works council. What this means in practice is that he has to accept, as one of the parameters of his job, the need to secure the agreement of employee representatives to certain types of decision. Probably this is no more than an institutional recognition of a situation which is already very widespread in British industry — there are certain decisions, e.g. on production rates and methods, on overtime or on manning levels, for which managers in many plants now have to get agreement from trade union representatives. Some managers deplore this situation and regard it as one of the reasons why the productivity of British industry compares badly with that of its European competitors[3], but it is a fact of industrial life which joint decision-making systems at plant level, whether through works councils or collective bargaining, have recognised rather than created. The point to be emphasised is that such situations and constraints do not alter the essential nature of management, which has always, like politics, been an 'art of the possible'.

Board-level participation

Shared control at board level is at the time of writing practically non-existent in the UK[4], though recommended by the Bullock Committee and now being tried on an experimental basis by the Post Office. The government in its White Paper has not gone as far as the Bullock proposals, restricting the proportion of employee representatives to one-third for the time being and providing the option of having these representatives sit on a separate supervisory board.

It could be argued that at board level, if at no other, management authority, and hence accountability, must be fatally impaired by having to accept joint decision-making. But boards already have to take account of a multitude of pressures and constraints, including legislation, consumers and trade union power. Thus one could claim that in formal terms shared control at board level does not alter the position of managers, even including executive directors, whose decisions are taken within, and as a result of, corporate policy decisions by the board. The fact that the joint board represents employees as well as shareholders would change the criteria for policy decisions, but not the process whereby such decisions are implemented through the executive hierarchy.

It seems, however, as if this argument may not be quite realistic. At present most boards are effectively controlled by executive directors, not by shareholders. Executive decisions cannot easily be distinguished from policy decisions, and the reality is that a group of managers has both the authority and responsibility for shaping the course of the company. In a 50-50 (or $2x + y$)[5] board of directors the conclusion seems inescapable that either the executive directors can no longer be held accountable for the performance of the company, or their accountability must include their success in persuading the other board members to agree to the policies which they judge to be necessary for the company's future.

It is difficult, therefore, to escape the conclusion that top management accountability for the performance and development of a company is likely to be seriously compromised by the existence of unitary boards with equal trade union representation, following the model proposed by Bullock. It should be noted that the two-tier board system of West Germany, even where there is 'parity' representation, seems partly to elude this difficulty. Here the 'board of management' composed of executive directors, is fully accountable for the running of the company to a supervisory board composed of representatives of shareholders, employees and certain third parties. Opinion in this country, as exemplified by the Labour Government's latest White Paper (Cmnd 7231), seems now to be moving away from the Bullock formula and towards a version of the two-tier system.

Direct participation: job design and meetings

Two of the most common forms of direct participation, job enrichment and workgroup meetings, create no problems for the managerial role. Job enrichment which enlarges the scope and autonomy of individuals simply means increasing the discretionary content of their jobs, extending the boundaries or 'prescribed limits'. Within the bounds of the enriched job the individual remains accountable to a manager for the way in which he uses his enlarged discretion.

The main problem that can arise is an organisational one: if the responsibility gap between manager and subordinate was adequate before the subordinate's job was redesigned it is likely to be too small afterwards, unless the manager's responsibility is also raised.[6] Under these circumstances the manager either has no job, or he has to encroach on his subordinate's discretion, effectively reversing the job-design process.

Workgroup meetings are a normal feature of participative management and do not detract in any way from the manager's responsibility for decisions. As long as he is held accountable by his superior for the work of himself and his subordinates the decisions taken at meetings must be treated as his own, however arrived at. (Even if he were to adopt a voting procedure in the interest of democratic leadership the 'majority decision' would still be his responsibility as long as he holds managerial accountability for the work of the group.) Such meetings can improve cohesiveness and co-ordination between group members, and provide considerable scope for shared decision-making, but they do not alter the ultimate responsibility of the manager.

Semi-autonomous work groups

The one form of direct participation which raises some new, and hitherto unexplored, issues of management accountability is the semi-autonomous workgroup, or self-managed team. The use of the word 'semi-autonomous' draws attention to the fact that such groups invariably function within a larger organisation which is hierarchically organised at higher levels, and cannot be equated with truly autonomous sub-contracting groups or 'gangs' such as exist in certain industries. Semi-autonomous groups must therefore come under the responsibility of an accountable manager at some point in the structure. Under normal circumstances a manager's accountability for the work of his subordinates is based on a series of one-to-one relationships, however much he may encourage his subordinates to operate cohesively as a group. For Jaques (1976), if a manager is to be held accountable for the work of his subordinates he must, as a minimum, have authority to assign tasks and allocate resources to individual subordinates and he must be in a position to veto the appointment of, or to 'deselect', subordinates whom he judges incapable of performing the work required.

What happens to this minimum managerial authority in the semi-autonomous group? A basic principle of this form of organisation is that the group as a whole, rather than any individual member, is accountable for the work to be done, and that tasks are assigned within the group by agreement between members, and not by decision of a manager or superior. In some cases, moreover, such groups may be self-selected (Blake and Ross, 1976), or, even where the initial membership is determined by management, recruitment and selection of new members is often made the responsibility of the group. It appears therefore that *individual* accountability to a manager does not exist in such a group, and that the manager responsible for its work is deprived of his main sources of influence, by not being able to allocate work in accordance with his assessment of individual competence or to hold individuals accountable for the performance of specific tasks.

What seems to happen in this situation is that the *group* is interposed between individual workers and their manager as an additional level of accountability. Each individual is accountable to the group, which in turn is accountable to the manager. The idea of an individual being accountable to a group is nothing new — it seems to exist in the relationship between a chief executive and his board. Examples of groups being corporately accountable to an individual or another group are harder to find, though not unknown. But how effective can these forms of accountability be at the 'shop-floor' level of the semi-autonomous workgroup?

The group's ability to hold its individual members accountable for their part of the work is not difficult to conceive. Groups, as is well known, are able to exert very powerful pressures over their members and often dispose of more effective sanctions than the individual manager, including the ability to 'de-select' members, or, as Searle puts it in Chapter 7, 'squeeze them out' by making their life uncomfortable.

It may be less obvious how a manager can hold a group jointly responsible for their work. But within existing hierarchical structures it is arguable that the group that does not produce the results required of it can, in effect, be 'sacked', by putting an end to group working and reverting to a conventional one-to-one style of operation. Thus the sanction, as far as the group is concerned, can be seen as being based on the members' desire to continue operating with group autonomy: if they are not committed to this then the basis for group accountability disappears and the system could be expected to revert to a set of individual manager-subordinate relationships.

Some managers might argue that the existence of the deterrent of ending group working does not really provide them with any positive way of controlling and guiding the work of the group so as to achieve the required results. They overlook the fact that the autonomous-team concept calls for a change in emphasis from the controlling aspect of management, now taken over by the group, towards the *facilitating* role which is always present among the tasks of management — the responsibility for creating conditions in which the group can work effectively. This point is taken up in the next section.

The management role in participation

Whatever effect employee participation in decision-making may have on the position of managers, it is clear that, without the active support and commitment of management, any system of participation is doomed to failure. The special problems which arise in implementation are examined in more detail in Chapter 15, here we want to look more generally at the role of management in making different forms of participation work. It seems that there are four areas in which management action is vital:

(a) initiating;
(b) communicating;
(c) providing resources and training; and
(d) adapting management styles and methods.

Initiating

Paradoxical as it may appear, most forms of participation other than collective bargaining, are in practice initiated by management. Some would see this as proof that employee participation is really an employers' confidence-trick, designed to wrest back some of the control exercised by workers through collective bargaining, restrictive practices and strikes.[7] Managers, governments and many 'middle of the road' trade unionists take a different view; acknowledging the need for some form of joint regulation, they seek institutions through which this can be achieved constructively, avoiding confrontation and the more damaging forms of conflict. Their aim, as Wilfred Brown once put it, is to have their strikes around the council table.

There is, after all, nothing very surprising about management taking the initiative in the introduction of new forms of participation, in the same way as for most other changes that take place in the organisation. Interpreting the needs and pressures for change and acting on them is an important part of management's job. What this implies, however, is that the decision to participate must not be taken as a grudging concession to government or employee pressure, but as a carefully considered step which takes account of the existing channels of participation (some form of employee influence over decisions exists in every organisation), the aims to be achieved by extending or formalising these channels, and which of the possible forms of participation is most likely to achieve those aims. In considering the approach to implementation (see Chapter 15), one of the most important questions will be how employees can be involved in decisions about the system and its development — while there may be no contradiction in management taking the initiative, there certainly would be in management-*imposed* participation.

Communicating

Whatever forms of participation are decided on, they will almost certainly depend for their success on management action to improve internal communications. This is inherent in the very concept of participation: to share in control at any level of the organisation or even to exercise more autonomy in their own jobs, employees need more information than before. It is unlikely that information which has not been required in the past will be automatically available through existing communication systems — hence the need for management action.

Improvements in communications throughout the organisation are particularly important in systems of indirect participation. The danger with such systems is that attention will be focused only on the information needs of representatives, leaving the bulk of employees whom the system is intended to serve no better informed than before. This is likely to result in committed representatives and disaffected constituents. Unless the latter are informed in good time about developments over which they may wish to be consulted, their participation may be not indirect but non-existent. The importance of creating additional communication channels is stressed in most of our case studies, and is a continuing problem which management does not solve once and for all. The experience of ICI Grangemouth is instructive: after years of successful participation their follow-up survey still showed the need for improvements in communications.

Initiatives to increase direct participation throw up their own information needs, usually for improved feedback on performance, which enables groups or individuals to learn from experience. This is clearest in the Morgan & Grundy example in Chapter 7, where a computerised information system had to be created to keep the teams informed about the results of their decisions. The same needs for improved feedback arise in cases of individual job enrichment, while some of the other forms of direct participation, such as work group meetings and briefing groups, are largely concerned with improving communications in both directions.

It is well to remember that good communications are not only, as some public relations experts would like to think, a question of presentation and information media, nor, as trainers might suggest, of communicating skills. While both of these are important, they are probably less fundamental to the quality of communications than organisation and management style. Organisation structures are full of communication blockages, which stop information from getting any further. They take the form of departmental boundaries and managerial reporting chains (with their built-in 'filters') as well as individual managers and specialists who restrict information to protect their own power and prestige. The more authority is concentrated at the top of the organisation, the greater will be the demand for lower-level participation (not least from managers), but the less information will be available at those levels. To make a success of employee participation may require more than briefing meetings and company newspapers; it may involve creating new lateral relationships, and more communicative managers.

Providing resources

From the experience of our contributors the chief resource required is management time, and the requirement is always underestimated. Some companies have found it useful to appoint a manager with special responsibility for getting the participation system under way; in other cases an existing department, such as personnel or industrial relations, has had to take the project under its wing.

But other resources which are equally important should not be overlooked. Representatives also need time away from their normal jobs, not only to attend meetings, but also to keep in touch with those they represent. They may need to be given opportunities to travel, to visit other sites or companies. Premises have to be made available for both formal and informal meetings. And the participation system needs proper clerical support — relying on a busy senior manager's secretary to produce minutes and agendas and circulate papers in his or her spare time may result in information being produced late, representatives being insufficiently briefed, minutes being published when they have become history, and the whole system losing impetus and running into the sand.

Adequate training for managers, representatives and members of semi-autonomous groups may be counted among the resources that the company has to make available if participation is to succeed. The special training requirements associated with participation are examined in Chapter 15, together with other aspects of implementation.

Adapting management styles and methods to the aims of participation

The view which managers take of the nature of their job can range from a conviction that it is necessary for them to control personally everything that happens in their area of responsibility, to seeing their task as facilitating the taking of initiatives by competent and trustworthy subordinates. Between these two extremes lies what is probably the most common view at present — that management is concerned with achieving maximum, or optimum, utilisation of the human and other resources of the enterprise, using strategies that include planning and control, consultation, shared or delegated decision-making and facilitation, as appropriate.

One important contribution to the success of systems of participation is a conscious examination of the assumptions

made about the managerial role at different levels of the organisation to see whether they are compatible with the aims of
participation.

As we have seen, participation systems are introduced with
many different aims in view. In broad terms these can be classified into three main categories. The first category is concerned
with regulating and structuring the inherent conflicts of interest between employers and workers so as to make industrial
relations more orderly and predictable for both sides. From
the employees' point of view this group of aims includes the
ability to protect themselves against management decisions
which threaten their long-term security and welfare, as well as
having a say in the short-term operational decisions which govern their day-to-day working lives. For management there is
the related aim of avoiding a debilitating series of *ad hoc* and
unpredictable challenges to managers' authority, and obtaining systematic sanction from employees for the normal 'right
to manage' through executive decisions within agreed policies.[8]

A second group of aims is concerned with improving the
effectiveness of the organisation, by making full use of the potential contributions of all employees, by eliminating costly by-
products of low morale, such as absence and high staff turnover, and by increasing all-round commitment to the official
goals of the enterprise. Such aims, again, are not confined to
management. The view that anything that benefits an
employer must therefore be against the interests of his employees, which seems almost to be taken for granted by many writers on industrial relations, is not necessarily shared by all
employees: on the contrary, there is probably widespread concern with the success of companies among their staff, and a
desire to be able to contribute to this success rather than have
one's ideas and experience ignored by short-sighted managers.

The third group of aims is not concerned primarily either
with industrial relations or with productivity and effectiveness, but with the 'quality of life' experienced by people working in the organisation. This includes the aspiration to make

organisations more 'democratic' (whatever that may mean —
cf. p. 8, and the commitment to participation for its own
sake, as well as the desire to create opportunities for greater
job satisfaction and personal growth and development within
the work situation. Again, this is an aim of many managers
who want to work in a humane and creative environment
rather than a restrictive and exploiting one, as well as of
employees who look to their job to satisfy more than their
economic needs.

For participation systems to be successful in meeting these
different kinds of aims, it may be important that managers
adjust their conception of their managerial role. Thus where
managers are committed to a 'controlling' view of their function (a view often instilled into first-line and middle managers
by the expectations of their superiors) participation systems
may be quite successful in the aim of regulating the conflict
inherent in such a stance and defining the limits of their authority, but to achieve effectiveness and 'quality of life' objectives
through participation, such managers will have drastically to
revise their view of their function and the behaviour that goes
with it.

The improvement of effectiveness through participation
seems to require as a minimum a 'resource utilisation' view of
management concerned to provide conditions under which
people can contribute fully and directly to the achievement of
organisational objectives. And when participation is explicitly
directed at improving the quality of life at work through providing opportunities for personal autonomy and growth,
managers need to learn to adopt a 'facilitating' and context-set-
ting view of their role: providing guidance, support and
resources, linking groups to their environment, but not personally directing their work.

Summary

The chapter looks at two related questions — the extent to

which employee participation in control and decision-making is compatible with management accountability, and the role of management in making participation a success.

Participation systems which are restricted to information giving and consultation do not seem to detract from management accountability. Joint decision-making systems may add an additional parameter to some managerial roles — the need to obtain agreement to certain decisions — but in practice this constraint exists already. A new situation seems, however, to be created by parity representation on boards of directors, because executive directors will in effect lose the almost total control which they exercise in many companies at present.

Among direct forms of participation the only one which creates serious problems for managerial accountability is the semi-autonomous workgroup, and this can be dealt with by recognising that the group itself constitutes an additional level of accountability between its individual members and the next level of management.

Management has an important part to play in the success of participation by initiating appropriate systems, by improving internal communications to ensure that employees are fully informed on all developments, by providing the necessary resources and training, and by adapting managerial styles and methods to the aims of participation.

Notes

[1] For example the unanimous voting works councils of the Glacier Metal Company, which give an effective veto over changes proposed by management to the representative of any group of employees.

[2] Where individual discretion has not been defined, as is often the case, implicit limits will either be assumed by job holders, in terms of the decisions which they sense as lying outside their authority, or the limits are discovered empirically, by trial and error.

[3] See, for example, 'Britain's Poverty: The Role of Union Power', report by Stephen Fay, *Sunday Times*, 5 March 1978.

[4] In the British Steel Corporation worker directors are in a minority on divisional boards and only one worker director sits on the main board (cf. Chapter 12).

[5] $2x + y$ refers to the formula proposed by the Bullock Committee, whereby equal numbers of shareholder- and employee-appointed directors are supplemented by a smaller 'neutral' group appointed by mutual agreement.

[6] Jaques (1976) distinguishes a number of discrete levels of responsibility in organisations: his research finding is that among the preconditions of effective performance and personal equilibrium at work an important factor is that a subordinate and his manager should be working at different but adjacent levels of responsibility.

[7] An example of this view can be found in Chapter 14, where Denis Gregory puts at the head of his list of trade union criticisms of 'work organisation' schemes, that they are invariably initiated by management (p. 258).

[8] Cf. Brown (1971) Chapter 16, who argues 'the need for clear institutions through which managers can obtain sanction from power groups [shareholders, customers, employees] for their use of authority'.

14 Trade union perspectives on participation

Denis Gregory
Trade Union Research Unit, Ruskin College

Introduction: union attitudes to participation

The first mistake which tends to be made when discussing or describing trade union attitudes to participation is to believe that among unions and their members there is a common view on the definition, desirability and means to achieve 'participation'. Indeed, if the critics of trade unions have serious doubts about the extent to which union aspirations and values fully reflect those of society at large, then a close study of the union movement's contribution to the current debate on democracy and participation in industry would at least go some way towards dispelling such fears. Merely in the context of evidence submitted to the Bullock Committee on Industrial Democracy[1] it is plain that wide and sometimes polarised differences of opinion exist between individual unions. Moreover, despite the TUC's considerable efforts to provide practical and unifying proposals to Bullock,[2] it is clear that a number of major unions still favour quite different approaches.

The word 'participation' is, itself, not helpful when attempting to generalise about trade union attitudes. There are, after all, many ways in which unions, their members, lay and full-time officials, 'participate' at workshop, plant, company, sector and national levels, in a variety of actions and systems which govern relationships between the employer and employee. There can be little doubt that collective bargaining represents a systematic and developing form of participation — *purposive*, in that it is a clear means to an end; *democratic*, in that bargaining demands are formulated with shop-floor involvement, whilst the negotiation process and final outcome are accountable and subject to the particular work groups' ultimate ratification; and demonstrably *effective*, in that both sides of industry in almost every case recognise collective bargaining as the optimal means of settling differences, initiating change and accommodating shifts in aspirations. To assume, as many have done, that 'participation' is somehow separate or separable from the most widespread existing system of participation, namely collective bargaining, is to accept a distinction which inevitably will conflict with the trade union view of reality.

This latter view is far more likely to be built around the essentially pragmatic factors highlighted above in relation to collective bargaining and made explicit in the form of three basic questions: will 'participation' (in whatever form) serve any useful purpose? To what extent will it increase the involvement of union members, in a positive sense, in decisions affecting the nature and security of their livelihood? And, lastly, will the proposals work? Despite the divergence of opinion between unions, their approaches to the issue of participation all attempt to satisfy these basic questions. The extent to which their conclusions vary is a reflection, on the one hand, of the political ideology which distinguishes individual trade unions, and on the other, of the differing views on the practical utility of current proposals for increasing 'participation' whether derived from Bullock, the EEC or the myriad options offered by new forms of work organisation.[3]

Union ideology and participation

The inference has already been made that the specific ideology of some unions is, or could be, a primary factor in conditioning their attitudes towards certain forms of participation. This would appear to explain the position of the AUEW, representing a left-wing viewpoint within the trade unions, who have said (AUEW, 1976) that they would oppose workers becoming a party to, and partly responsible for, decisions taken at board level in private industry, on the grounds that such participation would both legitimise and add support to capitalism, a system upon which they hold fundamentally Marxist views.

The TUC's continuing advocacy of worker participation in decision-making at all levels up to and including the board, both in private and public companies, may be seen as either realism or reformism according to one's ideological position. TUC policy does, however, reasonably reflect the middle ground in trade union thinking on participation and it is instructive to examine briefly how this 'centre' view has developed.

Since 1945 the theoretical arguments over the irreconcilability of union objectives with those of the majority of decision-makers in industry have remained; but it is fair to say that this concern has had a diminishing influence on TUC thinking as the postwar period has unfolded and experience has been gained of the potential and limits of both collective bargaining and public ownership. It is also clear that the TUC's attitude to participation has been shaped by events and developments within the economy and, in particular, the union movement's apparent impotence to influence the decisions which led to the considerable merger activity and changed the face of the manufacturing sector in the mid-1960s, with dire consequences for employment and job opportunities. More recently, perhaps as a consequence of the structural pressures which have persistently eluded the 'checks and balances' of collective bargaining, the TUC has argued that:

> collective bargaining is and will continue to be the central method of joint regulation in industry and the public services, but there are a number of specific questions of close concern to work-people which are not being effectively subjected to joint regulation through the present

process of collective bargaining, and additional forms of joint regulation are therefore needed, particularly as capital becomes more concentrated and the central decisions of boards of directors seem increasingly remote from any impact by work-people through their own organisation (TUC, *Industrial Democracy*, 1974).

It would seem that the TUC policy has overcome the question of principle which has bedevilled the debate on worker representation at board level by arguing that:

> ... the extension of joint control or joint regulation in any form, including collective bargaining is a *de facto* sharing of the management prerogative (TUC evidence to Bullock);

hence, board-level representation does not raise any new questions of principle for unions who are engaged in collective bargaining. However, despite the progression of TUC policy, many within the trade union movement remain doubtful, and it is significant that the key resolution on worker participation passed at the 1974 Annual Congress stressed that:

> any extension of trade union participation in industrial management shall be, and be seen to be, an extension of collective bargaining, and shall in no sense compromise the union's role as here defined.

The EEPTU, representing a right-wing trade union view, went even further when outlining to the Bullock Committee its conception of the union role, which, through collective bargaining they saw as being:

> to consider, contest, and oppose, if necessary, the exercise of managerial prerogatives ... It is not the responsibility of work-people to manage the enterprise, it is essential that trade unions retain their independence (EEPTU evidence to Bullock).

In summary, it can be seen, ironically, that the left wing and right wing of the trade union movement are united in their opposition to participation at board level. Their opposition is, however, founded upon fundamentally different ideologies. The left-wing trade unions, e.g. AUEW (TASS), reject any form of participation which would compromise their opposition to the system. The right-wing trade unions, on the other hand, more or less accept capitalism but stick to the traditional view that it is 'management's job to manage' and that the trade union role is to provide the checks and balances, independently, via collective bargaining.

In this sense participation at board level is seen as a challenge by the left-wing unions to their traditional *political* role and by the right-wing unions more as a challenge to their traditional *functional* role.

Union objections to managerial goals for participation

Many trade unionists doubt the sincerity of management offers of increased participation at whatever level in the enterprise. To the non-unionist this tends to appear as a typical trade union 'head-in-the-sand', negative attitude. However, a closer examination of employer contributions to the Bullock Committee reveals that, in terms of the criteria outlined at the start of this chapter, unions probably have far more justification for questioning the motivation of management offers than is generally recognised.

First, the CBI made it clear in the introduction to the evidence it submitted to Bullock, that it was interested in increased participation only as a *means* to an end and not as an *end* in itself:

> the facts of Britain's economic situation are such as to suggest that widespread changes are nevertheless needed in British Industry, and that these changes could be considerably assisted by an improvement in relationships between employers and employees through greater employee participation — *with the basic objective being an improvement in industrial efficiency* [my emphasis].

Second, the evidence goes on to suggest that participation

would only enable employees and trade unions to participate 'in the processes leading to decision making in enterprises', and that a central aim of participation would be to ensure 'that decision making in industry is, whenever practicable, with the acceptance of employees involved'.

The conflict between the CBI and trade union aspiration is sharpened considerably when a third issue, the question of control, is discussed. Indeed, it is on this issue that the whole debate really turns and the credibility of the CBI in the eyes of the trade unions finally shatters: 'the CBI considers that "the control of companies" is not something which should be radically changed by "means of representation on boards of companies". Radical changes in the control of companies are not acceptable to the CBI' (CBI evidence to Bullock).

While the issue of control is seemingly the major and most persistent stumbling block which lies between the majority of unions and industry's current decision-makers, there are other objections, based largely upon practical experience, which have a significant effect on trade union approaches to participation. These can be best illustrated by examining certain examples of approaches which fall under the umbrella of 'participation'.

Worker directors in the steel industry

Until the recent experiment launched by the Post Office, worker directors at the British Steel Corporation remained the single biggest postwar innovation in formally extending trade union representation into the boardroom. The scheme was agreed by the BSC and the TUC Steel Committee in 1967 and has operated, with a review in 1972, up to the present time. Yet the outcome is not regarded by the trade union movement as a success. Indeed, the best that can be said of the scheme is that it has provided numerous examples of pitfalls and mistakes which should prove valuable as indicators of 'things to avoid' in any schemes that follow in its wake.[4]

A number of factors have been identified as contributing to the failure of the scheme, as originally developed in 1967:

(a) initially the individual worker directors were selected and appointed by the BSC from a short-list supplied by the TUC;

(b) once appointed, worker directors were compelled to relinquish any trade union offices they held;

(c) the worker directors were appointed to each divisional board, and it quickly became apparent that such boards within the BSC management structure were largely advisory, with the majority of executive decisions being taken elsewhere.

TUC criticisms at the time of the review in 1972 stressed the overt management bias in the selection procedure and the damaging isolation of the worker director which resulted from his being forced to relinquish his union offices, and with them his regular and functional contact with the local union activists and ordinary employees. The remoteness and the ease with which the lone voice of the worker in the boardroom could be either swamped or thwarted by complex technical considerations have been amongst the most persistent of criticisms to emanate from unions associated with the scheme. The 1972 review went some way towards improving the selection procedure (although the chairman of the BSC still has the final choice of candidates) and revised the ruling *vis-à-vis* the holding of union offices. However, it would appear that this has made little difference to the isolation of worker directors or to the severe limitations which their minority position and the complexity of the BSC decision-making structure forced upon them.[5]

The position of the worker directors in BSC has of course been severely affected by their being tacit parties to the BSC ten-year development strategy, announced in 1973, which called for a programme of plant closures and extensive demanning, and, latterly, by the unprecedented world-wide slump in the demand for steel. Against this backcloth the inability of the worker director to offer more than token resistance on behalf of his special interest has been readily apparent to local trade union activists.

It can be seen, then, that the worker-director experiment at BSC has, in the general opinion of the unions involved, failed a number of key tests: the scheme has not added to the unions' ability to influence decisions, nor has it provided an avenue which could not have been achieved by more normal forms of union organisation (e.g., the works action committee). Despite this the worker director scheme has survived at the BSC, and, while union activists do not regard this particular form of participation with any great enthusiasm, it retains some support for the 'toe-hold' it provides unions with in the upper end of the corporation's decision-making structure. The Post Office scheme is a distinct improvement in that it provides parity trade union representation on the main board. However, it remains to be seen to what extent the 'distance' between trade union board representatives and various union officials and activists can be minimised. The ease with which information can be communicated back to the key sections of the various unions will obviously be critical in this respect.

Works councils and joint consultation

Considerable emphasis was placed on works councils or joint consultation as the appropriate form for the development of greater participation in many of the contributions to the Bullock Committee.[6] Such contributions, one suspects, could be attributed almost entirely to non-trade union sources. While joint consultation does afford a measure of participation, very rarely has it developed into anything in which unions have placed much faith.

The TUC in its policy document on industrial democracy noted that, in practice, where joint consultation and collective bargaining have existed side-by-side in a company, there has been a tendency for the two channels to merge as local trade unionists have attempted to synthesise the power of collective bargaining with the possibly wider, or at least additional, coverage of joint consultation. It is unlikely that such a process could be either stopped or reversed without joint consultation at plant level being given the sort of power (which employers have explicitly sought to avoid) which would either set it up in competition with collective bargaining channels, thereby inviting union opposition, or render it indistinguishable from existing collective bargaining, thereby frustrating management's own aspirations.

Proponents of joint consultation tend to hold out the example of the works council system developed in the postwar period throughout Europe (the German and Swedish models are most frequently cited), but it is apparent that such comparative exhortations have become less and less valid, not so much because of the major differences in the socio-legal framework which characterise the UK and individual European industrial relations systems (vitally important though these differences are) but more because of the rapidly growing shop steward movement in Scandinavia and other European countries.[7]

In short, many within the British trade union movement find it ironic that change towards the European example is advocated, when at the same time the industrial relations systems of these 'model' countries are themselves changing from within to resemble more and more our own present position.

Joint consultation may well persist as the only form of participation in industries and companies that are weakly organised by trade unions. Indeed, several recent instances can be found of large companies establishing works councils largely, one suspects, as a result of the Bullock debate. Nevertheless there is little reason to suggest any long term change from the position identified by Donovan that, as union organisational strength grows, so will the influence of joint consultation decline.

The simple reason for this again revolves around the exercise of power and influence. In the main, joint consultative committees in British industry have been shown to be without power and of little or no influence — criticisms which cannot be levelled with any justification at collective bargaining.

Work organisation

For the purpose of this chapter work organisation is defined as the conscious act of designing and structuring jobs and systems at the workplace in such a way that the individual worker and/or workgroup has an increased control over the *substance* of those jobs and systems. As such, the most committed advocates of new forms of work organisation argue that the trade union response at plant level, which in the UK has been one of seemingly widespread indifference, is greatly misguided. They suggest that experiments in work organisation offer more than mere collaboration in management-inspired strategies to head off industrial relations or production problems, and should be considered by unions as an integral part of the broader process of shifting overall economic control to a more democratic base.

Sadly, this latter contention does not stand up to the evidence which is available to us on work organisation experiments, both from this country and from elsewhere in Scandinavia and other European countries. Trade union criticism of such work organisation experiments centres upon a number of factors:

1 Work organisation schemes are invariably introduced as a result of a 'management' initiative.
2 While all sorts of altruistic motives are put forward, the real reasons for the experiments quickly become apparent and tend to fall into a narrow range of traditional management objectives. For example, Volvo's much-acclaimed new car plant at Kalmar, which incorporates autonomous workgroups and a radically different approach to the orthodox layout of a car plant, was so

designed to avoid the de-stabilising effect of alienation and dissatisfaction on the supply of labour. The success of the new plant is invariably measured in terms of reduced labour turnover and absenteeism and the fact that the company can attract native as opposed to only immigrant labour to work in the new plant.

3 The objectives of many proposed work organisation schemes have been perceived to conflict with traditional 'control' positions hitherto subject to variation only through a recognised bargaining process. Thus, where an experiment has required more flexible approaches to manning this has been seen by unions as a covert attempt by management to remove a restrictive practice (an element of union control) without cost or recourse to the established procedure.

It would, of course, be wrong to suggest from this list that unions were not interested in work organisation experiments or in the raising of job satisfaction and the improvement of worker motivation. There is a growing list of experiments within UK industry where unions and management have worked jointly to evolve new forms of work organisation with these objectives. Equally, it remains the case that the majority of unions involved view such experiments as being of useful but limited value as far as participating in, and extending their control over, major corporate decision-making is concerned. Moreover, it has been pointed out that there already exist a number of readily negotiable items which could and should be improved as part of any meaningful effort to improve the quality of working life, without the necessity for elaborate experimentation in work organisation.[8]

Any attempts to define those factors which are liable to make a work organisation experiment acceptable to a trade union has to be substantially qualified, primarily, because no two workplaces are alike (although superficially they may appear very similar) and, therefore, work organisation experiments have to be 'tailor-made' to fit local conditions, attitudes, custom and practice and *needs*. However, as a broad generalisation most unions will consider sympathetically proposals that:

(a) genuinely lessen boredom and fatigue;
(b) improve communications both horizontally and vertically between shop-floor groups and successive layers of management.
(c) make a material contribution to improving health and safety at work.

Unions have been, and are likely to remain sceptical of grandiose claims that the proposed changes are in the interest of greater democratisation, and, as this chapter has sought to emphasise, any changes which impinge upon traditional collective bargaining areas or lessen union control at shop floor level are likely to be resisted very strongly.

Recent legislation

From the point of view of facilitating greater participation by union representatives, both the Employment Protection Act (EPA) and Health and Safety at Work Act (HSWA) have some relevance to the issues under discussion here. Both pieces of legislation were seen by the trade union movement as a means of extending influence over the decision-making process, and in this sense both have fallen some way short of expectations.

Access to information is regarded by many active unionists as the acid test of management sincerity, since any proposed participation which does not involve a greater flow of information to the union side is seen to be a sham. Management fears regarding disclosure tend, publicly at least, to centre on the question of confidentiality. It is argued that individual trade unionists, perhaps unwittingly, would spread information which could damage the commercial position of the company. Against this it should be said that many individual union representatives are already privy to sensitive information, and no one has yet produced any hard evidence to show that such a position has been abused by a union to the detriment of a particular enterprise. Moreover, it is patently absurd to suggest that unions are not every bit as concerned to preserve the commercial integrity of the enterprise, since the validity and credibility of unions hinges as much on their ability to preserve employment as on their achievement of improved terms and conditions.

Information is clearly an important prerequisite for increasing union participation in decision-making, yet it is, perhaps, in this respect that the recent legislation has proved to be most flawed.

The final version of the Employment Protection Act has substantially qualified the notion of a statutory obligation to disclose, by requiring that unions must demonstrate that without specific information collective bargaining would be 'materially impeded'. Moreover, management is merely advised that greater disclosure would be good industrial relations practice. In addition, a number of loopholes are built into the Act and the Advisory Code of Practice which accompanies it. For example, information that would prejudice the competitive position of a company need not be disclosed. Similarly, if the company claims that the information would involve more resources and time in its collection and presentation than it is worth in the bargaining process, it can again refuse to disclose. There is a procedure laid down involving the Advisory, Conciliation and Arbitration Service (ACAS) and the Central Arbitration Committee (CAC) which is designed to give unions some power over employers who consistently refuse to disclose information and who would appear to be in breach of the Employment Protection Act. It is not known, at this point, however, how effective this procedure will be.

Despite its flaws, it is likely that unions will increasingly utilise the relevant sections of the EPA and its accompanying Code of Practice to enhance their collective-bargaining position. It is equally likely, as suggested above, that management's motivation in any proposal for increased participation will be judged by the information that such an initiative would make available.

The Health and Safety at Work Act 1974 contains, argu-
ably, direct provisions for extending union participation and
influence at the workplace over health and safety issues. Yet
even here, the prescribed regulations and advisory code of
practice covering the scope and functioning of union safety
representatives and joint safety committees, stop a long way
short of a real shift in the balance of decision-making power
on health and safety.[9] While the safety representative is
given statutory backing for the important rights of access to
accident sites and regular inspection of existing, and new,
plant and equipment, he/she has no authority, for example, to
instruct any part of the work force not to work a particular
machine or substance for fear of a safety problem. Moreover,
it is very clear that joint safety committees set up under the Act
are strictly advisory to management. Guidance notes issued as
part of a broader statement on safety representatives and
safety committees by the Health and Safety Commission have
made the point very succinctly:

> it is management's responsibility to take executive action
> and to have adequate arrangements for regular and effec-
> tive checking for health and safety precautions ... the
> work of the safety committees should supplement these
> arrangements; it cannot be a substitute for them [para-
> graph 8, p.39, Health and Safety Commission, 1976].

In gearing themselves up for the implementation of these
provisions (effective from 1 October, 1978) the TUC has made
strenuous efforts to develop ex-plant training courses which
will prepare the union member to become an effective safety
representative. (It is also the case that the more progressive
companies have reviewed with their unions their health and
safety arrangements and have themselves mounted in-com-
pany training exercises.) There has been an increasing recognition by individual unions that the safety representative should
also be a shop steward. It is clear that, by combining the two
functions, unions may be able to buttress the statutory lack of
authority of the safety representative with the authority and

control which the shop steward derives from the strength of workplace organisation. In this, their action is in no way inconsistent with the tendency, already described, for unions to merge purely consultative channels with the local bargaining system. It also neatly illustrates the central thesis of this chapter, that unions are not interested in participation without some increase in their own control and authority flowing from their involvement.

Conclusions

In conclusion, while collective bargaining as a participative system has its limitations, for example in dealing with multinational companies and in influencing corporate planning decisions, it does satisfy the conditions which unions lay down. It does extend union influence and it does increase the authority and control (albeit an authority of reaction as opposed to initiation) of the organised workforce. It must also be remembered that the scope and coverage of collective bargaining has widened dramatically in the last decade to embrace far more than the immediate wages and conditions of employment of the work force.[10]

It is worth while emphasising that at the macro-economic level, the NEDO industrial strategy and the forty-odd sector working parties which it has spawned are regarded as a successful and meaningful exercise in participation by the majority of unions involved. Management seeking clues at company level for appropriate and acceptable participative systems could do far worse than examine the objectives and information that are worked through at sectoral level to see if an equivalent exercise could not be carried out at company level.

None of the other systems of participation examined in this chapter fully passes the tests which unions have applied, and will continue to apply, to them.

For all these reasons it is submitted that collective bargaining will remain the central and dominant vehicle for union participation. Moreover, with the possibility of increased information disclosure, and the use of planning agreements to bring future decisions within the ambit of collective bargainers, it may well be that collective bargaining shows itself as being capable of shaking off its current limitations. The Government's recent White Paper setting out its intentions on industrial democracy represents a considerable 'watering down' of the Bullock Committee's recommendations and it is clear that the White Paper's proposals have recognised the need for a voluntary extension of participation through collective bargaining. At the time of writing it is not clear if and when the White Paper's proposals will be introduced into Parliament in the form of a Bill. In any event, it is apparent that an 'organic' growth of collective bargaining, as opposed to legislated culture and is, therefore, far more likely to be the chosen course of action.

Summary

There are many trade union views on participation, just as there are many ways in which trade unions and their members do in fact participate in companies, particularly in a collective bargaining context. The main tests unions apply to any form of participation are its usefulness, workability and the extent to which it increases their members' involvement in decisions affecting their livelihood.

Ideological union responses to participation range from the Marxist view that it helps to bolster up capitalism to the right wing's fear that it will weaken union independence in dealings with management. Between these extremes lies the TUC's view that extension of participation to strategic decisions is necessary and does not raise any new questions of principle. But trade unionists are opposed to the employer's view represented by the CBI that participation is purely a means towards achieving greater efficiency and that it must not lead to changes in the control of companies.

Trade union criticisms of some specific forms of participation are stated. Worker directors in British Steel have been remote from the shop floor and ineffective because in a minority and lacking access to the real centres of decision-making. Joint consultation through works councils has been a weak form of participation lacking in real power and influence, except where it has merged with collective bargaining. Changes in work organisation towards job enrichment and job design have been management initiated and directed at management objectives.

Recent legislation on Employment Protection and Health and Safety at Work, though falling somewhat short of trade union expectations, represents an advance and will be used by unions to increase their control over important areas of work. Overall, however, collective bargaining is likely to remain the main vehicle for increases in trade union participation.

Notes

[1] *Report of the Committee of Inquiry on Industrial Democracy*, Cmnd 6706, HMSO, London, 1977 (the Bullock Report).

[2] TUC, *Industrial Democracy*. Document adopted by Congress in 1974. Later editions include the TUC's evidence to Bullock.

[3] New forms of work organisation are taken to embrace 'job enrichment' and 'job design'.

[4] It is heartening that the Post Office scheme appears to have taken heed of a number of the lessons of the BSC experience.

[5] It is interesting to note that a recent Norwegian study of the experience of worker directors found that remoteness from the workgroup was the employee representatives' biggest problem despite the fact that they still held trade union offices. The study concluded that 'Board representation is an extension of the indirect bureaucratic forms of industrial democracy, and is no answer to demands about increased, direct

personal influence for the individual in his/her job'. (Qvale, 1977).

[6] The Bullock Report, Chapter 10, paragraph 3.

[7] See, for example, Commission on Industrial Relations (1974), Batstone and Davies (1976) and Berry (1974).

[8] For example: basic pay, hours of work, occupational pensions and health and safety; see Gregory and Hughes (1974).

[9] Despite, for example, the well-orchestrated protests of the CBI and EEF which may lead the casual observer to think otherwise.

[10] See for example the ICI wage claim for 1971 and the Ford wage claims for 1971, 1973 and 1977, published by the T&GWU.

15 Introducing Participation

Kenneth Knight

Director, Management Programme, Brunel Institute of Organisation and Social Studies, Brunel University

The Problem of Organisational Change

Systems of employee participation other than collective bargaining are, as we have seen, almost invariably initiated by management, like most other changes that take place in the organisation. But in this case this very normal and unsurprising facts contains a paradox. For in order to make participation a success, management will have to find a way of relinquishing its initiative, of sharing control. If management keeps the initiative and retains full control, it has, almost by definition, failed to establish genuine participation.

This can happen only too easily. British industry is full of examples of participation schemes which have either lapsed, been discontinued, or else live on as irrelevant rituals somewhere on the periphery of real life, which at the very least have largely failed to fulfil the hopes that had been placed in them. This danger is particularly great where a management, determined to remain firmly in control, sets up a joint consultation council which is 'consulted' only on matters of secondary importance. The fate of many of these councils may be one of the reasons which led so many trade unions to set their face against works councils generally, and which made them a political non-starter at the time of the Bullock Commission, in spite of the favourable reports from Germany and the Nether-lands.[1]

The problem of implementing employee participation, whether as an end in itself or to achieve other objectives, has to be considered in the same way as any other case of organisational change. There are always plenty of reasons why a change introduced into an organisation can fail to become effective. The objectives may have been unclear in the first place. The time and resources required turn out to be much greater than was anticipated. There is insufficient commitment to the change to make it work. There is resistance from those who see the change as a threat to their vested interests, as upsetting an existing power balance which they want to preserve. Or the new system simply fails to deal with the real problems of the organisation and gets pushed to one side at the first crisis.

It is also questionable whether every management that has introduced a form of employee participation has really wanted it to succeed. Some of these schemes may have been seen as internal public relations exercises, or as a way of containing employee demands. Perhaps the aim was not to start a fire but to put one out, to consolidate the *status quo* rather than create a new set of relationships.

How to fail

While there are no sure-fire recipes for success with employee participation, it is quite easy to provide guidelines for managements who do not want such a system to succeed. A set of simple steps, followed conscientiously, will almost guarantee failure:

1 Do not set any objectives for the system.
2 Be careful not to relate it to any pressing needs or problems either inside the organisation or from its environment.

3 Announce the introduction of the new system unilaterally — do not consult employees about it.
4 Make sure the system is associated with, and introduced by, a low-prestige figure or department in the organisation (e.g., personnel management in some companies).
5 Do not integrate the participation system with any other systems of management or industrial relations — keep it separate from normal operations.
6 Do not provide any additional resources for implementation, training or follow-up.

None of these prescriptions on its own is likely to be sufficient to ensure the collapse of the system — indeed one or other of them can be found incorporated in many a more-or-less successful implementation — but in combination they are almost sure to prove lethal.

Making success more likely: a set of interrelated choices

Will a simple reversal of these 'guidelines' maximise the chances of success? One would like to think so, but in practice the question is more complex. Implementation strategies do not come ready-made: they have to be tailored to fit the circumstances. A series of choices has to be made, which are related to one another, to the organisation's history and present situation and to the reasons for wishing to introduce participation. In broad outline the issues on which choices have to be made are these:

1 Whether and how to define the objectives of participation.
2 Whether to link implementation explicitly to pressing problems being experienced by the organisation.
3 How to give the system sufficient top-level backing and support without ruling out 'ownership' of the system at lower levels.
4 Whether to focus participation on specific issues and

problems, or to take a broad, unfocused approach.

5 Whether to plan and introduce the system 'unilaterally', based on a clear decision by management, or 'bilaterally' as a joint effort with employees or their representatives.

6 Whether to integrate the system fully into the existing management and representative system.

7 What resources should go into training and follow-up.

In the remainder of this chapter each of these questions is considered in greater detail.

Objectives

Whether or not the implementation of a change should be preceded by setting clear objectives is an old controversy. On the one hand 'if you don't know where you're going any road will take you there' — objectives are necessary for deciding which methods of implementation are the most appropriate. Against this, however, 'if you don't know where you're going you're liable to end up somewhere else', which might conceivably be a better place to be. In other words, by setting objectives one has a better chance of reaching the objectives set, but one may be forgoing other possibilities which were not obvious at the start.

As we have seen, however, within the broad framework of 'participation' we may be talking of a number of diverging objectives of both management and employees. The objective for participation may be to create a more stable and predictable set of relationships by obtaining unequivocal sanction of management authority within a jointly agreed policy framework (as in the Glacier system),[2] or it may be to enable employees to contribute to, and benefit from, increased productivity (as in the ICI example), or to increase the job satisfaction and scope for development of individual employees (as at Philips). In some cases there may be a combination of objectives. But an attempt to agree what they are and spell them out for all to see has a number of advantages.

The process of agreeing objectives might itself be the first step in participation. It can provide a basis for employees to judge management's sincerity (is there a hidden agenda?) and a criterion against which to judge later success. (Without such a criterion there is no basis for reviewing and improving the system and hence for a process of organisational learning.) It also enables judgements to be made about the appropriateness of the form of participation and of the method chosen to implement it. Employee representatives on the board may help to sanction company policy, but on the face of it are not the best ways of improving productivity at plant level, just as working parties looking at production methods are unlikely to have much effect on bad industrial relations. As for methods — job enrichment may be an appropriate means to greater job satisfaction, but redesigning a person's job with the help of everyone but himself may not be the best way to increase his sense of autonomy (a frequent criticism of the method advocated by Herzberg (1966)). The main potential dangers of having clear objectives at the outset are that these may inhibit other desirable developments, and that the system may lose impetus once the initial objectives have been achieved. Both of these dangers can be avoided by including at least one objective concerned with the future development of the system in accordance with the wishes of all the parties involved.

Pressures

One of the most widely agreed findings on organisational change is that success is a great deal more likely if a change corresponds to real pressures, both internal and external (cf. Greiner, 1967). The perception by people that there is a real problem, that something has to be done, that the change helps to meet a genuine need, is apparently necessary to overcome natural inertia and unavoidable resistance.

In some of our case studies such pressures were evident, and helped to provide the driving force for change. The Grangemouth plant at the outset was in such serious industrial relations trouble with its engineering workers, that closure loomed on the horizon, and the early steps towards participation were directly addressed to this problem. The change at Morgan & Grundy was preceded by fears of imminent 'breakdown'. In these cases the action taken was seen as a possible answer to serious problems. The same action taken at a time when these problems were less obvious, might have been pursued much less energetically and been less successful.

Where there appear to be no objectives, widely acknowledged pressures available to support a change, it may be possible to generate such pressures within the system by providing it with new data about itself. The survey undertaken in the local authority recreation department (Chapter 3) and the feedback of results to the staff involved is an example of such an approach. Indeed survey feedback is an old and tried method of generating pressures for change within an organisation — usually change of a participative kind (Mann, 1957).

External pressure can also be generated deliberately, as was done by ICI through the MUPS and Weekly Staff Agreements (Chapter 9), when substantial pay increases were offered but made conditional on the productivity improvements needed to pay for them. (In reality, of course, this was a way of translating into a convincing form the external competitive presures in world markets which were troubling top management.)

One possible argument against trying to link the introduction of participation systems to real and specific pressures on the organisation (apart from there being no such pressures in evidence — one of the best reasons for doing nothing) is that employees might cynically suppose that management is not really interested in their participation but merely in getting itself out of trouble. But this kind of reaction is hardly to be avoided, pressure or no pressure. At least where the problems are real there will be less temptation to look for various suspect, hidden motives on the part of management.

If participation is linked to pressing current problems there ought, however, to be some anticipation of what is to happen once these problems are solved. Is the organisation to revert to the *status quo*, or will the experience be used as a basis for a more permanent restructuring of relationships as happened at Grangemouth?

Patrons and change agents

The importance of top-management support is one of the commonplaces of organisational change. In most of the cases reported here that support was evident, from Lord Melchett and Lord Watkinson to David Searle and Geoffrey Richards, each the 'top man' over the relevant area of operations.

This point requires little comment. The top man's open and sustained support for a change is likely to increase its credibility with employees and to lessen the chance of obstruction from managers who disagree. In the case of participation, of course, top union support can be of equal importance, and many of the difficulties encountered by BSC's employee directors were related to the rather lukewarm initial support they received from the TUC and its Steel Committee.

The one obvious danger in the special case of participation schemes is that the system will come to be seen as the top man's 'baby', with other managers and employees going through the motions to please him, but with no personal identification with what is going on. The problem for the 'patron' is therefore how to give the system maximum support without appearing to take it over, how to generate the commitment of those whose participation or representation is the aim of the system.

While there are no definitive answers to this problem, it seems from the experience reported in this book that provided those participating in the system are able to have a part in working out the form of their participation and are in a position where they are able to take initiatives, and encouraged to do so, their commitment is secured. This may explain why managers are sometimes less committed to such systems with strong support from the top, than the participating representatives: they are more bound by the top man's wishes and, in contrast to representatives, less able to take initiatives within the system than outside it. There seems so far to have been only limited success in generating any commitment or sense of ownership among those who do not personally participate in the system,[3] and over-identification of the participation scheme with the head of the organisation may well increase the scepticism and alienation of the non-involved.

A closely related question is whether the introduction of a change as potentially far-reaching as some systems of employee participation requires the establishment of special 'change agent' roles. The need for such roles seems to arise from a number of factors. First, where senior or top management are the initiators of the change, they may simply not have the time to do the detailed spade-work which is required to turn ideas into realities. Our cases emphasise just how much time can be involved. Second, the organisation may lack the necessary knowledge, expertise or experience in generating alternatives and assessing practical options so as to develop a system best suited to achieving its objectives and foreseeing the problems that may arise. These needs, for expertise, and for someone to do the work, are the usual reasons for employing consultants, whether internal or external or a combination of the two.

There is, however, an additional function which is often performed by someone in a change agent role, and which has particular relevance to efforts to introduce employee participation. Where relationships between management and employees have become set into a pattern which combines elements of conflict, of negotiation and of collaboration, it is sometimes very difficult to break the mould in order to establish a new and different pattern of relationships. Every initiative made by either party, including an initiative by top management, is absorbed into the existing pattern and interpreted in terms of it. Under these circumstances it can be very useful, it may indeed be essential, to have a neutral and independent third party, who can play the role of an 'honest broker', and who can provide the actors with a detached view of their situation, a viewpoint which is right outside their existing relationship and which can be used as a point of departure towards a new relationship pattern. It is essential that such a third party should be perceived to be both independent — to be 'in the pocket' of neither party — and to have a full understanding of the problems of both. If he is seen as invested with considerable personal prestige, so much the better — his prestige will make it easier for the actors to move from their engaged positions towards his own more detached viewpoint, and will legitimise their movement towards a new definition of their relationship.[4]

Focused versus unfocused approaches

Should a participative system be introduced by focusing attention on specific issues and problems, or should it start off in an unfocused and open-ended way? Examples of focused approaches to participation are the semi-autonomous teams at Philips and Morgan & Grundy, concerned specifically with the organisation of their members' work to achieve concrete results, and the CAG and workgroups at ICI Grangemouth, concerned with finding ways to improve productivity. On the other hand the APGs in the local authority recreation department, the briefing groups at SNB, the Cadbury Schweppes works council structure and British Steel's worker director scheme are all unfocused, in the sense that these systems were not set up to look at specific areas but were given broad terms of reference which could include both issues of detail and the general running of the business.

From these examples it appears that the lower the organisational level, and the more direct the participation, the more likely it is that a focused approach will be adopted. But this is not the whole story. The advantage of relating a change to perceived pressures in the organisation and its environment has already been mentioned. But a corollary of acknowledging such pressures is often that the approach has to be focused on the specific problems which constitute the pressure points. Again, where the objectives of introducing the system have been clearly stated as an improvement in effectiveness through enlisting a wide range of employee contributions, a productivity-focused approach, as at ICI, has an obvious logic.

Among the advantages of a focused approach are that it is clear and comprehensible, provides unequivocal criteria of success and is basically practical. All of these are obvious sources of energy and generators of commitment.

The weakness of focusing on specific issues is that these may not be the ones which really concern employees. Management may be setting boundaries on the potential scope of participation, rather than allowing employees to decide on the areas in which they wish to increase their involvement. This kind of scope for greater co-determination is provided much more easily by an initially open-ended approach in which employees decide where they wish to focus attention. This type of approach, however, has its own drawback — the risk of losing steam, running out of energy. Where an unfocused approach is adopted it may have to be supplemented by various activities, such as surveys or working parties, which are designed to generate energy related to specific issues.

Unilateral and bilateral strategies

In implementing any organisational change, as in setting objectives, management has to choose between a 'unilateral' approach, in which the details of the change are worked out before the employees affected by it are brought into the picture, and a 'bilateral' one, in which problems are examined and changes planned as a joint effort.[5]

The main advantage of a unilateral approach is that management is better able to retain control of the change, and this is why it has in the past been the most popular way of implementing new systems and practices in British industry. Its main drawback is that it is unlikely to generate much commitment and indeed often leads to resistance, which has to be overcome by various pressures and inducements. A bilateral method of implementation, while on the face of it much more risky, has the virtue that it can arouse considerable commitment, even enthusiasm, in those involved in the change and thus is more likely to create a sense of ownership from the start.

The cases described in this book include examples of both strategies. The introduction of briefing groups at Scottish & Newcastle, of self-managed teams at Morgan & Grundy and even of the initial worker director scheme at British Steel employed, on the whole, a unilateral approach; while the formation of Action Planning Groups in the recreation department and the development of the consultative system at Cadbury Schweppes were based on a bilateral strategy. The development of participation in the Grangemouth works of ICI seems over the years to have employed a judicious mixture of both methods, with management taking a number of unilateral initiatives at the start, but moving more and more towards the bilateral development of new forms of participation.

In the introduction of participation systems the choice between unilateral and bilateral strategy is particularly difficult to make, but a number of the factors which will affect the choice emerge from our examples and the preceding analysis. Clearly, there are situations where a unilateral approach, at least at the outset, is the only one open to management. Where there is a history of conflict and distrust to overcome, management may have to take the initiative to begin with to try and convince employees of its own good faith. Again, where, as in David Searle's account, a revolutionary change is contemplated and the situation is judged urgent, a unilateral approach may be the only one possible. In such cases, however, there may well be a need for the change to include strong built-in inducements, as in the case mentioned, to generate energy and commitment, and it is interesting that David Searle reports lack of success with the new information system during the trial period before the new payment systems came into effect.

Where the form of participation is initially unfocused and the change is not a response to strongly felt pressures, there is a powerful case for adopting a bilateral approach either at the start or shortly after, for without it there is simply not going to be enough energy and commitment to keep the system going.

But whatever the initial approach employed, any system of employee participation must in due course become a bilateral approach to change — if it does not, it will be stillborn and ineffective.

Integration

The question of how, and to what extent, the system of participation is to be integrated with the normal operation of the organisation is one of the most crucial, and also one of the most difficult. The weakness of many of the older systems of joint consultation as well as some of the schemes of so-called financial participation has been that they had very little effective impact on the real decision-making processes of the enterprise. One of the most damning criticisms made of the earlier version of British Steel's worker director scheme, as well as of many of the German supervisory boards, was that the real decisions were made elsewhere.

It can be argued, indeed, that participation systems ought not to be integrated too far with the business of running the organisation. Managers must be left free to manage and trade unions to represent their members' interests — the function of the participation system being to provide a channel through which employee views can be expressed, so that they can be freely taken into account by managers going about their normal job of taking decisions and implementing policies. (Broadly speaking this seems to be the logic underlying the Cadbury Schweppes philosophy as expressed in Derek Williams's description of their system.)

Such a view probably represents the feelings of many employees of British organisations, who do not want to take any share in the responsibilities of management. The view of many active trade unionists who see an adversary system, in which all issues of concern are brought within the scope of the collective bargaining process, as the surest way of bringing effective pressure to bear is only a further step in the same direction and may lead to their opposing participation altogether.

The movement towards greater participation seems on the whole to be based on a different logic — a logic of involvement of the different interest groups with one another in place of their separation in an arm's-length relationship. Such involvement depends both on the structure of the participation system, and on the substantive decision areas which are brought within its scope.

The structure needs to be one which reflects as closely as possible the management and decision-making structure of the organisation itself. This will of course be conditioned by the original objectives of the system. Where they are concerned with the sanctioning of management authority, integration will take place mainly at the upper policy-making levels, as in employee-director schemes and company councils. Where the aims primarily concern the maximising of employee contributions to effective operations, the major forums for participation will be at the operating levels, in site and departmental groups and meetings. To achieve greater direct control and autonomy in the workplace requires integration at the level of the working group itself, or even at the level of the individual job.

In some of the more ambitious schemes attempts are being made to link these various levels into multi-level structures of participation which reflect the pattern of delegation of authority. A recent example of such an attempt is the experiment currently being tried in the Post Office which involves employee representatives on the main board, regional boards and area policy committees.

But while the mechanisms for participation may be integrated structurally, by reflecting, and engaging with, the different levels of the management structure the more important question is still whether such integration takes in the decisions that matter to employees on the one hand, and to the future of the organisation on the other. Here one may have to recognise two serious obstacles to any real integration of the participation system into the most important decision-making processes of the organisation. The time and experience required before representatives can make any real contribution to many business decisions is likely to be considerable, so genuine participation may be restricted on practical grounds. And at the same time, as was noted in the discussion of plant-level participation, trade unions may wish to keep the decisions that have a direct impact on their members within a collective bargaining framework.

So the choice of how far to integrate the participation system with the day-to-day as well as longer-term decision-making processes may be constrained both by the capacity of representatives and the willingness of trade unions, but such constraints should not be confused with criteria for deciding how much integration is desirable. There may be good reasons for overcoming the constraints, if only because failure to integrate may condemn the whole system to being perceived as peripheral, irrelevant and undeserving of serious commitment.

The German approach is interesting: through the Works Constitution Act of 1972 the degree of integration of the statutory works councils is fixed at different levels for different types of decision, ranging from information and consultation rights over certain classes of decision to co-determination rights on others, while a special financial committee appointed by the council is entitled to information on business policies and a range of financial issues.

In the context of the UK probably the most difficult question of integration concerns the relationship between collective bargaining, itself an important means of participation, and other forms of involvement. It is common, where new participative mechanisms are established, for management and unions to agree at the outset that the new systems should not deal with any topics which are normally subject to negotiation — as was the case with Scottish & Newcastle's briefing groups and the Cadbury Schweppes council structure. Trade unions tend to feel that they can get a better deal for their members through traditional negotiating practices, and may suspect management of trying to lessen their members' solidarity by a 'softening-up' process. Managers, by contrast, often fear that by importing the confrontational attitudes of the collective bargaining system, the collaborative aims of participation may be undermined.

In practice, however, it appears that such a restriction of the content of participation is often relaxed once a new participation system gets under way, because it proves both artificial and unnecessary. As we noted in Chapter 8, the trend at plant level seems to be towards merging the functions of collective bargaining and joint consultation into a single system of joint regulation. The logic of this process has been accepted for many years in the constitution of the Glacier Works Council, one of the longest-established systems of employee participation in British industry (Brown, 1971).

Indeed if the TUC's insistence on a single channel of representation is accepted and the employee representatives on participative bodies are also trade union representatives, there seems little point in splitting the functions of the single representative system in two — unless it is the symbolic point of distinguishing between the two processes of joint problem-solving and bargaining, and the different 'hats' the representatives may have to wear at different times.

In multi-union situations there is these days often a body, such as a 'combine committee', which brings together senior representatives from the different unions for a site or company, and this may well be seen as the natural body for other forms of participation. The strongest argument, however, for those who want participation to succeed, is that negotiating issues tend also to be the issues of greatest importance to employees, and their exclusion from any system of participation is the surest way of devaluing that system.

This is not to say that the process for dealing with such issues in the participation system may not be very different from that employed in negotiations. One of the advantages of some of the new participative mechanisms, as pointed out by Derek Williams in Chapter 11, has been the opportunity they have given to both managers and representatives to reduce the area of disagreement in a problem-solving context, before facing one another across the negotiating table.

Training and follow-up

The importance of training to most systems of participation is underlined in most of the cases described in this book. Successful participation requires not only changes in long-established relationships, but also additional knowledge and new skills, the lack of which may cause the collapse of the system.

To decide precisely what training is required and by whom, an initial training-needs analysis is useful. A helpful approach to such an analysis has been published by the Ceramics, Glass and Mineral Products Industry Training Board (1976). This distinguishes between the group of people actually involved in participation, and others likely to be affected by, or who can affect, the participating group, recognising that the success of any form of participation depends not only on the people who are actively involved in it, but also on their relations with the rest of the organisation. In the case of direct participation through job enrichment or teams, the attitudes of supervisors, managers, shop stewards and adjacent work groups may be enough to make or break the change, while in systems where involvement is restricted to a group of representatives, their efforts can remain largely ineffective unless they enjoy the full understanding and active interest of their constituents. (In one highly developed system of indirect participation, a senior union representative told us that most of the representatives were very committed to the system, but the work force regarded it as a failure.)

The primary needs which training has to meet in any new participation system are for knowledge and specific skills. Employees or their representatives can only play a meaningful role in decision-making if they have an understanding of the factors that affect the decision; hence both ICI and Cadbury Schweppes in our examples found it necessary to train representatives in various key aspects of the business, though one of the most intensive examples of business and managerial training has been the five-week BSC/TUC course mounted for the worker directors at the British Steel Corporation's staff college.

Managers, as well as representatives, may also have to acquire the new skills demanded by new systems. At a minimum, briefing groups and joint consultation call for well-developed communicating skills, as exemplified by the special training in briefing methods by Scottish & Newcastle Breweries, but beyond this managers may need to be given an opportunity to reassess their relationships with employees and representatives in the light of new approaches to participation: one example of the latter were the special workshops mounted in Cadbury Schweppes.

The next chapter describes in detail the planning and implementation of an extensive training programme for a new employee council structure. This draws attention to the need to equip both managers and representatives with basic committee skills and a full understanding of the participation system itself, as well as providing a range of relevant knowledge on manufacturing processes, business methods and the work of specialist functions. The account also throws some useful light on the problems of embarking on this type of training. The requirements for resources — mainly the time of managers, specialists and trainers — are considerable and often exceed expectations. Staff may be unavailable on the dates for which training is scheduled. Most important of all, participative bodies have minds of their own, and even if they initially agree to a programme they may later change their minds about certain of its components.

John Davis, the author of the chapter, puts forward the view that an important part of the training of management-union representative committees is some form of 'team-building' designed to enable them to operate as cohesive groups.

Not everyone, however, will agree with the view that such committees ought to learn to operate as 'teams'. One might even argue that the principle of indirect participation runs counter to the whole idea of team operation, through which representatives and managers start to identify common interests and a common frame of reference which weaken their links with their respective 'constituencies'.

The training programme described by Davis contained a number of events concerned with evaluation, which, when the time came, the committees proved reluctant to take up. This shows that while evaluation and follow-up by the participation bodies themselves seems a highly desirable approach, it can in practice be beset with political difficulties. An alternative approach is illustrated by the ICI Grangemouth and British Steel cases. In both, the task of evaluating the system was given to independent outsiders, who were given full access to all the people concerned. The results of these surveys demonstrate the vital importance of reviewing the workings of systems of participation. Both reviews revealed important deficiencies in the existing systems which led to significant changes being made. In the absence of such reviews, there is always a danger that a well-intentioned participation project will finish up as an ineffective public relations exercise which adds to the cynicism of employees.

Summary

The approach to implementing participation can make the difference between success and failure. While prescriptions for failure can easily be given, success depends on a number of interrelated choices which can only be made in the light of particular situations.

Issues about which decisions have to be made include the following:

1 The objectives of a change towards greater participation

can be clearly stated and agreed at the outset, or left to emerge.

2 The change can be deliberately linked to pressing problems experienced by the organisation in order to increase the energy devoted to making the system work. Alternatively it may be deliberately insulated from current concerns.

3 Top management must decide on the extent of its own involvement, considering both the danger of apparent lack of support and that of seeming to take over the system. A related issue concerns the use of external, and internal, 'change agents'.

4 The approach to participation can be focused on specific issues and decision areas, or it can be largely open-ended.

5 The initial strategy for introducing participation can be the unilateral one of management putting forward a fully worked-out scheme, or a bilateral approach of jointly designing the new system.

6 An important issue to be faced is whether the system of participation should be integrated as closely as possible with the normal processes of management decision-making and the collective bargaining system, or whether it should be kept separate from them.

7 Decisions also have to be made about the necessary training to be provided for representatives, managers and other groups, and about the need, and method, for evaluation and follow-up of the system with a view to discovering and correcting any deficiencies.

Notes

[1] But see a recent study of ninety works councils in the Netherlands, which reached the conclusion that these councils are easily manipulated by their management-appointed chairman (Hovels and Nas, 1977). In the German system, by contrast, works councils are not chaired by a management

appointee. Cf. also Chapter 14, p. 257.

[2] See Brown (1971), Chapter 16 *et seq.*

[3] This is suggested by the study carried out in British Steel by Brannen et al. (1976), as well as by contacts in other organisations.

[4] One of the best examples of this type of role in the context of a participative system is the role played by Elliott Jaques (1951) in the development of the Glacier Works Council.

[5] For a review of unilateral and bilateral change strategies, see Knight (1975).

16 Training for participation

John Davis

formerly Manager, Management Training, B.L. Cars Ltd.

The background to participation in Leyland

Well before the advent of participation British Leyland had
become increasingly concerned with its worsening industrial
relations climate, which was steadily resisting attempts to
nurse it back to a healthier state. Around fifty separate locations in the company, employing from about 300 to over
20,000 people, had differing, historically developed working
relationships and cultures. There were many areas where some
form of worker involvement was practised, but they were not
related in any formal company-wide way. Employees 'participated' in the determination of wages and conditions, but bargaining arrangements were almost as many as the number of
separate plants; systems of works committees and councils
also existed, but again in no formal, company-wide organisation, and often these committees had their roots in the bargaining system based upon conflict rather than co-operation. In
some plants job-evaluation schemes involved management
and shop-floor workers in reaching agreement about various
aspects of work, and throughout the company many other
arrangements existed for 'consultation'. From this complex
array of different practices one point clearly emerged; as
things were arranged they were not, in fact, improving industrial relations.

In 1974 the company formed a management working party

to review those practices and to make some recommendations as to how employees might be involved to better effect in the affairs of the company. Additionally, there was some concern about the company's preparedness to meet any future legislation on employee participation. In this environment of changing social, industrial and statutory needs the working party began its task. Before it could be completed, however, the company's situation became more critical, the Ryder investigation took place and the eventual results included a major re-organisation of British Leyland into four main areas — Leyland Cars, Truck and Bus, Special Products, and International. The Ryder Report specified that the first two of these areas were to have formal systems of employee participation.

It says much for the preparatory work done, as well as the urgency of the situation, that only two months after the first meeting of the Leyland Cars *ad hoc* committee (thirty-two representatives of the thirteen recognised trade unions, and a management team), agreement had been reached as to the constitution of the Leyland Cars employee participation system. The agreement was signed by unions and management on 28 October 1975.

The system

> The overall purpose of the participation system is to increase the effectiveness of the operations of Leyland Cars to the mutual benefit of all its employees. A structure of Joint Management Councils, Committees and Conferences will allow representatives of employees to contribute to the solution of current problems and to the formation of future plans. The structure is designed to replace any purely consultative machinery which may presently exist.

Thus reads the first paragraph of the agreement which defines the shape, relationships, roles, constraints, responsibilities and terms of reference of the company-wide system.

The structure (see Figure 16.1) comprises three levels covering the thirty-two manufacturing units (plants), and six divisions of Leyland Cars. The base is the Plant Joint Management committee, at the next level is the Division Joint Management Committee and at the top of the hierarchy is the Joint Management Council. Of the six divisions, three constitute groupings of similar types of manufacturing units — 'Body and Assembly', 'Power Train and Foundry', and 'Service and Parts' divisions — while three have no manufacturing base and operate in a similar way to plant JMCs. The system allows an optional lower-level JMC at the shop or department level. Plant JMCs and the non-manufacturing division JMCs meet monthly, manufacturing division JMCs quarterly, and the Joint Management Council 'at least four times a year'. Twice a year there is a conference involving every member of each of the committees and council.

Each committee is chaired by the senior executive of the operational area and its management members are nominated by him. These invariably include those responsible for finance, personnel and other key functions. There are between six and fifteen employee representatives on each plant JMC, depending on the size of the plant. These 'constituency representatives' are drawn from both staff and hourly-paid areas, and in line with the recommendations of the Ryder Report are shop stewards, senior shop stewards, staff representatives and senior staff representatives.

Employee representatives on the manufacturing division JMCs are elected by and from the representatives on plant JMCs. The same procedure is adopted to elect the Joint Management Council from division JMC employee representatives. Management members of the division JMCs and Council are drawn from division or group staffs, nominated by the appropriate chairman. A typical large plant Joint Management Committee would be about 23 strong, and the total membership of the 39 committees and council is about 800.

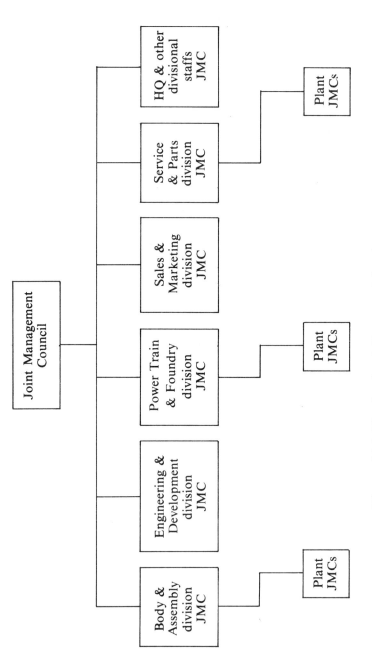

Figure 16.1 The Leyland Cars participation structure

JMCs discuss how to improve both production and the working environment, principally by focusing on current performance, production programmes, communications, environmental matters, and capital allocation, providing the particular topics are not within the orbit of the collective bargaining system. Specific matters for discussion — the JMCs agenda — are drawn from performance or situation reports, or can cover items submitted to the secretary of the JMC from any source.

Potential training needs

If the employee participation system was to succeed it would need more than a signed agreement, a fair wind and good intentions. A thorough understanding of the system, and what it was designed to achieve was vital. Reacting to the obvious need to know and comprehend the employee participation agreement (and via that document the participation structure, rules of procedure, roles, and so on) was a fairly conventional training aim. However, it was also obvious that such an important step in a new direction needed far more than conventional activities. If training operated in its usual reactive way, as training needs became clearer the opportunities of significantly affecting the chances of success would disappear.

The approach that training took was, in fact, proactive rather than reactive. During the development of the participation agreement, training became involved in the emerging picture. A dialogue was opened between training and the managers responsible for the development, implementation and communication of the system. A review of approaches taken by other companies both within the UK and elsewhere was initiated. What was learned was applied to what was understood about our own company culture and other special circumstances. The outcome of these activities was a fairly extensive identification of the likely concerns, difficulties and problems we might have to face in operating the system, and how these might be dealt with through a programme of training and development.

The first and already stated need was to understand thoroughly the nature of the system, but other needs emerged as the picture became clearer. Managers and employee representatives would be entering a new situation, in new groupings, taking part in activities which would demand different skills and attitudes. JMCs were to operate as working teams, using team strengths, expertise and experience to resolve their problems. Old attitudes of opposition and confrontation had to be converted to trust, co-operation and openness. These attitude problems would be as likely to apply to management as to employee-representative members of committees, and they would not disappear overnight just because of the introduction of the participation system. In this new situation, then, old barriers had to be removed and new relationships forged.

Members of JMCs, drawn as they were from management, staff and blue-collar areas, would have significantly differing experiences, skills, education, background and abilities. Properly harnessed, many of these differences would provide team strengths, but others would hinder effective team operation. The ramifications of these differences had to be recognised and carefully assessed. If people were not to feel inadequate, and therefore act defensively, they had to have the opportunity to make up knowledge gaps without any embarrassment to themselves.

The work of the committees and Council would need to be carried out according to the same model if they were to relate properly to each other and to the organisation and its needs. It was therefore important that everyone should not only understand what they were to do, but understand it in the same way.

The vast majority of the people involved in the participation system, and the work of the JMCs would be those involved in the day-to-day activities of plants. They would tend to have a very pragmatic view of things. Whatever training might be provided, it would need to be demonstrably relevant to their needs, particularly to that of effective committee operation.

Training would have to be of a very practical nature, and must in no way be perceived as 'academic'.

JMCs were precluded by the agreement from using the voting mechanism to arrive at committee decisions. The participation agreement demanded a genuine attempt to achieve consensus while underlining the fact that 'executive responsibility rests with management'. Simply put, committees were to 'make' decisions, management was to take them. The ability to influence the shape of a particular decision would rest not on weight of numbers, but on argument, experience, knowledge and understanding. Initially at least the major influence on decisions would probably come from management members unless there were real and successful attempts to search out ways of incorporating trade union representatives' experience and knowledge in discussion and decision-making. The need to build team skills would be of paramount importance to avoid both the idea and the fact of representatives merely 'rubber-stamping' management decisions.

Other, more obvious, assumptions were made about needs, including the importance of understanding such fundamentals as financial controls and performance information, the way the facets of the manufacturing systems are interdependent, and the roles and responsibilities of various staff functions. The training approach to cope with all these potential needs would have to be one which used team-development principles wherever possible, and provided each committee with an opportunity to 'settle in' and begin working as a cohesive team as quickly as possible. It must provide the subject knowledge which everyone would need to ensure contributions to high-quality decisions, and it must be able to respond to requests from individual committees where they felt they needed additional information or knowledge.

The training plan

There appeared to be two alternative ways of organising training for participation. Either plant training departments could go their own way, determining for themselves what their participation training approach would be, or the central (Group) training function could take on the business of developing the material and training the JMCs. The former would not in all likelihood meet some of the assumed needs from a corporate standpoint, notably the need for a common understanding and interpretation of the system; while the latter could not have been resourced either in terms of trainers or facilities. There were other advantages and disadvantages which argued for and against the alternatives. In the event, the decision was not difficult to make.

Group Training, being closer to the developing situation and therefore having an early start in terms of understanding and familiarisation, would be responsible for producing core materials centrally; they would train plant training managers in the use of the materials (and at the same time 'test market' them) and supply the training package to the plant trainers, who would themselves carry out their own JMC training, presenting these core materials in a language and style relevant to themselves and their plants, supplementing them where necessary with local information. Group training would provide a back-up support to give advice or more direct help should it be required. Division JMCs would be trained by Group Training Staffs, as would plant JMCs in the event that no plant trainer was trained and available on the day.

By the time the participation agreement was signed, the proposed training sequence had been produced and discussed. It had been given the full support of the Leyland Cars managing director and other senior managers, many of whom had been involved at some stage or another with the formulation of the proposals. When the explanation of the employee participation system appeared in the corporation's house journal the proposals for training were ready for implementation. Within a week of the agreement being signed the first step had been taken.

Very briefly, the proposed training sequence (Figure 16.2)

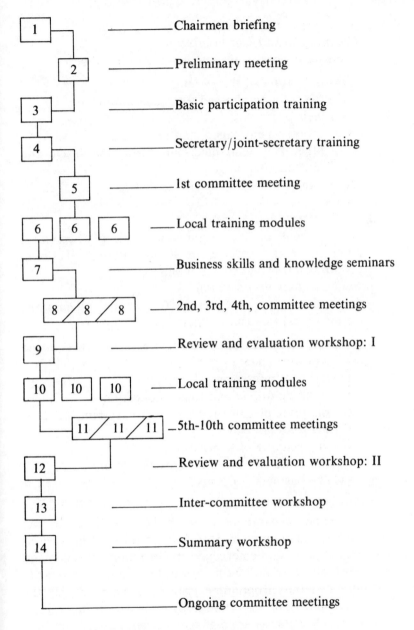

Figure 16.2 Proposed training sequence

was presented in the following way:

1 *Committee chairmen briefing*

A one-day workshop to acquaint chairmen with:

(a) the nature of the system;

(b) the training planned for their committees;

(c) their own roles;

(d) problems envisaged, and possible solutions;

(e) other key items emerging during the design and introductory stage.

(Note: three workshops were needed to cover all chairmen.)

2 *Preliminary JMC meeting*

Appointment of the committee's officers (Secretary, Joint Secretary and Senior Representative). Training proposals presented for discussion.

3 *Basic participation training*

A two-day activity for each JMC (including all committee members) to ensure understanding of:

(a) the total participation structure, including sequence and time span;

(b) terms of reference;

(c) standing orders and their implications;

(d) the principles of the participation system;

(e) the roles and rules;

(f) the meaning of 'consensus';

(g) the value and benefits of participation;

(h) key business concerns.

4 *Secretary and Joint-Secretary training*

A one-day programme to teach the skills, methods and procedures required by JMC Secretaries and Joint Secretaries, and ensure emergence of a common approach and working format. Secretaries and joint secretaries attended this programme only as pairs, to enable the development of a joint strategy to deal with this role.

(Note: Secretaries are management nominess, Joint Secretaries are employee representatives. They carry out the

normal committee secretarial role, including communicating to the shop floor and others, via brief minutes.)

5 *First committee meeting*
An operational meeting, attended by the trainer if
requested, not to become involved in the content of the
meeting, but to observe the process, provide feedback
on the meeting to the JMC and help identify concerns
and learning needs.

6 *Training modules*
Locally derived training modules, each of about half a
day to answer specific requests from committees. (The
fact of learning together subjects that they have requested
and which are therefore non-threatening, might further
cultivate the team identity.)

7 *Business skills and knowledge seminars*
Separate activities totalling between five and six days, to
give training in skills of importance to committee members. Areas to be covered:

(a) problem analysis and decision-making;
(b) financial control and information;
(c) communications;
(d) functional specialisms (personnel, sales and marketing, quality, systems, etc.).

It was thought that this training might be carried out in
committees or, if preferred, by the two constituent groups
— managers and representatives — who might not wish
to expose their lack of knowledge in these areas to each
other.

8 *Second, third, and fourth committee meetings*
Operational meetings.

9 *Review and evaluation workshop: I*
A one-day workshop for the whole committee to review it
working practices and styles and to evaluate its effectiveness.

10 *Training modules*
Locally derived modules each of about half a day to

answer particular needs identified in the previous work-shop. (The concern was to ensure that the system responded to learning needs that committees identified for themselves.)

11 *Fifth to tenth committee meetings*
Operational meetings.

12 *Review and evaluation workshop: II*
A one-day workshop for the committee to review again and evaluate its working practices and committee behaviour.

13 *Inter-committee workshop*
A one- or two-day workshop for the committees to compare notes on progress, operating methods, problem solutions and so on. (An opportunity to learn from one another for greater effectiveness.)

14 *Summary workshop*
A two-day workshop to provide each joint management committee with the opportunity to:

(a) assess its progress so far;
(b) assess its strengths and weaknesses;
(c) assess its skills;
(d) decide if it wished to modify its working pattern as a result of the inter-committee workshop;
(e) arrive at a consensus decision as to how it should now operate as a committee to optimise its effectiveness (after a year of working together there should be a feeling of collective identity).

The full sequence was scheduled to take place over the first year of operation, at which time the system itself would be reviewed. The initial stages (1 - 5) had specific time-targets for completion, while other stages were 'timed' by their sequential relationship to monthly meetings.

The overall training plan was presented to JMCs at their inaugural ('Preliminary') meeting in mid-November 1975, and was accepted as an approach to which JMCs could subscribe.

Implementing the plan — and the system

The training proposals were to prove a valuable aid in implementing the system. Besides establishing a level of understanding of the system, they provided JMCs with a non-threatening arena in which to test out their understanding and new working relationships.

The first step was to train the trainers, and this was carried out in sufficient time to provide the JMCs with basic training early in their life. Plant and other group trainers underwent a two-day familiarisation with the package, during which they were able to voice their concerns, both about the training materials and methods, and about the participation system itself. It was clear that they would need to train JMCs in new group skills. For most trainers it would be the first time that they had had to train groups as disparate as those including directors, managers, shop stewards and staff representatives. The package included a series of practical exercises, integrated with supporting inputs and discussions describing the system itself. The JMCs discussed and approved how the agreement was to be interpreted, what it meant in operational terms, the benefits that they and the company could expect. A discussion of what the JMCs saw as their key operational or business concerns provided an input to their next meetings.

JMC Secretaries and Joint Secretaries were trained, as planned, in pairs, working on various exercises designed to develop skills in note-taking, interpretation, the production of an agreed 'record' of the meeting and the compilation of a meaningful agenda. Emphasis was placed on the need to develop a joint strategy to enable each pair to both participate in and record the content of JMC meetings, and share in the responsibilities of their secretarial duties. During these exercises, and more particularly the feedback sessions, as much attention was paid to bridging potential attitude gaps, and resolving differences in expectations and understanding of what was required, as to the more technical aspects of the role.

The first modification to the plan was in the area of business skills training. This segment of the plan was separated into three parts: the first (Module A) was a 1½ day programme describing in simple terms the manufacturing processes in the company, and aspects of work closely related to manufacturing. It also described how the company was organised. For many people this was to be the first time they had seen how their work might be related to the whole, and the programme was designed using this simplified picture of aspects of manufacturing, as a backcloth to discussions intended to draw on and develop individuals' experiences and perceptions, to add to group knowledge and understanding and to further the development of the team identity. (Most JMCs have completed this element, and others are scheduling it as opportunity allows.)

The second section of this training (Module B) was itself divided into five parts, dealing with key functions in the company — finance, personnel, quality, sales and marketing, and systems. These functions were meant to develop the material themselves (programmes to last between a half and one and a half days), with whatever help they might need from group training. In the event training has been more heavily involved than intended in the development of some of the material, and the inability of already overstretched functional specialists to spend time on these activities has been a problem. One by-product of this functional involvement in participation training has been the opportunity offered to explain for the first time to large numbers of people what the functions are set up to do, and what contribution to the business they make. A second by-product has been the development of valuable induction material for general use with new employees. Module A, for instance, has been run on over a dozen occasions for non-JMC groups, and is scheduled for more. It has also been used in graduate induction programmes. The quality module — the first 'B' module to be completed — has been used as a quality-induction package. Parts of the personnel 'B' module — dealing with legislative aspects — has been incorporated into other training programmes. The preliminary work done on the other modules is seen by functional heads as ultimately providing the same facility.

The third section of business skills training (Module C) is a 1½-day programme dealing with 'Decision-Making and Planning in Groups'. It is not intended to equip JMCs fully with a disciplined committee skill in this fundamentally important area, since this would be impossible in so short a space of time. The intention is to demonstrate that a disciplined approach is both necessary and possible, and to give a foundation to such an approach.

Two years down the participation road has seen less than one-third of the JMCs complete Module C, though it is still being scheduled. In place of the planned 'B' modules, most JMCs , recognising their need to understand how various specialists work — particularly, but not exclusively finance — have had their needs serviced locally (at Stages 6 and 10). Plant specialists, generally the functional head, have given presentations to JMCs on topics of interest and concern. For instance, the finance function in most plants has given a half-day presentation explaining how its function is organised in the plant, the work it sets out to do and the meaning and derivation of local performance and status reports. Some JMCs have visited other plants to see other manufacturing operations as a means of adding to their understanding of the wider working environment and working relationships.

JMCs have, by and large, been more reluctant to undergo review and evaluation workshops. Perhaps they have considered the exercise to lack relevance, since such workshops might be seen as not dealing with real issues of plant importance. However, where this workshop has taken place it has reduced group frictions in the constituent groups. Workshops have included structured opportunities to identify problems of major concern in terms of either the JMC operation or its internal relationships. In mixed syndicates of managers and representatives problems or concerns have been identified, discussed and agreed, and discussed again in full plenary sessions. The trainer's role here has been to ensure that concerns are brought into the open and expressed even if they cannot be immediately resolved. The final workshop activity has always been that of action planning, with the emphasis on what the JMC can accomplish for itself, underlining its activities as a co-operating team. Much more work needs to be done to sell this approach to the JMCs who, may view an exercise which apparently does not add materially to what they know as being of relatively low priority.

On the recommendation of the Joint Management Council the second review workshop was replaced by another workshop designed to look outwards at the system itself, which was rather ponderously called the Participation Review Questionnaire Analysis Workshop. This activity arose from group training's involvement in the design and anaysis of a questionnaire, at an early stage in the training programme, which was eventually sent to every member of every JMC, canvassing views, opinions and attitudes related to the participation system. The workshop provided JMCs with their collated, analysed responses to consider, as well as those of all the other JMCs. They were to develop a team answer to two simplified questions. What strengths and weaknesses are there in the system? What changes would your committee recommend? Questionnaire responses indicated that nearly 75 per cent felt that they needed training to help them handle the business information they were dealing with. Naturally enough, trade union representatives felt this need much more keenly than management members of committees, though by no means exclusively. The approach adopted, of training committees together as whole working teams, was supported by the responses relating to the felt need for help 'to become a cohesive committee'. Only 25 per cent of the respondents felt that they needed no help.

The inter-committee and summary workshops have not yet taken place. The principle reason is, I believe, a lack of resources (time, money, people, facilities and opportunities) rather than unwillingness. The difficulties of finding opportunities to get JMCs together for training has proved one of the most taxing, since JMC management members include key personnel, almost invariably the plant's 'top-team', who are vitally necessary to the day-to-day running of the plants. The system, however, is ongoing, and therefore opportunities exist to maintain the approach and fulfil the intentions. In fact, JMCs are tending to continue to work their way through the training sequence proposed.

Conclusions

The original training plan had to be modified as time went on to respond to the developing needs of the system, and to take account of inaccuracies in our original assumptions. The time-scale of the training format was changed; in many cases plants have developed their own training packages (using Stages 6 and 10), where the original intention was that they should be developed by group training or other group functions. The second review and evaluation workshop was replaced by a workshop designed to look outwards at the system itself. But in fact 'formal' training has been only part of the total activity. From the outset we saw training as including briefing, informing, instructing, monitoring, evaluating, observing, giving feedback, coaching, counselling, analysing and discussing behaviour and actions. The model and its operation established the credibility and usefulness of the trainer, and gave JMCs someone to whom they could turn for a relatively impartial view of things. Trainers have been involved as observers in live JMC meetings in order to feed back to the committee an analysis of what was going on (or more usually, what was going wrong).

Particularly through the mechanism of working wherever possible with real issues during training sessions, of making those sessions participative, and including action planning as part of the format, the trainer has been a catalyst to action and to continuing action. He has operated as arbiter and interpreter on occasions, as peace-maker, and as pace-maker. Training has attempted to provide the necessary pressure on the system to more forward constantly, or at least to help prevent movement in the opposite direction.

Some have been less than satisfied with the progress of the participation system, believing the factional arguments and fallout which occur from time to time to be a measure of failure. But it must be recognised that even with the wholesale, total commitment of everyone to the new system, instant metamorphosis would have been impossible. Thirty years of developing relationships could not be turned around overnight — nor in a couple of years! Change programmes have to start from a base in reality.

What we have learned from our experiences is that, like any other company investment, the time and effort invested in participation requires constant servicing. Resources must be allocated to provide that servicing. Attention must be paid to the system and the problems in it. Training is one way of supplying some of the necessary attention by providing first, a platform for the expression of concerns, and, second, an arena for suggesting and testing ways of resolving them.

The need to provide opportunities to increase knowledge and understanding of the basis of business decisions is imperative. Failure to do so can lead to frustration, 'opting out', latent or manifest opposition to or distrust of those with the knowledge, or to committees able to deal only with issues of 'teas, toilets, or towels'.

The process, too, of decision-making in teams is not one which committees automatically understand. We felt that the development of team skills was obviously fundamental to the success of team- (or committee-) based systems. An effective committee comprising members who genuinely feel themselves to be part of a team is fundamental if the system is to survive and resolve the conflicts of interest which must inevitably arise from time to time.

Finally, the trainer must adopt any and every role which will enable him to provide the necessary skills, information and understanding. Participation is first and foremost a learning process for all concerned, and the trainer's job is to make that learning possible.

Summary

Following the Ryder Report, as well as earlier work by a management working party, a formal system of employee participation was introduced into Leyland Cars. The system was agreed by a committee of managers and trade union representatives, and involved joint management bodies at plant, divisional and group level.

A training plan was drawn up by the group training department, aimed at training the 800 or so members — both managers and trade union representatives — of the thirty-nine joint management committees, making use of both central and local training resources. The main training needs identified included a full understanding of the participation system, the ability to work together in a committee setting and the attitude changes this implied, the provision of the commercial, financial and operational knowledge required for meaningful participation in decision making, and an introduction to problem-solving and decision-making skills.

The chapter described the implementation of the training plan and the problems which led to modifications on the way. The time-scale proved to be optimistic, and the resources required were not always available. The plan to include review and evaluation workshops was not taken up by most of the committees. Other parts of the plan, however, were successfully completed, and the concluding section discussed the role of training in employee participation.

17 The Future of Participation

David Guest

Lecturer in Personnel Management, London School of Economics and Political Science

Despite the Labour Government's stated intention to legislate and the proposals contained in the 1978 White Paper, it might be tempting for some to believe that in the UK worker participation was a fashion of the mid-1970s, a passing response to economic crisis which in time will be replaced by another fad.

Taking this view, some of the management initiatives described in this book could be seen as a reflection of this fashion, perhaps a hasty response to the Bullock Committee but without any deeper or lasting significance. The aim of this final chapter is to argue that such a view is mistaken.

Three perspectives

Before identifying the pressures which are likely to lead to further growth in participation, it is useful to look at the major directions in which development is possible. A review of the case histories in this book and of the chapters on management and trade union concerns, suggests three perspectives on participation, corresponding to three possible directions for future development.

The first perspective sees participation in terms of *involvement*. This is the viewpoint of many employers and closely reflects the current policy of the CBI. It is based on three basic premises: namely, that employers and employees have a shared interest in the success of the enterprise; that no changes in the structuring and control of organisations are required; and that management should be left to manage with a minimum of interference from unions, government or other interest groups. The purpose of participation is therefore to increase the involvement of workers and their commitment to management policy and practice.

For workers or their representatives, the gains from forms of participation associated with this view are likely to be better information, a greater opportunity to discuss a range of issues and policies and, nearer the shop floor, some opportunity to engage in problem-solving as well as the possibility of increased involvement and job satisfaction. For management, the gains can be described in terms of increased co-operation, less resistance to change and possibly a better quality of decision-making.

To the cynical trade untionist, many of these employer initiatives may have the appearance of old wine in new bottles. Works councils may look like a revival of joint consultation; briefing groups and problem-solving groups are similar to well-tried communication devices and job redesign can sometimes seem to be a means of increasing efficiency. Similarly, profit-sharing schemes may have an appearance of novelty, yet, like other management initiatives on participation, make no concessions on control over most of the crucial decisions. In the light of this analysis it is not altogether surprising to find that most of the cases described in this book, some of which quite clearly fall within this perspective, were initiated by management. It is management that seems to have most to gain. At the same time, the lack of union initiatives in the development of most forms of participation becomes more understandable.

A second perspective sees participation in terms of *control*. This is a view which is advocated by large sections of the trade union movement and is based on the assumption that the central goal should be a sharing of power and control over the full range of organisational decisions. This may be restricted to the power to challenge decisions made by management or may extend to a sharing in the process whereby decisions are formulated. At the centre of this perspective is a challenge to managerial control, though this only infrequently extends to ownership. The preferred forms of participation are collective bargaining and, to a lesser extent, worker director schemes where worker representatives have parity representation.

This approach, based as it is on an assumption of differing interests and objectives of employer and employee and varying levels of mistrust and competition, has nevertheless succeeded in extending worker rights and union control over various kinds of decision. It is questionable, however, whether such an approach, on its own, will be sufficient to meet the individual aspirations and social pressures of the coming years.[1]

Given the situation outlined in the first chapter, in which a whole range of different hopes and desires seem to be crystallising around the issue of participation, any approach which is based exclusively on an employer- or trade union-dominated perspective is likely to prove inadequate, and what we are in fact seeing is the emergence of a third *combined approach*, based on the recognition that different forms of participation can and should co-exist in different and indeed the same organisation. Such a pragmatic approach, largely reflected in the government White Paper, favours flexibility and the importance of choice, and tries to take account of a wide variety of local circumstances and objectives.

The future

A recent 'Delphi' study, collecting the views of experts on likely developments over the coming years, suggested that by the mid-1980s, participation would not be a topic of heated debate because it would be well established and largely taken for granted by all sides in industry.[2]

The reasons why interest in participation has grown in recent years seem likely to become more rather than less valid.

The search for an accommodation of the interests of employer and employee will continue; and, as the range of issues over which agreement has to be reached is extended both by law and by a changing power-balance, so the need to work together effectively becomes more pressing. Without this the goals of increased satisfaction and productivity will become even harder to attain.

Pressures for participation

What, then, are the key pressures, issues and interests that are likely to affect the direction of developments in participation? The first is the possibility of government action. The Bullock Committee, the government White Paper and the prospect of the legislation which could lead to worker directors has undoubtedly provided a major stimulus to debate and new initiatives. Many of these management initiatives can be viewed, partly at least, as reactions, designed to forestall the introduction of worker directors by providing alternatives.

In practice, this has often meant that proposals concerned with a redistribution of power and based on a control perspective have been met by a response from employers aiming at greater commitment to organisational goals within a perspective of involvement. Hence, favoured approaches have included profit-sharing, information-sharing, joint problem-solving and job design. From an employer's point of view, such strategies may be viewed as an entirely rational response which could help to deflect government and trade union pressures.

As the threat of legislation along the lines of the Bullock proposals has receded, some of the urgency has gone out of the debate. The government White Paper[3] therefore serves a dual function both in pointing the possible way ahead and in maintaining the impetus of the debate.

Leaving aside legislation, there are other kinds of pressure to which managers must respond and which are likely to encourage the development of participation. One is the development of collective union power with which management at all levels must come to terms. A relatively recent feature of this is the growth of white-collar unions, including representation of managerial and professional workers.[4] This may lead to developments at all levels representing a fundamental challenge to control over corporate policy. Already there are illustrations of this, such as the Lucas shop stewards' combine which seeks to challenge the product and marketing strategy of Lucas, arguing that the manufacture of different, non-military products is an alternative to factory closures. Increasingly, it seems that the challenge is to the control rather than the ownership of the enterprise; and, while based on a recognition of the need for efficiency and investment, it primarily seeks to safeguard the interests of employees. From this point of view, typical employer initiatives are viewed as welcome but still rather marginal.

While the challenge from within the organisation concerns control rather than ownership, the question of ownership is likely to continue to be an issue. Profit-sharing may remain an area of secondary interest, but more significantly, the increasing influence of pensions funds will become more apparent in the 1980s. Already unions are strongly represented in the management of these funds and they will become one of the dominant, if not the most dominant, of the institutional investors. There is no sign that the growth of union involvement in the management of the funds has done anything to reduce their concern for profitability. However, it does help to diminish the negative image of capitalists controlling enterprises even if it still leaves open the potential conflict between the interests of capital invested from outside the enterprises and labour employed within. This opens up interesting new possibilities for unions to extend their influence over the development of participation and indeed a range of other activities in the organisations in which these funds invest. (It also of course, raises the danger of new kinds of inter-union conflict.)

A third factor likely to maintain pressure for participation at the level of the shop and office floor and to some extent at plant level, is a growing awareness of the available possibilities. As cases of participative practice become better known and as the workforce at all levels becomes less tolerant of routine low-discretion work and authoritarian management, so the demand for more flexible organisation and workgroup autonomy is likely to grow. Given developments in technology, the evidence that changes in job design can improve both job satisfaction and productivity is likely to prove appealing. Against this must be set the fact that many workers, typically including those in the low-skill jobs, do not at present seek greater involvement in their work and prefer to let the union safeguard and advance their interests.

A further motive for participation which has been frequently discussed and is likely to become more rather than less urgent is that many current organisational goals associated with innovation, growth and profitability can only be achieved with the consent of the workforce, both because of the dependence on their positive contribution and because of their negative power to block managerial initiatives.

Finally, although the role of management is often of necessity reactive, it would be wrong to lose sight of the considerable positive influence that can be exerted by key executives with a strong personal belief in employee participation. Several of the cases illustrated in this book developed out of an initiative of a chief executive. This is true, to a greater or lesser extent, of Cadbury Schweppes, the British Steel Corporation, Scottish & Newcastle Breweries and Morgan & Grundy. Each illustrates how a chief executive's belief in the involvement and potential contribution of employees at different levels led to an initiative on participation.

For all these reasons we feel that there is likely to be a continuing extension of participation over the next decade. Inevitably this implies a certain view of society, which has to take account of the reality of such problems as limited economic growth, high unemployment and a growth of protectionism. On the positive side, there is likely to be an increased acceptance of the need for a balance between efficiency and satisfaction and between the needs of the worker and the economy. There may also be a growing emphasis on the wishes and aspirations of individuals as a counter to the corporatist tendencies of trade unions and companies.

The need for flexibility

These trends seem to support the view underlying the government White Paper, that there is a need for further developments in participation but that the approach ought to be a flexible one.

The need for a range of strategies for the development of participation is highlighted by an analysis of the contexts in which it might be developed. Variations in organisational culture and history, the differing and changing power structures, the differing perceptions of those involved and change in technology and markets all point to the need for a variety of possible approaches from one organisation to another and even within one organisation over time. A lesson from the debate on the Bullock Report, as well as on the EEC's draft Fifth Directive, is that there are several paths ahead and no single one is acceptable to all. Even within one organisation of any size different approaches might be appropriate, and in rapidly changing environments the forms of participation that become established will, like all organisational systems, require constant review.

Returning to the three perspectives outlined at the start of this chapter, the most likely way ahead is the flexible middle path, the pragmatic view, which can accommodate established approaches like collective bargaining, as well as less familiar ones such as worker directors, works councils and autonomous workgroups. Sometimes these will be combined, sometimes one or other will dominate, at other times they will co-exist.

The management response

For management there are today two broad responses to participation. One is the traditional, rather negative one of seeing it as another challenge to managerial rights which should be opposed, deflected or met with minimum action. This, by and large, is the view adopted to date by the CBI. The alternative is to identify the pressures for more participation and use them as sources of energy for change, to view them as an opportunity to take a positive step to establish a new set of working relationships at all levels in the organisation.

It seems that the established interests of both employers and unions will need the impetus of legislation to adjust their traditional view of relationships. It might be better for many organisations if the various interest groups sought to clarify their goals and to harness the energies and pressures that exist to the achieving of these goals. Sometimes participation will be the most appropriate strategy, both as a means of progressing towards a new relationship and for maintaining that relationship on an effective basis. A central purpose of this book, however, has been to highlight the range of approaches available and to suggest that there is no one best way of putting participation into practice. There are no panaceas and the problems must be faced by the managers and workers within each enterprise.

Summary

In this final chapter we have outlined three perspectives on participation which might also indicate directions for participation in the future. The first perspective, favoured by sections of management, sees participation in terms of involvement, the second, favoured by many unions, sees participation primarily in terms of power. Thirdly, there is what we have termed a combined approach which is more flexible and accepts the co-existence of various forms of participation.

Looking to the future it is argued that the pressures for an extension of participation are likely to continue. The main pressures include the possibility of legislation; the development of union power; the growing awareness, among all levels of workers, of the potential benefits of participation; the need to obtain employee consent to change and innovation; and the belief in the value of participation among a number of chief executives. Given this range of pressures it is argued that a flexible approach is necessary and that managers should view participation as an opportunity to be welcomed, rather than as a threat to be opposed.

Notes

[1] These two contrasting perspectives have long been recognised by students of industrial relations (see, e.g., Fox, 1971), yet it is perhaps suprising how they have crystallised within the debate on participation.

[2] The same study also gave some indication that a parallel development might be a levelling-off or even a decline in the power of trade unions. See Guest (1977) for a report which refers, briefly, to some of the results of this particular study.

[3] *Industrial Democracy*, HMSO, Cmnd. 7231, London, 1978.

[4] It is perhaps a surprise to many people that quite senior managers often feel that they do not participate fully in 'managerial decisions'. One illustration of this was provided by a survey of senior managers in West German organisations working under co-determination (Hartmann, 1974).

Certainly any argument about exclusion from participation on the grounds of limited knowledge and expertise becomes increasingly tenuous as managers join the ranks of potential participants.

Bibliography

ADAIR, J., *Training for Leadership*, Gower Press, Farnborough, 1978 (originally Macdonald, London, 1968).

ARGYRIS, C., *Integrating the Individual and the Organisation*, John Wiley, New York, 1964.

AUEW, *An Investigation into the Scope of Industrial Democracy*, Amalgamated Union of Engineering Workers, 1976.

BANK, J, and JONES, K., with the British Steel Corporation Employee Directors, *Worker Directors Speak*, Gower Press, Farnborough, 1977.

BATSTONE, E. and DAVIES, P.L., *Industrial Democracy : European Experience*, Two reports prepared for the Bullock Committee, HMSO, 1976.

BELL, D.W., *Financial Participation — Wages, Profit-sharing and Employee Shareholders*. Industrial Participation Association, Devonshire Press, Torquay, 1973.

BERRY, A.P. (ed), *Worker Participation — The European Experience*, Coventry and District Engineering Employers Association, 1974.

BLAKE, J. and ROSS, S., 'Some experiences with autonomous work groups', in WEIR, M. (Ed), *Job Satisfaction : Challenge and Response in Modern Britain*, Fontana/Collins, 1976.

BLAUNER, R.R., *Alienation and Freedom : The Factory Worker and his Industry*, University of Chicago Press, Chicago, 1964.

BLUMBERG, P., *Industrial Democracy : The Sociology of*

Participation, Constable, London, 1968.

BRANNEN, P., BATSTONE, E., FATCHETT, D. and WHITE, P., *The Worker Directors*, Hutchinson, London, 1976.

BRAVERMAN, H., *Labour and Monopoly Capital*, Monthly Review Press, New York, 1974.

BROWN, W., *Organisation*, Heinemann Educational Books Ltd., London, 1971.

BULLOCK REPORT, *see Report of the Committee of Inquiry on Industrial Democracy, 1977.*

BURNS, T. and STALKER, G.M., *The Management of Innovation*, Tavistock, London, 1961.

BYE, B. and FISHER, J., *Shop stewards' attitudes to industrial democracy.* Paper read at Society of Industrial Tutors, Conference on Industrial Democracy, Barnsley, 1977.

CERAMICS GLASS AND MINERAL PRODUCTS INDUSTRY TRAINING BOARD, *Participative Practices : A Guide to Training Implications*, 1976.

CLARKE, R.O., FATCHETT, D.J. and ROBERTS, B.C., *Workers Participation in Management in Britain*, Heinemann, London, 1973.

CLEGG, C.W., NICHOLSON, N.N., URSELL, G., BLYTON, P. and WALL, T.D., *Managers' attitudes towards industrial democracy*, Medical Research Council Social and Applied Psychology Unit Memo No. 169.

COATES, K. (ed.) *The New Worker Co-operatives*, Spokesman Books, Nottingham, 1976.

COMMISSION ON INDUSTRIAL RELATIONS (CIR), *Worker Participation and Collective Bargaining in Europe*, CIR Study No. 4, HMSO, 1974.

COPEMAN, G., *Employee Co-ownership and Industrial Stability*, Institute of Personnel Management, London, 1974.

DAVIS, L.E., 'The coming crisis for production management: technology and organisation', in DAVIS, L.E. and TAYLOR, J.C., *Design of Jobs*, Penguin Books, Harmondsworth, England, 1972.

DERBER, M., 'Cross-currents in workers' participation',

Industrial Relations, 29, 1970, pp. 123-136.

DONOVAN REPORT, *see Report of the Royal Commission on Trade Unions and Employers' Associations 1965-68,* 1968.

DRINKWATER, A., *Industrial Democracy : Company Views and the Bullock Committee.* The Administrative Staff College, Henley-on-Thames, 1976.

EAGLE, F. and WEST, A., 'Opening moves in participation', *Industrial and Commercial Training, 10*, 5, May 1978.

EMERY, F.E. and THORSRUD, E., *Democracy at Work,* Martinus Nijhof Social Sciences Division, Leiden, 1976.

FAY, S., 'Britain's Poverty : The Role of Union Power', *Sunday Times,* 5 March 1978.

FORD, R.N., *Motivation Through the Work Itself,* American Management Association, New York, 1969.

FOX, A., *A Sociology of Work in Industry,* Collier-Macmillan, London, 1971.

THE FUTURE OF COMPANY REPORTS, HMSO, Cmnd. 6888, 29 July 1977.

GENNARD, J. and ROBERTS, B., 'Trends in plant and company bargaining', *Scot. J. of Political Economy,* June 1970.

GOODRICH, C.L., *The Frontiers of Control,* Pluto Press, London, 1975.

GREGORY, D. and HUGHES, J., 'Richer jobs for workers?', *New Society,* February, 1978.

GREINER, L.E., 'Patterns of organisation change', *Harvard Business Review, 45* 3, May/June, 1967.

GUEST, D., 'Motivation after Maslow', *Personnel Management, 8,* 3, March 1976, pp. 29-32.

GUEST, D., *Work and Careers in the Years up to 2000,* Institute of Careers Officers, Stourbridge, West Midlands, 1977.

GUEST, D. and FATCHETT, D., *Worker Participation : Individual Control and Performance,* Institute of Personnel Management, London, 1974.

HACKMAN, J.R. and OLDHAM, G.R., 'Development of the Job Diagnostic Survey', *Journal of Applied Psychology, 60,* 2, 1975, pp. 159-170.

HARTMANN, H., 'Managerial employees — new participants in industrial relations', *British Journal of Industrial Relations, XII,* 2, 1974, pp. 268-281.

HEALTH AND SAFETY COMMISSION, *Safety Representatives and Safety Committees, HMSO, London, 1976.*

HERZBERG, F., *Work and the Nature of Man,* World Publishing Company, New York, 1966.

HERZBERG, F., MAUSNER, B. and SNYDERMAN, G., *The Motivation to Work,* John Wiley, New York, 1959.

HERZBERG, F. and RAFALKO, E., 'Efficiency in the military : cutting costs with orthodox job enrichment', *Personnel,* November-December, 1975.

HESPE, G.W.A. and WALL, T.D., 'The demand for participation among employees', *Human Relations, 29,* 1976, pp. 411-428.

HOVELS, B. and NAS, P., reported in *International Management, 32,* 10, October, 1977, p. 16.

INCOMES DATA SERVICES IDS, *Profit Sharing 1,* IDS Study 160, London, 1977.

INDUSTRIAL DEMOCRACY, HMSO, Cmnd. 7231, London, 1978.

INDUSTRIAL RELATIONS REVIEW AND REPORT, 'Guide to employee share ownership, Part 1 — Profit Related Schemes', London, December 1977, pp. 2-6.

INGHAM, G., *Size of Industrial Organisation and Worker Behaviour,* Cambridge University Press, 1970.

INLAND REVENUE, *Profit Sharing : Tax Relief.* A consultative document, Inland Revenue Press Office, London, 1978.

JACKSON, S., MACFARLANE, I. and OSTEL, A.,
1. Pilot study into improving the effectiveness and assessing the impact of procedures to communicate a business information statement on the Grangemouth Works, 1976.
2. Communication of the 1977 Works/Departmental Plans at Grangemouth. 1977.
3. Communication of the 1977 Works/Departmental

Plans. A follow-up study. 1977.

(Three reports to Imperial Chemical Industries Limited).

JACOBS, E., ORWELL, S., PATERSON, P. and WELTY, F., *The Approach to Industrial Relations*, Anglo-German Foundation, London, 1977.

JAQUES, E., *The Changing Culture of a Factory*, Tavistock Publications, London, 1951.

JAQUES, E., *A General Theory of Bureaucracy*, Heinemann Educational Books Ltd., London, 1976.

JESSUP, G., 'The case for shop floor participation', *Department of Employment Gazette*, June 1977.

KNIGHT, K., 'Organisational Change Strategies', unpublished paper, Brunel Management Programme, Brunel University, 1975.

KNIGHT, K., 'The employee survey — handle with care', *Journal of General Management, 4*, 2, Winter 1976/77.

KLEIN, L., *New Forms of Work Organisation*, Cambridge University Press, Cambridge, 1976.

LIKERT, R., *The Human Organisation : Its Management and Value*, McGraw-Hill, New York, 1967.

LINDHOLM, R. and NORSTEDT, J.P., *The Volvo Report*, SAF, Stockholm, 1975.

McCARTHY, W.E.J. and ELLIS, N.D., *Management by Agreement*, Hutchinson, London, 1973.

McGREGOR, D.M., *The Human Side of Enterprise*, McGraw-Hill, New York, 1960.

McGREGOR, D.M., *The Professional Manager,* McGraw-Hill, New York, 1967.

MAHER, J.R., *New Perspectives in Job Enrichment*, Litton Educational Publishing Co., 1971.

MANN, F.C., 'Studying and Creating Change : A Means to Understanding Social Organisation', 1957. (Reproduced in HORNSTEIN, H.A. et al., *Social Intervention*, The Free Press, 1971.)

MEIDNER, R., *Employee Investment Funds,* George Allen and Unwin, London, 1978.

OPPENHEIM, A.N., *Questionnaire Design and Attitude*

Measurement, Heinemann, London, 1966.

PARKER, S.R., *Workplace Industrial Relations, 1972.* Social Survey Report, London, 1974.

PARKER, S.R., *Workplace Industrial Relations, 1973*, Office of Population Censuses and Surveys, Social Survey Division, SS1020; London, 1977.

PATEMAN, C., *Participation and Democratic Theory*, Cambridge University Press, 1970.

PAUL, W.J. and ROBERTSON, K., *Job Enrichment and Employee Motivation*, Gower Press, London, 1970.

PYM, D., 'Exploring Characteristics of the Versatile Worker', *Occupational Psychology*, 39, 1965, pp. 271-8.

QVALE, T., 'Improved Quality of Working Life, Bureaucracy or Productivity? Experience with board level worker representation in Norway', paper presented to a conference 'Productivity and the Quality of Working Life', arranged by the European Association of Productivity Centres, The Hague, December, 1977.

RAMSAY, H., 'Participation : the shop floor view', *British Journal of Industrial Relations*, XIV, 1976, pp. 128-141.

Report of the Commission of Inquiry on Industrial Democracy, HMSO (Cmnd. 6706), London, 1977 (The Bullock Report).

Report of the Royal Commission on Trade Unions and Employers' Associations 1965-68, (The Donovan Report) HMSO (Cmnd. 3623), London, 1968.

RICE, A.K., *Productivity and Social Organisation : The Ahmedabad Experiment*, Tavistock, London, 1958.

ROEBER, J., *Social Change at Work : The ICI Weekly Staff Agreement*, Duckworth, London, 1975.

TAYLOR, J.C. 'Experiments in Work System Design : Economic and Human Results'.
  (a) Part I, *Personnel Review, 6*, 3, Summer 1977, pp. 21-34.
  (b) Part II, *Personnel Review, 6,* 4, Autumn 1977, pp. 21-42.

THORSRUD, E., 'Job design in the wider context', *in* DAVIS, L.E. and TAYLOR, J.C., *Design of Jobs*, Penguin

Books, Harmondsworth, Middx, 1972.

TRIST, E.L., and BAMFORTH, K.W., 'Some social and psychological consequences of the longwall method of coal getting', *Human Relations*, 4, 7, 1951, pp. 13-38.

TRIST, E.L., HIGGIN, G.W., MURRAY, H., and POLLOCK, A.B., *Organisational Choice*, Tavistock, London, 1963.

TRADE UNION CONGRESS, *Industrial Democracy*, TUC, London, 1974.

TRADE UNION CONGRESS, *Evidence to the Bullock Committee*, TUC, London, 1976.

URSELL, G., WALL, T.D., CLEGG, C.W., NICHOLSON, N.N. and BLYTON, P., *Shop Stewards' attitudes towards industrial democracy*, Medical Research Council Social and Applied Psychology Unit (in preparation).

WALKER, K. and GREYFIE DE BELLECOMBE, L., 'Worker Participation : the concept and its implementation', *International Institute for Labour Studies Bulletin*, No. 2, February, 1967.

WALL, T.D., and LISCHERON, J.A., *Worker Participation*, McGraw-Hill, London, 1977.

WALTON, R.E., and McKERSIE, R.B., *A Behavioural Theory of Labour Negotiations*, McGraw-Hill, New York, 1965.

WILKINSON, A., *A Survey of Some Western European Experiments in Motivation* (unpublished report), Institute of Work Study Practitioners, Enfield, Middlesex, 1971.

WILSON, N.A.B., *On the Quality of Working Life*, HMSO, London, 1973.

WOODWARD, J., *Industrial Organisation: Theory and Practice*, Oxford University Press, 1965.

WOODWARD, J., (ed), *Industrial Organisation : Behaviour and Control*, Oxford University Press, 1970.

WORK RESEARCH UNIT, *Bibliographies 1-9, Developments in the Quality of Working Life* (by industries), Department of Employment, London, February, 1978.

WREN, A., 'Participation through added value', *Industrial and Commerical Training*, 7, 6, June 1975, pp. 233-38.

Index